Different
by Design

Edward B. Howell

amacom
American Management Association
New York • Atlanta • Boston • Chicago • Kansas City • San Francisco • Washington, D.C.
Brussels • Mexico City • Tokyo • Toronto

Library of Congress Cataloging-in-Publication Data

Howell, Edward Beach, 1924–
    Different by design / Edward B. Howell.
        p.   cm.
    Includes bibliographical references and index.
    ISBN 0-8144-0321-2
    1. Insurance, Architects' liability—United States.   2. Insurance,
Engineers' liability—United States.   I. Title.
HG8053.6H69   1996
368.5—dc20   96-5995
                                                                    CIP

Printing number

10   9   8   7   6   5   4   3   2   1

This book is dedicated to my wife, **Jo**, and daughter, **Melinda**, who must have been wondering, "Where is he going now?"

Contents

Foreword

Fate, which in the context of my comments means an unexpected occurrence that changes the course of one's life, affects everyone's life. Sometimes the fateful event has a disastrous consequence. For Napoléon, fate was the rain that fell on the battlefield of Waterloo the night before he attacked the allied forces arrayed against him. If the field had not been muddy he would have been able to move his cannons to an advantageous position early in the fray, but he was forced to wait until the afternoon after the sun had dried the turf to move his artillery. By then it was too late and he lost the battle.

My own fateful event, less dramatic and certainly much less meaningful than Napoléon's defeat at Waterloo, nevertheless was important to me personally because it had much to do with the subsequent years of my career as an insurance agent.

In early 1971 I received a telephone call in my office from structural engineer James R. Libby. Jim was a client of mine and had come from a meeting of the Consulting Engineers Association of California where he listened to a speaker by the name of Ed Howell who told the audience about a new insurance company that was going to be "Different by Design," Design Professionals Insurance Company (DPIC). Jim thought that what Howell said made sense and suggested I call him in San Francisco to see if there was a chance our firm might represent them in San Diego. After a subsequent meeting I became DPIC's exclusive insurance agent in San Diego. As a result of my affiliation many good things happened to me, the benefits of which I continue to enjoy to this day.

The highlights of the good things that happened to me can be summarized as follows:

- I represented DPIC, an insurance company that has no peer in the field of architects'and engineers' professional liability insurance and, arguably, no peer in any other type of insurance. Quality is essential to any sales or businessperson who wants to meaningfully distinguish himself or herself from the competition. DPIC represents quality at its best.
- I reached a degree of professionalism because of the training, discipline, and commitment required by the DPIC program and plan of operation, such that my capabilities surpassed those of any of my competitors.
- By getting to know many of the DPIC agents, who with few exceptions were the finest group of insurance agents with whom I have

ever been associated, I developed some important lifelong friend-ships.

- I also made some important money from doing business the DPIC way.

These things I have mentioned can be considered the foundation and structure of my DPIC experience. Like a building, the attractiveness of the edifice occurs when it is completed and is not only a thing of substance, but when designed effectively, also a thing of beauty.

The beauties of the DPIC experience are multifaceted. One of them is the spirit of the Company and its agents working together (not, of course, without some occasional disagreements between agents and Company personnel) with a harmony seldom found in the traditional insurance company–agent relationship. This unique involvement was rewarding to me. The caliber and camaraderie of the DPIC agents, which I previously mentioned, was evident and began in 1975 when a group of pioneer agents, including Rollo Jacobs, Irv Page, Jim Hurley, Jim Atkins, and this writer journeyed to New York City and state in September of that year to complete four or five long-form professional liability insurance applica-tions per day so that DPIC could take over a book of insurance business being abandoned by another insurance company. The friendship-bonding from the New York experience resulted in these agents, and subsequently others, getting together periodically to help each other become more pro-ficient in the handling of design professionals' coverages.

One of the early DPIC agents' meetings was held at the International Hotel, Maui, Hawaii. The beauty of the DPIC experience was never more ev-ident. It was dusk and we were enjoying a luau in the hotel's garden when suddenly there were flowers falling from the sky. Some of us thought, "Wow! This guy, Howell, really has contacts!"—until we heard the "Thrump! Thrump! Thrump!" of a hovering helicopter as it passed overhead.

Another attractive aspect of DPIC is the appearance of second genera-tion agents who are either working with or replacing their seniors or fathers. It is a second generation experience of my own that I want to relate, because it was an interesting and important moment in my DPIC involvement.

Shortly after, my son Jeff joined my firm, and I took him with me on a client call to familiarize him with the DPIC lore and way. The client was a small architectural firm. I presented a written proposal and then de-scribed in detail the advantages of the DPIC service and coverages to the two principals of the firm. At the conclusion of my presentation the archi-tects made a decision on the spot to place their insurance with us and DPIC even though the premium would be close to 40% higher than their existing policy. This, to me, was a home run with the bases loaded: There was a new account for our firm, Jeff learned that quality and dedication can mean more than price, and my stature in my son's eyes as a person who knew how to make a sale was confirmed.

—Frank G. Cavignac

Preface

It may seem to many that things in the business world just happen, and that may often be the case. There are times, though, when this is not the case, and what is described on the following pages gives a glimpse of one business situation that followed a well-planned effort to create a business entity distinct from most. For the founders of that company, Design Professionals Insurance Company (DPIC), set out to be different, Different by Design.

This book is anecdotal, in that the happenings are biographical and one man's recollections. No doubt others who lived through the founding of the insurance company DPIC will remember things wholly differently from my perspective. Oh, well, it can't be helped. Time dims memories, and although I kept copious notes during visits with underwriters, lawyers, reinsurers, architects, and consulting engineers, most of those notes were not available, since my loving wife, Jo, in a moment of spousal pique, put them in a bin marked GARBAGE. Their destruction may have improved the quality of the depicted life. Most of this book is my memory's best recall. Therefore, if you find portions that are incorrect or incoherent from your vantage point, please keep it mum.

E.B.H.

Acknowledgments

I am grateful to Alan R. Gruber, chairman and CEO of Orion Capital Corporation, for making this book possible. I am glad that he thought the subject worth memorializing and that he and Orion Capital Corporation were willing to foot the bill for gathering old, dusty data spread far and wide. Without the aid of Peter G. Kelly, Esq., I do not know if our company would have survived to be memorialized. He gave support when others looked the other way. His candor and practiced eye on this work made it better than it might otherwise have been. Thanks also must be given to the present and past employees of Kemper Corporation who dredged through their records to come up with facts about happenings almost 30 years old. They have given unstintingly of their time in reconstructing the views of the events that happened before and during the formation of the Design Professionals Insurance Company (DPIC). Special thanks goes to Hiram L. Kennicott, Jr., Arthur D. Webster, Ron Seaver, David Mathis, Harry Marcus, and John Ryan. Employees of DPFC-DPIC who aided in this effort were Bernard P. Engels, Elliott Gleason, Florence H. Whitmire, Peter B. Hawes, Richard P. Howell, and former employees, Scott A. McKown, David Coduto, and Joe McQuillan, Esq. Wini Waggoner made available the summarization report on the Asilomar Conference, "Professional Liability—The Public Interest, Who Benefits? Who Pays?" authored by her late husband, Eugene B. Waggoner. That report detailed the historic meeting on design professionals' liability March 16–21, 1972. This made it possible to correctly report on the event. Thanks, Wini! (Did anyone ever thank Gene for the wonderful job he did?) My sister, Mary Lou Wynne, was a big help in resolving the debate over correct language form, usages, and other important minutiae connected with the high babble of the English language.

I am indebted to H. Felix Kloman, now retired, but formerly a principal and vice president of Tillinghast, a Towers Perrin company, where he wagged his finger at the insurance industry, saying things like, "Gentlemen, curb your dogs!" He deserves special plaudits for many reasons; for example, for his support, challenging ideas, and courage in facing the rascals down.

Thanks, too, to former Directors of DPIC and personal friends, James R. Rush, R. Neal Campbell, Wesley G. McCain, and William L. Shannon. They helped with claims histories, details about board meetings, and other company formation dates and memorabilia.

Of extraordinary help in the editing process was former DPIC employee, Elizabeth A. Korver: She deserves special commendation. She attempted to keep my language grammatically correct, spelling reasonably close to accurate, and the punctuation in those areas where it belongs. Thanks Liz. Thanks, also, to Sheila Dixon who took up where Liz left off; did Liz become bored with the work? Jeanne Hotchkiss, assistant vice president of communications, Orion Capital Corporation, deserves a medal for her fine work in bringing order out of chaos.

Not to be forgotten is the help my wife, Jo, gave in sorting out pages, proofing garbled language, and putting up with hours of complaints about chapters being too long, or too short, but never *just right*; just like in *Goldilocks*.

Chapter 1

Setting the Stage

On April 30, 1962, Rantoul, Illinois, was struck by a climatic anomaly. Lightning was flashing steadily, causing an eerie green glow that turned the dark day almost light. Torrential rain and hail were driven by fierce winds (some said "tornadic") so strong that automobile windshield wipers failed to make vision anything other than a vague blur. At nearby Chanute Air Force Base, the anemometer whirred, and smoked, and its bearings locked when the wind passed 76 knots (87.4 miles per hour), making wind speed measurements impossible.

At about 1:30 P.M. Tahiko Laukkanen pulled her wind-buffeted automobile into a grocery store parking lot. She clutched a plastic scarf around her head, struggled to control the car door as the wind tore it from her grip, then slammed it and sprinted for the grocery store's entry. A deluge of rain obscured her vision and soaked her clothes. At the door she wrenched at the handle and pulled with all of her strength, but the door remained firmly closed. She stared in disbelief at the sign that said PULL. On the other side of the glass door she saw the store manager, Mr. Walker, rushing toward her, his face contorted in anguish. In his hand he held the keys that would unlock the door. From behind her someone screamed, "Look out!" Then she heard a crash, and a numbing pain hit her. She slipped into a red, then black, oblivion that spelled disaster for Tahiko Laukkanen.

Rantoul's local paper reported that a concrete and brick pylon, which at one time held up a PIGGLY WIGGLY sign, had collapsed on Tahiko Laukkanen and on the store manager, Walker, as Mrs. Laukkanen tried to open the door that had been locked against the wind. Walker died almost instantly.[1] The medics thought Mrs. Laukkanen died in the ambulance and stopped administering oxygen halfway to the hospital. When they arrived at the hospital, an alert nurse noticed that her iris contracted when exposed to a light. They began emergency procedures immediately. Mrs. Laukkanen remained in intensive care for two weeks slipping into and out of a coma. Finally, it was diagnosed that she would remain a brain-impaired, incontinent paraplegic for the rest of her life.

The Engineer

Charles N. Debes, a professional engineer who, along with his employee, Harry N. Cordes, ran a small multidisciplinary* firm in central Illinois, related his own tragic story of the incident to me following the meeting of Consulting Engineers Council of Illinois in 1967.

"It wasn't anything that we did. Heck, the contractor didn't even follow our plans and specifications. We specified hollow concrete block. He used lightweight aggregate hollow concrete block with fine thermal qualities but no strength. Its shear strength[†] isn't nearly as great as standard hollow concrete block. Standard hollow concrete block has a safety factor 50% greater than that of lightweight aggregate block. He left out the two courses of brick we designed for the fascia and substituted a single course of cut limestone. He didn't put in any of the steel we specified. Our design met code. Besides, our design was for a different location. They used our plans without telling us. We would never have designed a pylon like they built. They can't do that and hold us liable, can they? That just wasn't our work!

"The contractor's foreman told Harry that the only reason they used lightweight aggregate block was because the building materials yard had a whale of a special sale on it, and they thought it would be okay to use it for a wall that was not load bearing. In other words, they made a major change in our design. The court said that we should have specified the standard-weight concrete block for the failed pylon with "particularity." Cheez! Does that mean we should have had signs on the plans for every course of concrete block saying, 'This is standard concrete block—use it'? They used it on the rest of the structure. I don't know, Mr. Howell. I just don't know about this thing called justice. I've had to come out of retirement to work to try to pay off the judgment—over $200,000. The other defendants paid up front and got an agreement of nonsuit, whatever that is.

"Oh, and let me tell you about the insurance. We finished our plans and specifications in May of 1958—for another store. They wouldn't even hire us to do the fieldwork, just took the plans and gave them to their contractors. For years I carried professional liability insurance. Never had a claim. Then I retired. On April 30, 1962, that damn thing blew down. You'd think our statute of limitations would have protected me, but it had a fatal flaw. It didn't say how long after our work was done that action needed to be filed. I called my insurance guy. He said he'd 'look into it.' Didn't hear from him so I called again. And do you know what? He said there was no coverage because the claim had to be made during the currency of the policy, not when the work was done. I was shattered!"

---

* Usually mechanical, electrical, and structural engineering, but may include virtually all design disciplines.
† The strength to lateral loads, such as gusting wind.

I tried to explain to Charlie Debes about *occurrence* and *claims made** coverages, but he wasn't even slightly interested. He felt that when he retired, someone ought to have told him that the coverage was no longer in effect. I explained that many insurance people weren't even aware of the fact that claims made coverage had to be maintained until after death and probate in order to be safe. Debes went on:

"And, oh, let me tell you about my attorney. He's a nice enough guy. He may know his law, but I just think he wasn't aggressive enough on this case. He kept telling me I didn't have anything to worry about, but look what happened! Why couldn't he get into evidence the information about the storm? The Department of Commerce said it was a freak storm. Kind of like an act of God. Why should I be liable for that? The Consulting Engineers Council of Illinois tried to file a brief as *amicus curiae* (a friend of the court) and the appeals court wouldn't look at it. Said it was a jury question, a question of fact that the jury could have reasonably found us liable. They said our negligence need not be the only cause nor even the nearest in order to find us liable. If this is the way it is for engineers in private practice, we're crazy to stay in business!"

A Crazy Business

Indeed, this was the way it was with consulting engineers and architects in private practice. Their professional liability nightmare was to visit them about a decade before doctors were to be engulfed in their own malpractice maelstrom. We (Alexander & Alexander, Inc. [A&A], insurance brokers, and American Motorists Insurance Company [AMICO], a Kemper subsidiary) had been in a program of professional liability loss prevention and insurance for consulting engineers a little under four years when I met Charlie Debes in 1967. Although his story was tragic and seemed uniquely strange, it wasn't atypical. Claims were being made in ever-increasing numbers, with proximate relationships to the design professionals' skill extremely dubious. Failure in their professional proficiency did not seem to be the primary cause for claims.

The psychological trauma of professional liability claims against professionals has a devastating effect on the individuals involved. The finger of accusation destroys their sense of well-being and inevitably causes them to fall into deep depression. Even in our short, four-year involvement with this weighty problem, we knew of suicides, stress-related heart problems, psychological dysfunction, and flight from the profession—all triggered by the

---

* *Occurrence* coverage insures against claims for property damage or injury caused by a sudden and unexpected event during the currency of the policy, no matter when the claim is made after such a sudden and unexpected event; *claims made* coverage is for claims that are made during the currency of the policy and not after it has expired.

accusation that somehow, in some way, the failure in professional performance led to a seemingly unrelated loss.

Sure, in retrospect you can always find a "you should have." For instance, as with Charlie Debes: "You should have never taken an assignment in which you didn't perform the full scope of services; that is, you
should have performed the construction review to make certain that your
plans and specifications are, in general, followed." But the fact of the matter is that there were major failures in the overall design-construction system that had not been there 20 years before. And these failures were
becoming waking nightmares for professionals like Charlie Debes.

What had changed? Why, with historical suddenness, had this professional liability phenomenon visited virtually our entire nation? Why were
other countries, such as Japan, virtually free of this legal virulence? Could
we expect more instances of liability being found against consulting engineers when their professional performance's proximate relationship to any
loss might be tenuous at best?

One author laid the fault at President Truman's feet because on January 31, 1950, he decided to go ahead with the development of the hydrogen
bomb,[2] creating "the age of anti-technologists," that is, a public distrust of
all things scientific. While that date was close to the time when the claims
began to emerge, it seems likely that, as with the causes of war, the claims
were the result of highly variable factors. No single event or series of events
can explain the change in public and legal attitudes.

Our job at A&A and AMICO was to find answers to these complex
questions so that the enervation caused by professional liability claims did
not hamper the productivity of these vital professional people. We didn't
know what was happening or why. We did know that construction was a
complex process—far more intricate than most people believed. After all,
construction brings together a multitude of disciplines—mechanical, electrical, civil, structural, acoustical, architectural, geological, interior design, and
many others—that must be coordinated with precision. Then, too, there is a
diversity of people involved, each bent on furthering his or her particular job
or agenda. Machines, tools, and materials must be moved onto and off of the
job site in a synchronized way. Accidents must be avoided or paid for by the
party or parties at fault. Time must be watched with a critical eye since each
moment wasted costs someone money. It's no wonder that there are break-
downs, conflicts, and recriminations. The mystery is why they became so
emotionally charged and commonplace when they were so rare prior to
World War II.

Long, Long, Long Ago

At Meidum, Egypt, about 5,000 years ago, a pyramid was built that had design flaws. The pyramid failed and may have killed as many as 5,000 peo-

ple.[3] Its design departed from the concepts of the great Egyptian designer, Imhotep, in several respects. The result was a pile of rubble so huge that it was taken as a natural hill by many who saw it centuries later. Deductive analysis indicates that the lateral forces on the structure were too great for the angle of inclination, resulting in a slumping and collapse. This catastrophe caused the populace to shun the site for centuries[4] because of the ill omen it seemed to portend.[5] There is no evidence as to what may have happened to the designer, but the superstitious nature of the people at that time probably led them to conclude that the pyramid failed as a result of spiritual factors, not through the fault of the designer.

Designers on other contemporary projects, however, took note of the Meidum failure and changed their designs to avoid a like fate. The Bent Pyramid of Egypt is probably an example. Archaeologists noticed that the lower course of construction block was angled at approximately 54°, much steeper than the other pyramids in Egypt, but maybe akin to the Meidum Pyramid. The designer (not thought to be Imhotep) was obviously looking for a spire that would reach for the sky. About halfway up, the angle was dropped to about 43.5°, giving the pyramid its bent look. He also changed the type of stone. While archeologists were excavating at the bottom of the pyramid, huge amounts of stone rubble were uncovered, suggesting that its constructors had difficulty dealing with the steeper slope and lost control of their heavy loads which crashed at the base and turned to rubble, maybe even causing loss of life. The design received a change order and the easier, time-proven gradient of 43.5° was commenced. Also, a more consolidated type of stone was substituted. Was this caused solely by a design error? Probably. Was there any form of retribution? We can only surmise, but it was an era in which the code of kings held sway, and it may be that the parties involved lost their lives or limbs at the whim of the Pharaoh.

One can imagine the irate Pharaoh reproachfully addressing his designer:

"What do you mean, Saski, that you have to change the angle? Didn't you tell me that the increased angle would cause the sun to glint off the surface and that this would please the gods in the next world? Wasn't it you who convinced me to try an approach different from the one used by other Pharoahs; to use the greater angle and a different stone? Now, you say the construction is going badly and that you want to save me from needless expense by using the safer, better angle of 43.5°. You also want to change the quarry to one further from the building site, one with finer-grained stone? A more expensive act I cannot imagine. Do you take me for a fool—a buffoon to be trifled with on this holiest of structures that will ease my travel into the next world? Perhaps your severed head on an altar would placate the gods who confounded our construction problem. What would you say to that?"

Even in those ancient times argument may not have been a designer's strong suit, and he could not point out that his head upon the altar wouldn't change the fact that the steeper pyramid side angle increased the lateral load factor beyond Egyptian structural capabilities in 2000 B.C.

Engineering and architectural failures have been mentioned specifically in ancient history, for example, in the Code of Hammurabi (eighteenth century B.C.).[6] The attitude of that era was very much "an eye for an eye." If your failure in design (or construction) caused death, then you could be put to death by the wronged party. If you built a dike and it failed, flooding your neighbor's field, you had to pay for the resultant damage.

Retribution for design errors may have remained severe in the centuries that followed. In 480 B.C., Xerxes, King of Persia and son of Darius the Great (historical name: Darius the Builder), ordered a bridge to be built across the Hellespont, a narrow strait in northwestern Turkey (now called the Dardanelles). It seems that the Greeks had been annoying Xerxes with border disputes and revolts. To put an end to it, he needed to move his huge army across the Hellespont. Since his father Darius had built a bridge across the Bosphorus River, Xerxes may have reasoned that he could do the same across the Hellespont. This would enable him to loose his huge army against the errant, quarrelsome Greeks.

The first bridge built was destroyed by a storm, so Xerxes ordered the beheading of the engineers and builders, some 500 souls.[7] It may be assumed that Xerxes' builders and designers had families, friends, and fellow workers who were deeply and eternally affected by the harsh treatment meted out by the tyrannical leader. How this influenced their future design behavior may be guessed. We do know that the next bridge built had cables of flax weighing 50 pounds per foot! Papayrus cables were added as guys, connected to some 674 galleys acting as pontoons.[8] The cables were stretched across the Hellespont on the galleys, followed by planking perpendicular to the cables. Brush was then laid down and earth was piled on it to create a roadway. This bridge did not fail.

Was the second bridge overengineered (that is, had excess components and safety factors in the design)? The beheadings make it likely. Xerxes, like his modern-day counterparts—project owners—did not understand that one-of-a-kind engineering structures on the leading edge of technology often fail or have component failures. Failures teach,[9] and without them progress would be stifled. Xerxes' attitude may have bought him extreme engineering reticence in the future, which in the long run cost more than it gained him. In any event, his incursion into Hellas (Greece) ultimately failed miserably, largely because of the enormous logistical problems connected with trying to field 150,000 troops and hundreds of hungry horses. Xerxes will be remembered more for his despotic tyranny and failure to tend to details than for his appreciation of the art of design.

In Roman and Greek times, the designers seemed to be immune from recriminations due to design errors. At least the copiously recorded chronicles of construction implied that details of design were art forms—not subject to scientific certainty. When things went wrong, it was the gods having their fun. A failure was "too bad, but that's fate," rather than something that should put the designer in jeopardy.

The water supply of the city of Rome is an example.[10] The intricately designed water system had constant structural failures that required full-time maintenance crews. In addition, the leakage was prodigious. Some estimates are as high as 20%. (How much is lost to leakage in our modern cities? One water official for a West Coast city admitted to 7%.) The Roman designers sought to improve the integrity of the system by *puddling* the leaking cracks with a mixture of limestone and wood ash to seal the leaks with a temporary blockage—a method still used in New England in the nineteenth century—but to no avail. The water conduits were lined with a cement that cracked and spalled (chipped), destroying the containment integrity of the flumes (inclined channels for conveying water). Still the Roman officials looked upon leakage as we view internal combustion engine pollutants in our atmosphere; that is, it can't be helped. It's just part of the system.

Long, Long Ago

In medieval times, Gothic cathedrals became very popular, with their robust columns and artistic flying buttresses. Each city tried to outdo its neighbors by experimenting with designs to increase the height of the naves and spires. Great sums of money were required to build these structures. People might be starving, but the construction of the cathedrals would continue. The higher the cathedrals got, the more they cracked, sank, and collapsed. Each failure taught the designers lessons in design and construction.[11] When cathedrals did fail, the attitude appears to have been benign, explained away as "God's will." Maybe it was.

Long Ago

A design error of historic proportions was committed in 1624 by Henrik Hybertson, a Dutch naval architect and designer of the *Mayflower*. King Gustave II Adolf of Sweden commissioned Hybertson to design four warships that were to be the most decorated and heaviest armed in the then-known world.[12] The first ship, the *Vasa*, was completed in 1628. The vessel was beautifully carved, painted, and gilded, and it was huge by standards of the time. She displaced 1,400 tons (the *Mayflower* was 400 tons) and had a sail area of 3,800 square feet. Her armament was awe-inspiring: two decks of twenty-four cannons, and other ordinance providing a gross weight of 80 tons of bronze. Her mast towered 160 feet above her keel. She was a fearsome fighting machine, enough to start any naval buff's heart pounding, especially King Gustave II Adolf who said, "After God, it is the Navy which will determine the future prosperity of our country."

In the spring of 1628, the *Vasa* was towed from Blasieholmen Island, where she was built, to the naval dockyard at Stockholm. There her ballast was loaded with care, her cannons secured in place, and crew and soldiers assigned as her complement. Late on August 10, 1628, with bunting flying, a bevy of women and children on board, speeches made, and a festive air hanging over the harbor, the *Vasa* set sail to join the Swedish navy at Alvsnabben and take her rightful place as the most beautiful and dangerous warship ever constructed.

A slight breeze was blowing, with some gusting. Not a mile out, a heavy gust of wind caught her topsails and, within minutes, the *Vasa* had heeled over so that her lower (open) gunports were under water. The chilly sea flooded her almost immediately. The *Vasa* sank within minutes, with a heavy loss of life (approximately 400 persons were on board, most of whom were on the main deck). She came to rest, with her hull on the bottom, in 150 feet of water. Her masts protruded above the surface with top spars pointed at drunken angles, like a grim obscene gesture. The festive air ceased.

A board of inquiry was called the next day. Since Hybertson had died some time earlier, the board sought to blame the sailing master, the second in command, and the hand responsible for stowing the ballast. All vehemently disclaimed any culpability. It seemed that there had been a gross design flaw, but King Gustaf II Adolf had **approved** the design himself and had even set some dimensions. In view of this circumstance, the board of inquiry reasoned that it was best to close the inquiry without reaching any conclusions. Even then approving, as now, may have shifted some of the liability, but, of course, "The King can do no wrong" (Sir William Blackstone, circa 1765).

Keeping this loss in mind, and remembering that the same designer planned the *Mayflower*, you have to wonder if the *Mayflower* contained the same design flaws.

In third grade our teacher told us the story of the *Mayflower*.

"Children, you have no idea how much privation the Pilgrims went through in order to colonize America. They set sail on August 15, 1620, on board the *Mayflower*, accompanied by a smaller vessel, the *Speedwell*. They were forced back twice by storms with gale-force winds and heavy seas. All on board were violently ill, and many decided to give up the trip. The *Speedwell* was found to be unseaworthy, so her provisions and passengers were loaded onto the *Mayflower*. Over 100 passengers, plus a crew, were crowded into a space just 26 by 64 feet. They set sail again and were a few days out before they once more ran into high winds and mountainous seas. The Pilgrims complained of the tipping, pitching, and yawing of the *Mayflower*; virtually everyone on board was nauseated, vomiting, and disoriented. One of the *Mayflower's* main beams split, and many feared that she would be torn asunder. After repairs were made on her midship beam, they decided to continue on their voyage in spite of the oppressive conditions. They truly placed their lives in the hands of God.

"Things were so uncomfortable in the tipping, careening vessel that the captain and the leaders of the colonial company feared there would be mutiny. This fear led to the development of the *Mayflower Compact,* a document which, when signed, required obedience to any government formed by the colonial company.

"On November 20, 1620, the Pilgrims sighted land and with prayers answered, they went ashore the next day to praise God for their salvation. They had set sail for Virginia, but because of the vile pitching, rolling, and lack of navigational control of the *Mayflower,* there was no thought of continuing on to their original destination."

Can it be that Henrik Hybertson miscalculated the center of gravity on the *Mayflower* as well as the *Vasa,* and, had he not done so, would we be eating corn pone, grits, and ham for Thanksgiving? If the *Mayflower* had turned turtle as the *Vasa* did, we might celebrate Octoberfest today instead of Thanksgiving. Fate is a curious thing.

Evolution

Errors in design continued until recent modern times with no evidence that the designers were given anything but pity for the failures that ensued. In English common law the widest breadth was given architects and engineers for their design indiscretions. First, they were liable only to their client for any damages. Second, it seemed they had to have been grossly negligent or criminally culpable before they were required to pay damages.

All through the nineteenth century, the laissez-faire attitude continued with respect to design errors. Since it was the century of railroads, there were thousands of design errors, but they were treated as part of testing the limits of new horizons. Today we marvel at some of the rail structures, particularly bridges and tunnels, that were built to carry the silver ribbons of steel across the United States, Europe, and Asia. "How could they have done it?" you ask. The designs were complex, dangerous, sometimes as frail as match houses, but they worked!

We are awed at magnificient structures such as the Vienna Opera House. Following its first construction in 1873 it was found to be replete with omissions in the design.[13] The story goes that on the opening night, a very famous conductor was hired to lead the orchestra. He did so with a flair, bringing the house to its feet with "Bravos!" The intermission was announced, and *"Mein Gott,"* the audience screamed. There were no restrooms!

There were other failings in the structure, such as differential settlement or cracking of walls—so many that one of the architects, Eduard van der Null, could take the criticism no longer. After a short time he ended his life with a pistol ball. The other architect who worked on the design, August von Siccardsburg, died in disgrace soon after, some said of a broken heart due to the continuing belittling of the design.[14] Still there does not seem to be any record that damages were sought from either designer or their estates.

More recently we have had our share of design problems that have been treated in a fairly benign way. The crash and burning of the *Hindenburg* was one of these. This catastrophe led to a mild inquiry, but no horrendous liability as might be expected today. Then there was the St. Francis dam failure in southern California in 1926. Some 600 people were killed. The engineer of record was William Mulholland, a public works official who would not deign to seek private sector geotechnical help for the dam's design. Several foundation inadequacies were noted after the catastrophe.[15] Even so, they named a street in Los Angeles after Mulholland. His water district employers were sorry about the debacle, but those were the breaks, weren't they?

Another sensational tragedy was the collapse of the Tacoma Narrows bridge on November 7, 1940. It was a long (2,800-foot) suspension bridge, theoretically designed within the state of the art at the time of its failure. Whether it was state of the art is still hotly debated, both by structural engineers who lived at the time and by those born since.[16] It is known that the Washington State Bridge Authority was forced by Eastern banks to hire a highly acclaimed New York designer, Leon S. Moisseiff, because they did not trust the expertise of West Coast designers. This rankled the local Washington state engineers who later liked to say, "We told you so!"[17] It is interesting to note that a University of Washington professor of civil engineering and structural design lectured on the bridge's probability of failure at about the time it swung, bucked, and crashed into the Tacoma Narrows.

The bridge was called "Galloping Gertie" by all who crossed her. People joked about being seasick at the end of a crossing, largely because of her tendency to buck and sway. Adventurous folks would go on the bridge just for the trip—up, down, and sideways. Today the argument rages over what caused the collapse and, indeed, whether some of our other suspension bridges contain the same design faults.[18] Yet, there is no report of anyone seeking redress from Mr. Moisseiff, and his reputation as a bridge designer remains unsullied.[19] As an interesting historical footnote, the insurance agent for the bridge District, Hallet R. French, was so certain of the bridge's infallible safety that he pocketed much of the bridge's insurance premium and earned himself a stay at Walla Walla state prison.[20]

Modern Times

Our short foray into the history of architectural and engineering design errors seems to suggest that in most of human history such flaws were treated as part of the learning curve and, although unfortunate, were not something that brought down the world on the designers' heads (notwith-standing Xerxes and his harsh retribution for a failed bridge).

The suggestion that the changes in the public's perception of liability were the result of the development of the H-bomb seems too simple. The date seems correct, because it was about 1950 that claims against technical professionals started mounting, so much so that the American Institute of Architects initiated a program of professional liability insurance under the guidance of Victor O. Schinnerer & Company in 1956. However, other events happening in our country[21] at that time may have had an equal or more pronounced effect upon societal behavior.[22]

Some factors that need to be considered are:

- *Dramatic changes in moral perceptions.* There are those of us who are still gasping at the sexual revolution, the movies with scenes long thought forbidden, the explosion in drug use, and the runaway in-crease of white-collar crime. America seemed to have a new code of ethics, one that permitted excesses in moral deportment, which might include suing your neighbor over trivia, and certainly your designer if things didn't come out *just right.*

- *The mega-growth of the construction industry.* Huge jobs were every-where and there were not enough contractors to handle them. Long-standing friendships between the design teams and contractors were ruptured as new builders with low bids spread out across the country seeking jobs to fill their coffers.

- *The litigation explosion.* My being a lawyer by training (admitted to the Wisconsin Bar in 1950), may have led to my belief that the litiga-tion explosion may have had a major measure of influence on de-signers, doctors, lawyers, and products liability claims. It became easier and more rewarding for plaintiffs to sue all kinds of business-people during the 1950s and this has continued. Doctrines with tremendous implications, such as breach of implied warranty, strict liability, and death of contract disclaimers, were dreamed up and successfully tried by plaintiffs' attorneys. The new legal theories swelled, twisted, and contorted tort law into a three-ring circus that resulted in the "deepest pocket" (i.e., the party having the greatest resources) paying for almost any kind of bodily injury or property damage.[23]

These factors may be just the tip of the iceberg contributing to design-ers' liability problems. Obviously the problem is extremely complex and begs for major changes in social and human behavior before the enigma will abate. One overall idea suggests itself: There is rampant immorality in our business workplace feeding the notion that anything you can get away with is acceptable. That idea is having a devastating effect on our designers and other professionals.[24] The unfortunate truth is that the great majority of our professionals and businesspeople are honest and well intentioned, but their image is distorted by a few who have quirks of immorality. The public tends to make the illogical conclusion from these few that the specific proves the general. It does not. Our professional designers are producing high quality work and should be protected from spurious claims.

Chapter 2

Discovering Loss Prevention

We are all controlled by the world in which we live, and part of that world has been and will be constructed by men. The question is this: are we to be controlled by accidents, by tyrants, or by ourselves in effective cultural design?

—*Burrhus Fredric (B. F.) Skinner, 1972*

The insurance industry's tarnished image got that way largely because of the same malaise that struck most service industries following World War II in a rapidly expanding economy. It had too much business volume and too little time to do the job right. Insurance companies, banks, construction companies, medical services organizations—virtually all service industries burgeoned. They grew so fast that they had to shortcut some of the services they sold. Things had to be rushed just to stay even with the demand. Banks had long lines of customers in a hurry to be served. Doctors had waiting rooms bursting with patients (and Doc's prices went through the roof). Subdivisions swept over the countryside and people fought for the houses. Much of the world's population demanded goods and services in endless quantity and endless variety.

Most corporations became preoccupied with a *short term, bottom line* mentality; that is, do anything to make profits and do this even to the exclusion of customers' wants or needs.

While the insurance companies were doing this, what were the U.S. automakers doing? What about law firms, pharmaceutical houses, and other companies? Publicly traded corporations in particular placed bottom line thinking in the forefront because managements' income is usually tied to the stock price to earnings ratio. If the stock price goes up, so does income; conversely if it goes down, in theory, there is less money for management to take home.

In this hurry up and grab the cash environment, insurance companies and all other service industries almost *had* to become impersonal. It was either resort to computer-produced form letters, long lines, and drive-in claims handling facilities or turn business away, something the bottom line couldn't stand. As a result, it was not long before policyholders viewed insurance companies as selling fungibles, that is, one company's insurance policy was pretty much the same as another's, like grains of rice in a sack. They were all the same, all impersonal. They didn't seem to care because if they drove one customer away there were two others to fill the void.

As young people were hired to service the insurance business, they followed the role models of their supervisors, characterized as "rushed indifference." They learned that drowning in paper was a normal condition of their employment. So it became de rigueur to treat the customer in a hasty-get-rid-of-the-problem manner; to use the easiest way out, whatever it might be. They just didn't know any better. There was no one to teach them that there might be a better way, a way that paid careful attention to the policyholders' wants and needs. It seemed that the success-through-service culture that had built up during the depression was lost.

Most insurance companies tried to distance themselves from the unattractive image through glitzy, yet somehow homely, advertising that focused on safety and appealing family themes. They endlessly chanted the differences between themselves and their competitors. But was anyone really listening? Flamboyant claims of caring and concern just didn't add up to the type of service the public was receiving.

In this negative environment, an insurance salesperson had a hard job trying to convince a potential policyholder that his company was somehow different and better. The public had become so jaded by constant hype about services and products that they were just not buying what they were being told. Claims of financial quality and stability, better service, faster claims handling, or anything else that might lead them to make a decision one way or another were dismissed as sales puffery. Selling property and casualty insurance had become rough, discouraging duty.

Selling Property and Casualty Insurance

In the early 1950s my family and I were living in Seattle. I was trying to sell property and casualty insurance in a tough buyer-resistant environment. I worked for a large direct writing* mutual†, the Employers Mutuals of Wausau. It was a good company. From what I could determine, all of the employees wanted to deliver better insurance service at a fair price. Their

---

* An insurance company that does not sell through independent agents or brokers, but has its own sales force.

† A company owned by the policyholders as opposed to stockholder ownership.

philosophy was based on a heritage that encouraged them to act in the service of others. They believed, as I did, that they were making a contribution to society by helping to reduce worker-related injuries, but also providing financial redress when an injury occurred. Conveying this philosophy to sales prospects, however, was a task that felt equal to the climb up Mount Everest.

The Employers Mutuals of Wausau was started by a group of forest products employers in Wisconsin in 1911 when the first state workmen's (now workers) compensation law was declared constitutional. They started their own insurance company because they were either unable to purchase workers compensation insurance or they thought it was too expensive. The prosaic insurers said of the new company, "You'll lose your shirt!"

In fact, there was considerable risk, because the fledgling company had little capital and surplus (retained earnings) and virtually no loss experience as a basis for premium rates. It had, however, several constructive ideas that, in retrospect, looked like genius. For example, all of the participating employers agreed to use intensive means to reduce losses by protecting their employees from injury. They did this through loss prevention engineering: hardhats in the forest were mandatory, all workers wore steel-capped boots, power saws had guards to keep errant human limbs from being sliced, and yelling "Timber!" was required during the felling of all trees. Dozens of other methods were used as well, all aimed at preventing work-related injuries.

The Employers Mutuals of Wausau wrote its first workmen's compensation policy on September 1, 1911, for the Wausau Sulphate and Fibre Company. It still insures the same company under its new name, Mosinee Paper Corporation. Employers Mutuals also had a tough-minded manager, Hans J. Hagge, who believed in its ultimate success with a missionary's zeal. Known to all who worked for him as "Mister" Hagge, he served as a model for the employees to emulate, and he saw to it that they didn't lose sight of their objective: Reduce worker-related losses.

While detractors hooted, these hard-driving pulp, paper, and timber men of Employers Mutuals set about their task of coping with the workers compensation problem with dedication and vigor. Careful underwriting,* loss prevention engineering, and enlightened claims management (it pioneered rehabilitation and industrial hygiene) led Employers Mutuals to a profit its first year and it paid a dividend to its policyholders from that year until at least 1970 when I lost track. The hooters had been wrong.

By the 1950s the Employers Mutuals of Wausau† had a price advantage

---

* Making an assessment of a risk to determine whether it fits the company's standards for acceptance as a policyholder. Literally, taken from Lloyds of London's practice to use a slip describing a risk (usually a ship) and having the various insurers sign on the bottom of the slip if they were willing to take a part of the risk; thus, they "underwrote."

† Now the Wausau Insurance Companies is a subsidiary of the Nationwide Group, Columbus, Ohio.

over many of the stock insurance companies because of its fifty-year record of uninterrupted dividend payments. Yet, selling it as *the* company to an insured was not like falling off a log. The sales training manuals admonished: Meet all of the prospect's objections. If a prospect says, "Well, I'm not sure about the company's financial condition," meet that objection by saying, "Our company Best's* insurance guide rating is A+ (excellent). That is the highest possible." By meeting their objections, you can make the sale.

Unfortunately, that was not generally the case. Logically you'd think that people would buy at a better price from a stable insurance company, but price differential was a small factor in their buying decision. There is a mystique in getting orders that seems to be quite independent of conventional wisdom. I learned early that trying to sell insurance on the basis of price alone is a fool's errand. Certainly, price is a consideration, but it ranks below several others. Potential policyholders seemed to want something more than a good price and a good Best's rating. Their questions seemed to say to me, "Yes, but what else will you be doing for me?" Finding the right answer was a puzzle.

When I first started selling insurance in Seattle, I learned that you had to sell something other than a piece of paper with writing on it if you wanted to pique the interest of the potential policyholder. Since the state had a monopoly on workers compensation insurance†, I concentrated on other lines; one insurance line that seemed to be neglected by many agents and brokers was fidelity bonds. Employers Mutuals taught us that "Knowledge is earning power," and I believed that. It had a training manual on fidelity bonds as well as advisors who could fill in the voids from their personal experience. I became a local expert on fidelity bonds and took to the field.

My first few calls revealed a common misconception: "I don't need fidelity coverage. I trust my employees. We're like a family here. No one would steal. Besides, my system is foolproof." It was obvious that if I were going to sell any fidelity bonds, I'd have to develop a new approach. It went something like this:

Howell: Mr. White, I'd like to talk to you about fidelity coverage.

White: Don't need it. I have full faith in my employees. Most of them have been with me for over 10 years. If they were stealing I'd know it by now. My system is foolproof.

---

*The company that rates insurance companies by their financial strength and policyholders' satisfaction.

† Some states run their own insurance companies to provide workers compensation coverage, to the exclusion of private sector insurers. In 1956 eight states operated monopoly workers compensation insurance funds.

Howell: Mr. White, I'm sure your employees are, in the main, honest. But things happen that you don't know about that might affect their behavior—sick children, divorces, and unexpected expenses may change attitudes. If I can show you how someone might be stealing from you, will you then reconsider the coverage?

White: You mean you think you know more about my business than I do? I think you're wasting your time. There are no holes in my check-in system. In the laundry and dry cleaning business (his company was very large with about 10 outlets) everything has to balance. But if you can study my setup without upsetting everyone, go ahead.

Howell: Thanks, Mr. White. Why don't you introduce me as an office equipment salesman. That way no one will get upset.

Then the fun began. Every study of control systems I conducted revealed that the systems had holes in them. In White's company, all items brought in for cleaning or laundering had sequentially numbered work slips. These slips followed the items to be cleaned or laundered throughout the process. The customer was given one copy of a three-part set with which they reclaimed the cleaned item, one copy followed the work onto the floor and returned on the cleaned, packaged item, and one copy was filed for production control. When the customer came in for the cleaned item, an employee had access to all three. These could be stapled together and VOID written across them as if the job had been stopped due to expense or some other consideration. This could be done only on large orders such as drapes or blankets. The money paid by the customer could then be pocketed.

When I showed this exposure to White he said, "You win. I'll buy the fidelity bond." We paid on it a year later when the system failed as predicted. The culprit had worked for White for eighteen years and had given herself a $100-a-week "raise." White was in shock, but she cried and complained about the expenses she had in raising her children as a single parent, and he forgave her.

By using this approach I sold a flock of fidelity bonds.* This experience taught me that selling a service related to the insurance coverage made it easier.

St. Louis, Where Things Happen

In 1956 the Employers Mutuals of Wausau transferred me from Seattle to St. Louis, where Employers was a large writer of workers compensation coverage and where prospects were said to be better.

---

* It never ceased to amaze me how much white collar-crime was being committed. The Seattle claims manager of Employers Mutuals of Wausau told me, some years later, that virtually all of the coverage I had sold had claims made against them within three years!

Demographers say that Cincinnati, St. Louis, and Milwaukee (in that order) are the toughest cities in the United States in which to change peoples' buying habits through sales effort. Even so, I was excited about the potential, and I set about the task of selling workers compensation coverage. I found out immediately that business people in St. Louis were some of the nicest in the country. They were unfailingly polite and attentive. They just didn't want to leave their current agent or broker for a relative stranger making untested representations, even for a possible 15% savings on their workers comp or a 10% savings on their comprehensive general liability* premiums. Where St. Louis was concerned, the demographers knew their demographics.

To help loosen these bonds, Employers Mutuals advised its sales force to offer prospects insurance surveys on a no-obligation basis. The surveys would be a kind of a report card on the coverages the prospect had in place. Was the coverage adequate, fairly priced, and so forth? As before, Employers Mutuals' philosophy of "Knowledge is earning power" provided us with the necessary tools to conduct such surveys. The company had prepared preprinted survey sheets that simplified the exercise. There were checklists for various types of businesses that made surveying relatively painless as well as accurate. Want to survey a bank? Pull out the bank survey sheets. How about an auto dealer? Just pull out the prescribed sheets.

It became evident to me that it was difficult to become expert in all types of risks. It was more effective to be expert in a specific business field. Because Employers Mutuals was already strong in the construction industry, I chose this field and studied it from all angles. The task was relatively easy because I'd had earlier construction experience in the U.S. Army 173rd Engineer Combat Battalion for a number of years, and I knew how construction problems could defeat even the most skilled manager. It wasn't long until I felt fairly proficient in the coverages for contractors, ready-mix dealers, timber companies, home builders, and most other areas of the construction trades. Like most in the sales force I knew that to be effective in sales I had to be thoroughly knowledgeable about my prospects' businesses. Many of us who were interested in construction and related industries joined the Associated General Contractors as associate members. We also joined the Associated Home Builders, subscribed to the *F. W. Dodge Reports* for construction bidding information, read the *Engineering News Record* magazine, and avidly perused the *Daily Journal of Commerce* which listed jobs for bid, bidders, and other items of interest. In essence, we immersed ourselves in the construction industry culture and became *one of them*.

I still wasn't fully convinced that we could *really* affect loss ratios with our loss prevention engineering, but I stuck to the script and approached

---

* Coverage that would protect against liability imposed by law, or assumed under an indemnifying provision of agreements, for damages because of bodily injury or property damages arising out of insured risks and hazards in connection with the insureds conduct of business.

something on the order of eight to ten risks per day. We were being paid on a draw plus commission. If we got orders, we made money. Promises didn't count. (We had a saying, "It counts as an order only if you can spend the commission at A&P.") That gave us the impetus to make dozens of calls with the hope that sheer numbers would translate into orders for coverage. It didn't.

Most of the sales force were pretty hard up financially, but we saw that we could make money if we just learned how. We had a good model in Charlie Beeler, a senior salesperson who was doing very well financially and seemed to be able to get orders when no one else could. He was generous with his knowledge and helped the younger salespeople all that he could.

Besides Charlie we had a thoroughly enlightened underwriter by the name of Sam Alcorn.* They taught us about retrospective rating plans and how to use the Retrospective D[†] formula to be more competitive. In essence, they used the policyholder's dividend (which was not guaranteed) to absorb any penalty. For example, if the maximum were 117.5% (the 17.5% being the adverse losses penalty) of the standard premium, and that percentage were multiplied by 85% (Employers Mutuals had been paying a 15% policyholder's dividend for over 50 years) the result would be 99.9% (just about exactly the standard premium). Thus the risk that the policyholder was taking was very slight. This was a powerful stimulus to pursue loss prevention activity.

Retrospective rating plans had a distinct advantage over standard premium discount rating plans for the larger workers compensation risks, particularly if the policyholder's management believed that it could reduce its losses through loss prevention engineering, and if it effectively implemented it. These rating plans provided distinct monetary incentives for a company's management to reduce claims frequency and severity in order to increase profitability and competitiveness. This was, and is, especially true in construction, where every point means the difference between getting a job and losing it. A reduction in claims might mean a premium return. More losses might mean paying a penalty premium. Tie that to a company's bonus system and you've got middle management's attention! It was a wonderful sales tool because most stock (as opposed to mutual) companies could not compete with us effectively.

The insurance industry runs a service called the Workers Compensation Rating Bureau that collects loss information on all employers and pub-

---

* Sam was to become a well-known figure in the insurance industry. He joined a brokerage company in 1959, rose in its ranks, and finally was made a senior vice president of Bayly, Martin & Fay. It was bought by Sperry and Hutchinson Co., the green stamp company. He was very active in the Society of Chartered Professional Casualty Underwriters.

† A rating plan that charged premium after the fact (may be written on a one or three years basis) based upon the actual losses that the insured incurred. A basic premium is charged + losses x a loss conversion factor (that is, a factor that reflects loss adjustment expenses and loss expenses) + taxes, subject to a maximum and minimum to develop the total premium.

lishes a modifier for every insured within its jurisdiction. This factor is applied to workers compensation rates based upon the individual loss experience of the employer. One employer in the same classification might be
required to pay more (or less) premium per employee due to its experience.
Each employer also has various classifications that are published for the
type of work the employees are doing, and the rate for each type of work is
governed by the exposure (as shown by historic loss data collected on each
type of work; a steel erector, for example, has a greater exposure and a
higher rate than a typist).

The Bureau modifier for a particular employer could be acquired with
a simple phone call. The Bureau, however, would give you loss runs showing what actual losses had been incurred only if you had a letter of autho-
rization from the insured employer. Even so, when we made sales calls we
were armed with the modifier and had a substantial subject to talk about
with the employer. We tended to call on those employers whose modifiers
were adverse because we knew that they might be paying more for their
workers compensation coverage than their competitors and thus be receptive to anything that might enable them to reduce their expenses. By reducing their workers compensation coverage costs, we would increase their
competitive edge.

Another addition to my service quiver was the review of the general
and special conditions of a construction job to make certain that the necessary insurance was in place to conform with the contract's terms and conditions. It was shocking to learn that most contractors would take on jobs
without the slightest attention to the insurance conditions. The requirements for builder's risk* insurance would stipulate that it should be "all
risk," without sufficient definition as to what was meant by "all risk." Did
"all risk" include flood, earthquake, and acts of God? Often I found that
contractors didn't even have completed operations coverage to protect
them against liability if property damage or injury (e. g., a door falling on
someone or a drain backing up) were to ensue after the job had been completed. Worst of all, they would sign contracts that made them liable,
under a hold harmless and indemnity clause, even for the sole negligence
of the indemnitee, that is, the owner. Many insurance companies refused to
write such coverage, but the contractors seemed oblivious to that fact. It
was challenging to try to find where there was inadequate protection.
Most often their current agent or broker benefited from my service, but
that's life.

---

* The coverage placed in effect during the course of construction; also called COC insurance;
tends to be a difficult coverage to properly design because of the many nuances of different
constructions sites.

Contractors: An Easy Sell?

The contractors liked being told how their insurance was doing, but most of them would listen politely and act unconvinced. They didn't want to rock the boat. Earlier I mentioned that people in St. Louis were polite and attentive—well, not always. One employer I called on put me through a gut wrenching, but edifying, experience. When I stepped into this contractor's office, I should have known there was something wrong. The secretary looked absolutely terrified; not just scared, but more as if she had just looked death in the face. When I said I wanted to see the owner, she scuttled off with deep concern written on her face, muttering incantations, her eyes wide with trepidation. She showed me into the boss's office with a vague wave of her hand. The exchange with the owner went something like this:

Howell: Good morning, sir, may I have a few moments of your time to talk about your workers compensation coverage. I notice from the Rating Bureau that you're paying a 34% debit.

Contractor: No! Can't you see that I'm busy? I've already got workers compensation insurance—don't need any more. Especially from a guy who's probably never done a day's work in his life. Now, get lost!

Howell: Yes, sir, I can see you are busy. Perhaps there's a better time, if you could please tell me when.

Contractor: Well, jeez H cripes! Come back at 6:00 on Saturday morning. If I'm not here, just wait!

Howell: Thank you, sir.

On the next Saturday at 6:00 A.M., I was in his construction yard. He showed up at about 6:15. He was covered with cement dust from head to toe as usual. (Had he slept that way?) He looked madder than a Barcelona bull on fiesta day. He came out of his pickup truck with muscles bulging and mouth going a mile a minute. He was built like an M-1 tank and used every ounce of his 225 pounds in a pose that would have been labeled *Intimidation* if he were a painting in the St. Louis Museum of Art.

Contractor: Why, you S.O.B.!!! I told you I had plenty of insurance. Now, get the hell out of here, before I throw you out, and don't come back—EVER!!!

Hey, what a challenge! He wouldn't even talk. I let him cool down for about two weeks and went back one day at about 5:30 P.M.. (Contractors put in long days, doing their paperwork in the evenings and equipment maintenance in the early morning.) I hoped he would be too tired to bluster. Would he hit me?

Howell: Hi there. Are you over being mad? I say that because the last time I saw you, you were really sore. I know it wasn't me 'cause you don't know me well enough to be that sore—not at me anyway.

Contractor: Well, I'll be damned! I used all of my best anti-salesman tricks on you, and here you are. All that insulting language, and you come back for more. What do I need to call you to scare you off? So, I told you I had all the insurance I need. What do ya wanna do, twist my arm?

(He flexed his huge biceps, and I cringed.)

Howell: No, I'd just like to collect all of your insurance policies, get a letter to the Rating Bureau for your loss records, and do a no-obligation insurance survey and claims analysis. If I can figure out how to cure your 34% debit, I hope you'll give me your business. Also, the next time you get a job, I'll review the general and special conditions to make sure your insurance coverages are adequate.

Contractor: Well, you're probably wasting our time, but okay.

We got out all of his policies and found some major omissions, but more important were his workers compensation losses. They were almost all back injuries. He was doing heavy concrete work, so maybe that wasn't too unusual. However, I did a chronological spreadsheet on the claims, and the losses grouped periodically like a tidal chart—waves, due to claims frequency, were distributed evenly throughout the year. Claims seemed to bunch up about every six to eight weeks. It was a puzzle. What would make the claims suddenly appear in groups with such regularity? I pondered it for a couple of weeks and then took it to one of Employers' older loss prevention engineers, Jim Miller.

Jim: Easy, rockin' chair money.

Howell: What do you mean?

Jim: Don'tcha know anything? Your guy is in concrete work, right? He hires when he's got work and lays off when the job is done. The jobs last about six to eight weeks. Just before he lays off, the guys know about it, and they get really bad backaches. You should know that at least 14% of the workers comp claims have elements of fraud in them—maybe more. The guys collect workers compensation for back injuries and sit in rockin' chairs humming tunes, like "*Wabash Cannon Ball.*"

Jim went on to explain how they would set up cameras in the backs of fake laundry trucks trying to get pictures of the malingerers bowling, roofing their houses, climbing trees, and other types of activities. He said that they were only partially successful, but he told some humorous tales about catching some of the goof-offs doing pretty far out things while contending that they had bad backs. Like the guy who entered a rodeo and rode a bucking bull. They took movies of that.

"The trouble is," Jim concluded, "medical people can rarely tell if the injured employee really has a bad back or is just faking it. It makes back cases the toughest to adjust. That's why they are the most suspect for fraud."

When I returned to see my concrete contractor at 6:00 A.M. on a Saturday with the survey and the claims analysis, his jaw went slack and he kept muttering, "I'll be damned. I'll be damned." He changed his way of doing business, hired a smaller, almost permanent, crew, and stretched his work into a longer period so that he never had to have layoff periods. It worked. The claims stopped and his modification went from a debit to a credit in less than two years. We got all of his insurance coverages (except performance bonds). He then would tell anyone who'd listen what a genius I was. I never thought it was necessary to tell him that the genius was Jim Miller.

Yes, But Just What Do Loss Prevention Engineers Do?

I was really curious about what a loss prevention guy could do with a contractor in order to reduce the chance for workers compensation or general liability claims, so I asked one of the other loss prevention guys, Roy Wenneman, to take me on a survey. What a surprise! We drove up to the construction site and parked. As I rose to get out of the vehicle he said, "Wait a minute! We do much of our work from here. Just look at the job. How's the housekeeping? It looks fair, but they need to tighten up. Look at that spilled lumber pile with timbers that might trip someone. How about that crane lifting material over a public thoroughfare with no street level guard? Did you notice those two guys going onto the job site without hard hats? The rolled-up plans mean they're probably architects or engineers. They know better than that. Notice the welder on the tenth floor operating without a spark-arrester screen. Most course-of-construction fires are the result of welders' sparks. He could burn the whole job down. Look at the wind-borne particulates from the sprayed on fireproofing (at that time asbestos). They'll get claims from the neighbors for that. I give this guy's management a C."

This was all before we even got out of the car. Once we started walking around, even more evidence of lack of safety control became obvious: unguarded, open stairwells; power sources not properly grounded; no fire extinguishers where they should have been; lack of respirators for the welders; and other safety violations. I asked Roy, "Is the usual job like this one?"

"Unfortunately," he replied, "this guy is average. He's got a lot riding on getting the work finished. Sometimes they let the reward of completion interfere with their safety judgment. Contractors are risk takers. They try to pull off things that you and I would never undertake. They make money by taking chances, with our money. That's where we have a problem, but that's why we can sell insurance."

Roy took me to a job where they had done some blasting. He had done a preconstruction survey in the construction site's neighborhood, drawing pictures and taking photographs of every building within the block and noting cracks in the foundations, walkways, and walls. He left copies with the building owners. Even so, the Company's phone started ringing at the first blast. A householder outside the preconstruction survey zone yelled into his phone, "You're ruining my house! Get someone over here, I want to make a claim!" This was a job for the loss prevention people, like Roy, not claims; maybe they could forestall a claim.

Roy asked me, "Hey, Ed, do you want to see some real, honest-to-goodness magic? Just like a rabbit from a hat?"

"Hey, Roy, sure. If you think you can pull off a magic trick or voodoo, I want to see!"

Roy was a patient man. No matter how perturbed the claimant, he remained calm and reassuring. "Don't you worry, sir, if our insured caused any damage, we'll fix it." Then he'd set up his brass pins. They were brass rods with flattened ends. By balancing them on end, he created a vibration sensing system of several different length pins that would fall over if they received even a slight jar. With different lengths they would respond to different groundwave frequencies. Roy jumped lightly on the floor and all the pins would fall over. He then said to the claimant, "I guess the jolt that you think caused the cracks was a lot bigger than my jumping. Is that right, sir?"

"You, bet. It was tremendous!" the claimant replied.

"Okay." Roy retorted "At 1:00 P.M. a charge is going to be set off that the logs show is the same size as the one you're complaining about." Roy then set up the pins and sat watching them. At 1:00 there was a loud, "Crump!" but the pins didn't even teeter. Roy looked at the claimant, who looked very distressed.

"It's some kinda trick. How do you explain them cracks in my plaster. They weren't there before the blasting! And that's fer sure!"

"I don't know," Roy responded. "Do you have a broom I could borrow?" The claimant looked surprised, but brought Roy a broom. Roy took one straw out of the broom, went over to the cracked wall, inserted the straw lengthwise and twisted it. Pulling it out, he ask the claimant, "What's that on the straw?"

"Looks to me like cobwebs," the claimant replied.

"Exactly," Roy retorted, "and notice they have dark dust on them. They must've been in that crack for a long time. Do you think maybe that crack was there for a long time, but you just didn't notice it until the blasting started?"

"Wull, I'll be!" the potential claimant retorted, "I'd never have believed it if I hadn't seen it. I just never noticed them cracks before. I guess the joke's on me!"

As we left, Roy grinned and said, "See, magic, just like I said."

Another claim was averted*, and I got a valuable lesson in loss prevention: Never, ever take the obvious for granted. This lesson came into valuable use some years later.

How the Network Works

The network theory works in property and casualty insurance sales. My difficult-to-get-to-know concrete contractor introduced me to his ready-mix supplier, who introduced me to some river contractors (the Mississippi and Missouri rivers require constant nudging to keep them in line), who introduced me to some railroad tie manufacturers. On my own I met some home builders, mechanical contractors, and steel erectors and succeeded in developing a client base.

Because railroad tie manufacturers were in the timber industry, Employers Mutuals' underwriters were familiar with their exposures. Not many people know that St. Louis once was the U.S. center for railroad tie manufacturers and hardwood floor producers. Millions of railroad ties were produced annually (pressure treated with creosote) and shipped to the various trackages throughout the country to replace worn-out ties or to become new railway rights-of-way. Nor do many people know that these manufacturers have fierce workers compensation problems (backs again) from lifting ties and wrestling logs out of the woods. Those ties weighed 110 pounds apiece—backaches are real.

The peculiar thing I found was that the tie cutters worked as independent contractors. Often they were families who liked working in the woods, which was wholly understandable since the flora and fauna of the Ozark Plateau are enchanting. What was remarkable was the fevered pace at which the tree cutters worked and the long hours they put in—12 to 14 a day. The trees they cut were tough, resistant white and red oaks, so formidable that if you hit a knot wrong you'd end up with a screaming, slashing, runaway chain saw back in your lap.

These trees towered in the deciduous forests and were the crop of the toughest bunch of people I have ever encountered. Most of them had fingers or toes missing, but that didn't slow them an iota. They all had different techniques for snaking the logs out of the woods. Some used mules; others built Rube Goldberg type winch-and-pulley systems to get the logs to a staging area where they were rough-cut. The log base was sold to floor and barrel makers, the balance was used for railroad ties. The woodsman's uniform was bib overalls, sometimes with a T-shirt the color of an elephant under-

---

* Roy told me they weren't always so lucky. On one job the charge was improperly tamped, and the blast shook three houses off their foundations. "That's why we have insurance," he said with a philosophical shrug.

neath, but many times just bare skin was showing. My necktie was out of place so I stopped wearing it. Even so, they kidded me about my city clothes.

These handsome Scots-Irish, soft-drawled woodsmen worked so hard it was amazing. Blame their zeal on piecework, which was how they were paid. The workers compensation underwriter was upset with a piecework risk. It seems they felt that safe conduct went out the window when the workers income was determined by piecework. "Heck, they'll do anything to increase the money they make—even tie back the sawguards," was their thought. Maybe so, but it did not show up in Employers Mutuals of Wausau's experience.

The Missouri State Industrial Accident Commission* made the railroad tie manufacturers treat these woodsmen as employees, as opposed to independent contractors, for workers compensation reasons. If they were independent contractors the tie manufacturers would not have been responsible for their job-connected injuries. The Commission didn't seem to like an absence of workers compensation coverage based on (what they perceived to be) a legal technicality; that is, the contention that "They are not my employees since they are not on my premises, nor are they under my direction and control" (the test for an employee as opposed to an independent contractor). The Commission countered, "While they might not be under your immediate direction and control, they could be if you wanted them to be. In addition, you grade the ties—A, B, and C—and that gives you a modicum of direction and control. Your premises are anywhere you do business. That means the woods. We rule that they are your employees."

This edict made these risks ripe for a workers compensation Retrospective D program with its built-in incentive for reduction of losses. I suggested they buy such a plan from us, without knowing how we could reduce losses, and they bought the coverage. Then we talked the manufacturers into paying a no-loss bonus on each delivered tie, more pay overall on ties delivered in any given month if there were no workers compensation losses (other than minor medical claims). It worked.

River contractors had vicious workers compensation and employer's liability problems too, because they had multiple legal exposures. They not only had the state workers compensation law to contend with, but also Longshoremen's and Harbor Workers' coverage† and Jones Act coverage‡. The latter act was passed to give employers' liability coverage to

---

* The state appointed body that rules on workers compensation claims and exposures.

† A federal law passed in 1927 for injuries occasioned on navigable waters, but on jobs incidental to the operation of a vessel such as stevedores, ship painters, vessel repairmen, tallymen, freight handlers, adjustors.

‡ The Federal Maritime Act of 1920. Applies to seamen only, but covers injuries, as well as death, occurring anywhere within admiralty jurisdiction, which means all navigable bodies of water within a state or on the high seas. It covers risks incident to the seaman's calling, thus there is an overlap among Longshoremen's and Harbor workers and Jones Act laws; the plaintiff is allowed to invoke any statute.

members of the crew whenever they were injured, regardless of fault, whether it was caused by a fellow employee or even if there were contributory negligence.

These various laws created ambiguity as to what needed covering when. The courts called this a "twilight zone." For example, suppose a crew member of a vessel was burned while welding a rudder on shore. Workers comp claim or Jones Act? Not always clear. It was the same with the Longshoremen's and Harbor Workers exposure which differentiated between "local" employment and "nonlocal." For example, a dredge cutting a new channel would have workers whose job was "local" in nature—not subject to Longshoremen's and Harbor Workers' coverage—while an employee on a dredge working in navigable waters to clear a channel was deemed to be doing "nonlocal" work subject to the Longshoremen's and Harbor Workers benefits. How did they figure that?

The intricacies of this puzzle of words would make any defense attorney glow with the expectation of getting rich out of endless litigation. They often did.

The river contractors were incensed. They thought that the marine underwriters were charging what the traffic would bear for their marine insurance rather than fair rates based on losses. They contended that their experience on the river was very good to excellent. They contended that they paid their employees so well (30% above scale) for their labor-intensive work, the crews couldn't afford to get injured—so they didn't. (Does that make sense?) I talked with an independent marine insurance expert and broker, Jack Fleisch.

"Yes," he said, "they are paying too much for their protection and indemnity insurance (for Jones Act exposures), but there are so few markets, what can we do about it?"

"I don't know," I countered, "but let's try."

So I teamed up with Jack, who was well past retirement age (75 plus). "Oh, I love a good fight! The underwriters may put me on their 'prohibited list,' but what the hell!" Jack sang out. He was a true throwback to a different age. He wore high stiff collars, a pince-nez, a heavy gold chain on a tailor-made three-piece suit, and sometimes even spats. He was an outstanding maritime insurance specialist and had an impressive list of clients. Most of all, serving the needs of his clients came above all else.

Jack had an awesome grasp of his subject. When we were traveling to places such as Cairo (pronounced kay-roe), Illinois, he used to tell me about the history of marine insurance. He operated as an independent broker, housed with a large international insurance brokerage company. He stressed the constant need for utmost good faith in dealings between underwriters and marine insurance brokers. Time and again he would say, "Without utmost good faith in all of my dealings, I wouldn't be sitting here. I'd have been a has-been. Keep in mind, the marine insurance business would not have survived several centuries without the utmost good faith between the parties. Remember that, and practice that, and you can be a success in the insurance business. Without it, in my eyes, you are a nullity." He talked about particular* and general† average clauses and the Inchmaree clause,‡ but most interesting was his discussion of limitation of liability.§ It really captured my imagination.

Jack didn't like being forced to use one or two marine insurance underwriters that had a minimonopoly on river business. I, too, didn't like being locked out of this lucrative, challenging market. We concocted a plan: He would place the protection and indemnity‖ coverages (for Jones Act exposures) with a marine underwriter who was unable to write anything other than marine insurance, while I got the balance from Employers Mutuals. Our underwriter had to get home office approval, but after a series of phone conferences, with lots of talk about utmost good faith, it was arranged. We got the two underwriters to agree on which company would be responsible for the various exposures. The marine underwriter would take all Jones Act claims, and we would insure the balance. There was no written document between the underwriters—just trust.

A Jones Act claim was elective. The injured employee could sue under the Jones Act and wait for trial or he could take "maintenance and cure" under the state workers compensation law.# Instances of injured employees electing to pursue the Jones Act course were rare. Workers compensation was faster, better, and they didn't have to face the Federal Limitation of Liability Statute.** In our experience, the marine underwriter was called on to settle few property damage claims not associated with injured employees. Our experience with the injured crew members was also good. We had a winner.

---

* A partial loss caused by a marine peril, which has to be borne by the person upon whom it falls, since the other shippers would not receive benefit from the loss.

† A loss that is less than total that benefits all interests in a marine venture in proportion to how much their interests were preserved, such as a voluntary sacrifice of ship or cargo to preserve the interests of all. For example, when cargo might be jettisoned to lighten the ship to save it, all shippers would share in the loss of the jettisoned cargo.

‡ A clause named after the ship *Inchmaree*. This clause in a marine insurance policy provides coverage for cargo lost or damaged from bursting boilers, the breakage of shafts, latent defects of hull or machinery, or damage caused by errors in navigation or management of the vessel. Coverage may be extended by a negligence clause to cover claims of damage done by negligence.

§ A common law (British) doctrine that limits the liability of a ship owner to the value of the hull and cargo at the time of the loss; codified in 1601 by the British Parliament.

‖ A marine insurance package that includes third party liability for property damage, bodily injury or death, carrier's liability and employers liability (Jones Act) in a single policy form.

Valley Towing v. Allen; Mississippi Supreme Court, No. 41,028, held that state workers compensation was elective, only if the injury did not occur on a navigable body of water and was not "local" in nature. In such instances recovery had to be made under the Jones Act.

** The Jones Act enforces the common law doctrine of limitation of liability; that is, a plaintiff's claim is limited to the value of the hull and cargo at the time of the loss.

Jack and I wrote a bunch of insurance using this combination of carriers. The river contractors were ecstatic. The marine underwriters who had monopolized the coverages saw the light, dropped their rates, and sought to compete with us. But it was too late. Jack and I were heroes.

We received inquiries from other river traffic employers. One was a towboat operator. He wanted our combination insurance so, as with all of our river risks, we had a preinsuring survey done by the loss prevention engineers—in this case good old Jim Miller. He took a ride in the pilot's cabin of one of the towboats and came back absolutely wide-eyed. It seems that one of the helmsmen was approaching a set of locks on the Mississippi River (through which hundreds of millions of dollars of cargo passed each year), and he was steering the towboat, which was pushing barges two football fields long and loaded to the gunwales with oil, with his feet while he strummed, "You Ain't Nuthin' But a Hound Dog" on his guitar. It's a pity that we didn't get to write coverage for that risk. I would like to have seen seen his risky performance.

On December 24, 1960, our office was open just half a day. My sales year had been mediocre, yet between 8:00 and noon I got five orders from large contractor and tie manufacturing accounts! See, there is a mystique about selling. Occurrences like that make you superstitious.

The Critical Lesson

That year John F. Kennedy was elected president, and we all hoped that times would get better. Little did we know that times were about as good as they could get. Another event occurred that was to have a profound effect on my business career and subsequent events in the insurance industry.

I had been calling on one of the largest sand, gravel, and ready-mix dealers in St. Louis. Their loss experience, workers compensation, comprehensive general liability, and fleet were about as bad as they could get. The president of the company was a tough-minded, crusty guy who'd had every insurance pitch in the book thrown at him. He was also confined to a wheelchair, but it didn't seem to impede him. I kept calling on him with case examples in which we (Employers Mutuals) had turned around adverse claims situations. He wasn't buying it, not until one of their ready-mix drivers accidentally killed a little girl. That galvanized Bob (I'll call him) into action.

He called me in, saying that he would make the change from his current carrier and give our much-heralded loss prevention program a try. He gave me to understand that "I don't know why in hell I'm doing this, but I'll give you a shot. It better, by gawd, work or it will be your fanny!" His fleet had a debit modifier of 1.59, which meant that he was paying 59% more than many of his competitors with the same classification. His workers compensation modification was a disturbing 1.33, a 33% penalty. Between the two, he was spending most of his potential profit on insurance premiums.

Bob: Okay, what do want from us? Remember we have a business to run. There can't be too much disruption.

Howell: Well, we need your loss runs from the Workers Compensation Rating Bureau so we can analyze the claims. We'll see what they are, whether there are patterns and any areas of frequency, and suggest what might be done if there are. Also, we need to set up a loss prevention education meeting with your drivers and yardmen to enable our loss prevention engineers to conduct a seminar.

Bob: Hey! That's going to cost! I'll have to pay the drivers and yard guys overtime if they attend a meeting. Do you realize how much that will cost? What are our stockholders (mostly family members) going to say?

After he got over the shock, he agreed to all requests. The loss runs showed a high frequency of claims in the fleet from negligent backing. The drivers were putting their vehicles into reverse and pouring on the gas; they weren't posting a guide person outside the vehicle like they should. Claims ran $7,500, $10,000, and up. They acted like accidents were an every-day occurrence, just part of the deal. The claims added up to well over $150,000 for 1959 alone; prior years were bad too. The bodily injury claims were for a few rear-enders but, except for the claim in the death of the little girl, these didn't amount to much. There was frequency, however, which is considered bad news in the insurance industry. They say "frequency breeds severity," and it often does.

Their workers compensation losses showed another interesting trend under chronological analysis: At least 62% of all claims were filed on Mondays. "Oh, yes," said our claims manager, "we call that the 'Monday morning syndrome.' These guys fall while fixing the gutters on their houses on the weekend, or they spill water skiing and don't get medical attention until they report back to the job on Monday morning. Then they report a job-connected injury. Happens all the time. Gee, 62%! That's a lot."

Bob called the meeting of the drivers and yard people for a Friday evening after work at one of the big spaghetti houses out on Lindbergh Boulevard. It was one of those hot, muggy evenings that made St. Louis well known as the summer hell hole of creation. We said, "No beer, please," but the drivers largely ignored our entreaty and proceeded to follow their normal habits—not a propitious way to start a loss prevention program for drivers and yard people.

After the greasy pasta was consumed, runny ice cream (they invented "humid heat" in St. Louis) was served, and Bob introduced our loss prevention guy, Jim Miller. I stage-whispered to him, "Quick, Jim, do something. These guys are bored stiff!"

Jim got up and introduced himself. He said how terrible it was that so many losses had taken place and that they'd have to do better. He then showed one of those ten-minute driver's ed movies, like *Red Asphalt*. Jim's movie showed horror scenes of truck accidents with blood spewed around everywhere, legs and arms missing, that sort of thing. The sanctity of the family was highlighted, too, with music that really tugged at your heart. When the lights went up, Jim got up and started on his best rehearsed monologue. It must not have been good enough though, because Bob twisted his wheelchair up to the podium. The bored stares of the drivers showed little interest in the drama that was about to unfold before them. They all looked as if they wished they were elsewhere, disgusted with the entire proceedings. My seersucker suit was soaked through, and I felt like slithering out the door.

Bob grabbed the microphone away from Jim, glared about the room (Lordy, how that man could glare), and said, "What this S.O.B. is trying to get across is, the next guy that has an accident is fired! And the next, and the next 'til they stop. When you're fired, I'm going to print in big block letters on your personnel file FIRED FOR SAFETY INFRACTION! You can explain it when you look for a job elsewhere! If anyone has a problem with that, leave now! Also, anyone who files a Monday morning workers comp claim must submit it to me in person. Do you get me? If I don't like the smell of it, you're gone!" Then he glared at them for a full minute. It was a silent glare communicating more than a two-hour speech.

The stunned silence hung like a dark cloud until a union shop steward leapt up and yelled, "Now, wait a minute, Boss! That ain't in the contract. We'll NLRB [National Labor Relations Board] that. That's unfair!"

"You S.O.B.!" Bob roared, "Unfair! Unfair! I'll tell you what's unfair. It's that you above everyone should have done something about those losses before it came to this. How do you justify your existence if you don't protect these guys' jobs? What the hell do you want us to do, shut down the operation? We could make more money by investing our capital in U.S. Government securities! No, by God, you help or we'll quit!!!" He meant it. They knew he meant it.

The guys who were drunk were suddenly sober; the boredom was gone. The guys who weren't drunk were adding up their unemployment eligibility months. "Geez," I thought to myself, "what a brouhaha I've started. How do I get out of this one?" The shop steward jogged by me, glowered and said, "This is on your head, you insurance s——!" He meant that to be the worst kind of insult.

As it turned out, everything worked out fine. The union decided they'd better cooperate. Three firings later, the losses stopped. Absolutely! Within three years the ready-mix company got an award, complete with a plaque, from Employers Mutuals because of the "excellent loss prevention effort they had put forth."

Most important, though, was that I found my insurance religion—loss prevention will work if you get the attention of the person you're trying to convince to use it. It does work. Bob showed me that.

At last I had something real to sell, not just theory, but a demonstrable benefit of tremendous value. This discovery turned me from a so-so salesman into a hero, as in the line from *Death of a Salesman*, "If you get the order, you're a hero; if you don't, you're a bum." Suddenly I became one of the top salespeople in the office, all due to the discovery that eludes most insurance people: Losses can be reduced. Bob and his company proved it to me with such overwhelming evidence that I became a ranting and raving disciple of loss prevention as *the* way to make insurance work for the policyholder, not to mention to make a salesperson affluent.

Yes, selling property and casualty insurance is a rich, challenging, and remunerative occupation. You just have to know how to do it.

Chapter 3

Trouble on the Big Bend River: A Fictionalized Example of What Was Happening to Design Professionals in Private Practice

For 'tis the sport to have the engineer
Hoist with his own petard.

—Shakespeare, Hamlet

Shortly after noon Tom Smith returned to his office at Smith Engineering Company to find a telegram from Spence Davis, vice-president of plants and facilities of the Yellowstone Paper Company:

HAVE NOT RECEIVED YOUR CERTIFICATES OF INSURANCE. NEED THEM YOUR SOONEST. CHAIRMAN LIVID. PLEASE SEND THEM TODAY. URGENT.

"Damn," thought Tom. "I never did call that insurance agent. He's always so darn negative. Wonder why they want them so badly now?"

At 3:00 P.M. he had his answer. A man in uniform, complete with a badge, handed him a Summons and Complaint. The widow of a workman and an injured workman were bringing claim against Yellowstone Paper Company, Smith Engineering Company, and 12 John Does. They were seeking damages of $2.4 million against a project on which Smith Engineering Company was the engineer of record.

In the weeks that followed Tom Smith suffered a veritable hell. Yellowstone Paper Company demanded that he hold them harmless and protect them as agreed in the indemnity provision of their contract. His insurance agent warned him that it was unlikely he had coverage for that assumed liability, and he could not provide certificates of insurance in accordance with the contract Smith signed since he was seeking them after the loss. His insurance carriers also refused to name Yellowstone Paper Company as an additional insured on the workers compensation and professional liability insurance policies for the same reason. Neither would the comprehensive general liability carrier since claim was pending; they questioned whether Smith Engineering had acted in good faith.

Fueling the fire, Yellowstone Paper Company instituted an action against Smith Engineering Company, Emerald Construction Company, and several John Does. In their complaint against Smith Engineering, Yellowstone alleged not only professional negligence but also misrepresentation, something that Tom knew was not covered in his professional liability policy. Tom also heard that Emerald Construction's bonding company had filed suit against him for errors and omissions in his plans and specifications. He had not yet been served with that action.

How did it all happen? Tom Smith recalled that the catastrophic sequence had begun six months earlier when Spence Davis of Yellowstone Paper called. "Hello, Tom, this is Spence Davis. Our board of directors decided to go ahead with the project we talked about. I called you right away to tell you that the contract is on its way to you. Take a look at it and get it back as quickly as possible. It will save us an awful lot of hassle if you'll sign it and return it by messenger this afternoon. As you know, time is of the essence. We want to get things rolling. The minute I can report to the board that you are ready to proceed on their terms, the better it will be for all of us. Have your lawyer look at it if you want to, but don't slow things down. As a favor to me, try to do it today."

"Sure, Spence," Tom responded, "I'll get it right back to you. We're as anxious as you are to get started. I don't go for that legal gobbledygook anyway. My way is to shake hands and get on with the work. I'll try to get it back to you today or tomorrow at the latest. Don't worry. You can count on me."

Spence, relieved, answered confidentially, "I know I can, Tom. I don't want anything to hang this up. As you know, you and I have fought long and hard to get this project rolling. We have that one attorney on our board. He's a stickler for details. It will be just you and me working together anyway, but I appreciate your willingness to expedite."

When the contract arrived Tom read the terms and conditions. He found that the contract was different, not a standard form of agreement but a document that constantly referred to him as the "Contractor." It seemed to imply that he would be up to his ankles in mud doing the actual work as well as controlling construction. It set forth the scope of services in very broad terms, saying that "The Contractor [meaning the civil engineer] will provide any and all engineering services necessary to complete a wastewater treatment plant for the Yellowstone Paper Company at their mill on the Big Bend River." It also stipulated that "The plans and specifications are to be the sole responsibility of the engineer," and that "All construction review will be performed by staff personnel of Yellowstone Paper Company." The contract went on to set forth the time and manner of payment. In addition, it stipulated that "The plans and specifications will be owned by the Yellowstone Paper Company."

Another clause said, "Time is of the essence. Failure upon the part of the Contractor to perform in a timely manner will result in his being liable for resulting damages of whatsoever kind." It required that "a cost estimate shall be prepared and the Contractor shall redesign the facility for no additional fee if the bids exceed the estimate by more than 10%."

An indemnity provision stated, "The Contractor will hold harmless and indemnify the Company, its agents, officers, and employees from and against any and all liability, of whatsoever kind, arising out of the performance of the work described herein."

Nestled up to the indemnity clause was one titled "Insurance." It said:

Contractor will provide Owner with certificates of insurance evidencing comprehensive general and professional liability, workers compensation, and automobile insurances with limits of no less than $1 million combined single limit, including contractual, XC & U [blasting, collapse and underground] coverages, and a statement from the company or companies providing such coverage that they will not cancel or alter the provisions of coverage in any way without first giving the Owner 30 days' notice of such cancellation or alteration. Further, Contractor shall cause such policies of insurance to be endorsed naming Owner as an additional insured as respects the work to be performed under this agreement.

Following the insurance provision was a clause titled "Warranty" that stated: "The Contractor warrants that he will perform in the highest professional manner and hereby certifies that only professionals of extraordinary skill and capability will work upon the designs, plans, and specifications called for by this agreement."

There was an arbitration clause making arbitration the sole and exclusive remedy in the event of a dispute of "whatsoever" kind arising out of the performance of the work. Finally, the contract stipulated, "Following completion of the work, the engineer will certify that all of the work has been performed in exact accordance with the plans and specifications prepared by him."

Tom read the last statement with amusement: "In this Agreement, whenever the context so requires, the singular shall include the plural, and the neuter shall include the masculine and feminine. And the masculine shall include the feminine and the neuter."

That really struck him as funny. He chuckled slightly while he wrote a note to his project manager saying, "Bernie, look this over quickly. I promised to get it back to them this afternoon." He attached the note to the contract, sent it on to Bernie, and went back to more interesting things.

Later that day Tom got a phone call from his wife. She told him that their son Bill, a third-year engineering student, needed more money for a special course he wanted to take in soil compaction testing. Their lifestyle had already been squeezed by the expenses of Bill's schooling. They had even borrowed on their house to make certain that Bill got the best education possible because Tom hoped that Bill would take over the firm some day, although Bill wasn't enthusiastic about the idea because of the changing nature of construction. Even so, Tom told his wife, "Send him the money. We'll take a vacation some other year."

That same afternoon the executive committee of the Yellowstone Paper Company held a tense meeting about the project. Yellowstone's chairman was concerned that for the second year in a row unimpressive profits were showing up in the company's operating report. Further, the company was being forced into a wastewater treatment program that promised to erode profits even more. Nevertheless, the executive committee decided that they could just squeak by with the pending project and still leave the company in the black. They concluded, however, that deviation from the strict budget would cause the red ink to flow and the shareholders, particularly the institutional investors, to squawk.

During the coffee break a special messenger delivered the contract from Tom Smith to Spence Davis. When the meeting reconvened, Spence Davis announced to the executive committee, "Here it is, you guys. I have the contract from the engineer. At least one thing has gone smoothly. It's signed, and we're ready to go."

Chairman: What do you mean?

Spence Davis: I mean that Tom Smith has signed the contract and will begin work. He hasn't altered it at all. Not a scratch on it. I knew I could count on him.

Chairman: What do you mean count on him? You mean he signed that thing? I can't believe it! Anybody who would sign that contract has to be out of his mind! I expected him to alter it. Looks like the engineer we are hiring for this job is willing to sign anything that is put in front of him. We must have a real turkey!

Spence Davis: He's a good engineer. He's done work for us before and he's got a good reputation. I'd stand him up against any engineer in the country.

Chairman: That may be. But I can tell you he doesn't know a damn thing about contracts or negotiation, or he wouldn't have signed that agreement. It worries me that if he's careless with important matters like this, he'll be just as careless in his design. Mark my words, we'll have trouble on this job. I can smell it. I just can't believe that a professional would agree to that stuff. Our counsel said the only reason he put half of that boilerplate in there was to gain bargaining power. I'm worried.

Spence Davis: Relax. Tom Smith is true blue. He's an engineer's engineer and he'll do the job right.

Save a Little Bit of Money and Lose a Lot

It was true that Tom Smith was a good engineer. Moreover, the work that he did on the Yellowstone Paper Company plant was fine. The technology he used was some of the latest. It was going to save Yellowstone Paper Company a bundle on building costs, and the environmental considerations would please the state. But from the start he was sunk. To save money he was not given the job on a full scope-of-services basis. The people at Yellowstone somehow felt that their engineers were capable of reviewing the progress of the work to see that it was done in general conformity with the plans and specifications. It didn't seem to matter to them that their engineers were chemical engineers who had no experience in construction. They simply didn't realize that competent construction review was vital to getting the job done right. Their decision was an economy move aimed at reducing the cost of a job that had to be run under tight fiscal constraints. "Besides," they thought, "an engineer's an engineer, right?"

As consultants, Tom Smith and his firm had studied Yellowstone's wastewater problem and compared it with the technology that had been used throughout the world for coping with paper mill wastes. They came up with a system that used holding ponds for flocculent settling. Most of the water was recycled so that there was a continuous loop requiring very little makeup water. The final treatment of effluents was to be achieved in oxidation lagoons so that the discharge would be cleaner than the river water itself. Tom Smith was certain that the state pollution control board would approve the end result.

The cost estimate was well within budget. In addition, Tom Smith and his crew completed their work almost on schedule so that bids were let only a week or two later than was intended. Yellowstone was pleasantly surprised when one contractor, Emerald Construction Company, came in a whopping 21.5% below the other lowest bidder, and 23% under Tom Smith's estimate. This concerned Tom Smith. The work was fairly straightforward. It did not appear to him that there should be that much latitude in the range of bids. But everyone was so enormously pleased! He fell into the same euphoria as the rest and was happy that the job seemed to be off to a good start.

Tom Smith was unaware of what had transpired in Emerald Construction Company's office a month earlier. Kevin Riley, owner of Emerald Construction Company, was talking to his nephew Brendon, who worked for him. Brendon was six months out of engineering school and eager to please his uncle with his tremendous knowledge.

"Hey, Bren," Kevin prodded, "this is one job we have to have. Our cash flow is squeezed down to a trickle. So, sharpen your pencil and start doing the take-offs. I'll check your figures when I get back from Las Vegas." Kevin had recently divorced his wife of 30 years and married a young, gorgeous woman who loved to travel. Construction bored her, but she liked the money it made. After returning from Las Vegas, she and Kevin were planning to take a month's vacation in Hawaii.

Trying to sound offhand, Brendon replied, "No sweat, Uncle Kevin, I'll have this done in two, three days.

The trouble was that it did take sweat. Brendon liked to drink beer more than most, and he thought he could do that and work with figures too. He was bright and he tried hard, but he lacked the experience and discipline of his Uncle Kevin.

Brendon worked on the quantities and came up with a total amount. It looked good. When Kevin returned he was pleased. The job was just what they needed to start the old cash flow. He didn't have time to check the figures, though, and he told Brendon to get it typed and sent off with the performance bond.

When they were awarded the job, Brendon was thrilled. "Hot damn," he thought. "I may end up as president of this company yet!" His euphoric dream turned into a nightmare when he was told of Smith Engineering's estimate. He went back to his computations and, after three hours, he spotted it. There was a transposition: Instead of figuring on 10,000 yards of excavation and spoil, he'd figured it on 1,000. "What the hell do I do now?" he wondered. "Call Uncle Kevin? No, he'd blow his top." So he drank a beer. Then another and another and another.

Things began to unravel on the third day of construction. Tom was sitting in his office when he got an urgent call from his client. "Hello, Tom. This is Spence Davis. We've had some kind of mix-up. Kevin Riley, the head of Emerald Construction, just called demanding extras. He says that the soil borings we supplied him are misleading, and it's going to cost more to excavate those ponds than he originally thought. He's running into glacial till that contains some very large cobbles, and he said he didn't figure it. He's blaming us—well, I mean, you—because he says the logs that were available in our office didn't indicate cobbles. He's talking big money!"

Tom responded, "Now wait a minute, Spence. I think there must be some misunderstanding. We didn't perform any subsurface soil investigation. That was done by your other consultant, Mother Earth Technology.

Even so, their soil borings were for feasibility and percolation considerations, not construction. Besides, we had a legend on our plans and specifications that stipulated that the contractor was to visit the site and familiarize himself with the local conditions before preparing the bid. As far as we're concerned, if he wanted to know what was under the ground, he should have found out. That's not our duty."

Spence Davis's reply was not encouraging. "I hear what you're saying, Tom, but our chairman and the rest of our executive committee feel that you agreed to provide all of the engineering services necessary to complete this plant. They consider subsurface soil investigation to be one of those services. I thought I should let you know. Emerald Construction Company is asking for an extra that will wipe out the 21.5% they were low on this job. Someone is going to have hell to pay on account of it."

That night Tom Smith did not sleep well. It was the first of many sleepless nights. He worried about entanglement in a web that he could feel being drawn about him by the circumstances of the job. He worried, too, about his son, Bill, and the expenses of his education. What would additional expenses from this job do to his personal cash flow. His wife remarked on his nervousness and suggested he get a physical checkup. He blurted, "To hell with it!"

Two days later it began to rain. It rained and rained some more. On the third day of wet weather, Tom's telephone rang. The frightened voice of the construction foreman fairly yelled at him. "Mr. Smith. This is Joe Baldino, the Emerald foreman on the Yellowstone Paper Company job. We've got a problem. We put some temporary dikes around the excavation site at the job to hold back the runoff as you stipulated. You know, there's a prohibition against contaminating the river, but those dikes are not enough. Muddy water's running down into the river. Yellowstone's engineers don't know what to do; they're not quite sure how to interpret the standby facilities you drew. Brendon Riley doesn't know either, and Kevin's out of town. The dikes have breached in three spots and the water is running into the river. A guy from a fish hatchery downstream came screaming up this morning yelling about his salmonoids. He's as mad as I've ever seen anyone. You'd better get down here right away."

Tom was miffed at being ordered around and retorted, "Now wait a minute! We weren't hired to do construction review. Those standby facilities are perfectly simple. I'm not going to tell you guys how to do your job. If the people from Yellowstone can't help you on that problem, get Brendon to tell you what to do. I can't get into a problem that is purely construction. I hope you excavated the lower pond first. It should be adequate to take care of all the runoff. In any event, it's not our problem!"

Baldino was taken aback. In a hurt tone he said, "Well, this is a hell of a time to run out on us. It seems like your responsibility. That guy from the fish hatchery will be yelling at every government agency in the state. The engineering guys from Yellowstone are less than worthless. If I were you, as engineer of record, I would be concerned."

Tom Smith was concerned. He was especially concerned since much effort had been devoted to being certain that the construction site would not contribute to the turbidity of the Big Bend River, well known for its run of salmon. The paper mill had a bad enough name with environmentalists and biologists without adding more fuel to the fire by having a muddy construction site that would silt up spawning beds. If the newspapers got ahold of this, they would have a field day saying, "We told you so!" Tom thought to himself, "This would never have happened if we'd been on the job doing construction review. Damn 'em for reducing the scope of services to save pennies!"

Tom Smith wrestled with his conscience for almost two hours. He couldn't stand the suspense. He put on a slicker, got into his car, and sped to the job site. He could hardly believe his eyes. What should have been a wet, but well-drained, construction site was a morass. The lower pond which was set up to receive any runoff was separated from the rest of the site by spoil, a huge pile, that had been placed in exactly the wrong spot. The standby drainage system was not even in place. Workmen were standing around, hands in pockets, waiting for directions. No one seemed to be in charge. He yelled at Baldino, "Didn't you see in the specifications where it said, 'Any runoff into the river was to be potable water'?"

"Potable? Potable? What the hell does that mean?" roared Baldino.

Tom looked at him cooly and said, "It means you can drink it, you idiot!"

Whereupon Baldino leaned over, scooped up a handful of runoff water, and said with a sneer, "You mean like this?" as he drank the murky water. "Now, who's the idiot?"

Tom Smith was furious. How could this have happened? It was an extremely serious engineering problem, and he felt trapped. Worse yet, he felt compelled to do something about it. He tried. Lord how he tried! It was nineteen hours before the runoff stopped pouring into the Big Bend River. Even then, one man had been killed and another severely injured when an unshored trench collapsed on the two as they were hastily installing the steel corrugated pipe for the standby drainage system.

The next morning Tom Smith's employees noticed that his hands trembled as he drank his coffee. He missed an important meeting with another client when he was unexpectedly compelled to visit the Yellowstone job site. The other client left several messages for him to call. He noticed that there were two calls from Spence Davis as well. He was not up to returning the calls because he felt a deep sense of frustration and guilt about the horror that had happened at the job site. He just wanted to be left alone. But the newspapers wouldn't allow that. They kept calling, asking what was going on. They were unrelenting.

"How could I have been talked into doing it? Why did I agree to reduce the scope of my services? If only I'd been reviewing that job, none of it would have happened. Those two guys would be walking around and healthy," he muttered to himself. By 10:00 A.M. he was exhausted. He got up, left the office, and took a drive down to an old job he had done three years before that had gone smoothly.

A week later Tom Smith had ceased all engineering activities; his time was monopolized by lawyers. Not only was he being sued by relatives of the deceased workman, the injured workman, and his client, but, on the advice of his lawyers, he was going to start action against his insurance agent and insurance companies. They were denying liability based upon the terms and conditions of his policy. In addition, Bernie Atkins, one of Tom's key people, had heard a rumor that Yellowstone Paper Company had made a claim against the builder's risk insurance carrier. Yellowstone had taken out an "all-risk" completed value form, which included earthquake and flood. Yellowstone was contending that the damage to the job was caused by "flood." Atkins got feedback to the effect that the carrier denied liability and stated that the loss at the job was not the result of flood but due to errors or omissions in the plans and specifications, an excluded item. Although Yellowstone had named the contractor and the subcontractors on the policy of insurance, they had not named Tom. As a consequence, even if the carrier did pay on it, they might have rights of subrogation against him in the event that they were called upon to pay for the damages caused by the uncontrolled waters.

Kevin and Brendon Riley were also in trouble. Their bonding company had taken over the job and were talking about suing everyone in sight. Kevin explained to his new wife, Maureen, how he had lost his bondability and how that had "put me out of business." She turned her well-shaped back on him, took her newly acquired four-carat, canary yellow diamond, fifteen-carat ruby brooch, a Rolex, and a Mercedes 450SL and left.

Brendon was out of a job, so he had a beer.

Listening to Lawyers

Tom Smith's attorney, Harry Hendrickson, droned on, "But Tom, they're going to allege that this wouldn't have happened if you hadn't been a few days late with your plans and specifications. You signed an agreement that 'time is to be of the essence.' Do you know what that means? It means that performing punctually and completing your work precisely on the date you agreed was critical to your agreement. They're going to say that the project wouldn't have been caught in the rainy season had the job started on time. Then, too, they're going to point to the fact that you did not supply certificates of insurance or do the other things in regard to the insurance that you agreed to do. And how about your agreement to perform 'in the highest professional manner'? You used your ordinary engineers. You admit things were done just as you usually do, but that's not good enough for this contract."

Hendrickson explained to Tom that the way things stood, he was in a very poor defensive position even though his engineering had been up to par. It looked as if he had willfully breached contract clauses and contractually assumed responsibilities. This was also going to make it difficult to enforce his insurance policies since he had been careless about seeking their concurrence to insure the indemnity and insurance provisions of the contract.

Two weeks later Tom Smith had a heart attack. Struck down physically, he had to relinquish the management of his firm to others. This ultimately led to his removal from the mainstream of activity in his firm. Bernie tried, but eventually the firm went out of business.

When Spence Davis got word of Tom's heart attack he felt sick. He told the chairman, "It was so needless! It was really quite a straightforward job. Now the company is in a mess and poor Tom Smith, who just wanted to be a good engineer, is in trouble. I feel guilty, but I don't think there's anything we can do about it. It's up to the lawyers, now. And, you know where that will lead us."

It did.

Chapter 4

People in Trouble

Ask, and it shall be given;
seek, and ye shall find;

—Matthew 7:7

I started my 1961 insurance sales effort at the St. Louis office of the Employers Mutuals of Wausau with high hopes. After all, 1960 had ended on a soaring note, and I had some very good prospects near to closing at year end. Jack Fleisch, my marine insurance colleague, and I began looking at some international corporations that had complicated marine and workers compensation insurance problems. These corporations showed interest in our shared approach. In addition, I was making good headway with a large coal company, Peabody Coal. They liked the idea of a workers compensation retrospective rating plan. They just needed an okay from our loss prevention engineers in order to become a policyholder.

The warm winds of spring began blowing across the midwestern prairie in late March, and with them came particulates, oak leaf mold spores, ragweed pollen, and other asthma-producing substances that severely affected my seven-year-old daughter's health. My wife Jo and I watched our daughter Melinda gasping for breath, sometimes until four in the morning. It hurt. Her doctor recommended that we return to the West Coast where she had not been bothered by allergies. Other than that, he could offer no remedy. During World War II there was a popular song, *"We Did It Before and We Can Do It Again."* That song became our motto.

My employer was very understanding and said that the company could place me in a position in Los Angeles. This area, heavy with smog, did not seem a likely spot for a person with asthma. Returning to Seattle didn't seem to be in the cards either since workers compensation, my main product, could not be sold there. That left San Francisco. Employers Mutuals of Wausau was a direct writing company; that is, its own employees did the selling instead of independent agents or brokers, except in northern California and New York City, which were considered "broker" territories. Employers Mutuals dropped its direct writing ways in these territories since it believed the way to do business there was through selected independent agents and brokers. Thus, it became evident that I would have to leave Employers Mutuals and become a broker. The people at Employers Mutuals said they would help me in that regard, and Bill Polk of Marsh & McLennan said he would introduce me to his friend Pete Kelsy, the manager of the Marsh & McLennan office in San Francisco.

A date was set and I flew to San Francisco. I had paid my own way, so I felt free to call on all of the major brokerage companies—not only Marsh & McLennan, but Johnson & Higgins, Fred S. James, Miller and Ames (now part of Corroon & Black), and A&A, as well. A&A particularly attracted me because the office was relatively small; the manager, Jack Okell, was a handsome, dynamic guy interested in construction risks; and he was willing to hire me on the spot. They had an impressive book of accounts, and Jack liked dealing with the Employers Mutuals . It took a trip to Los Angeles and a period of prejob dalliance, but we finally agreed that I should start sales work for them in June of 1961.

Alexander & Alexander, Inc.

Starting with A&A was exciting. The first day there I arrived at 8:00 A.M., after a one-hour commute from Palo Alto. At the elevator an older gentleman and I did the "after you, no, after you" routine. Then we repeated it at the second floor, and it amused us both to the point of laughter. My amused acquaintance turned out to be the president of A&A, Sam Shriver, visiting from New York. After I was shown around, Shriver asked me to step into the conference room with him. He was soft spoken, impeccably dressed, and had kindly eyes that conveyed the message, "I'm here to help you." He said that he wanted to tell me a little bit about the founding of A&A and its philosophy. He gave me a short history of A&A, recalling that it had been started by two cousins, William F. Alexander and Herbert L. Alexander, in Clarksburg, West Virginia. William's brother, Charles B. Alexander, joined them a year later. Five years after they began, they invented the inherent explosion clause, to provide, for the first time, insurance protection for unexplained explosions (perhaps static electricity) in the gas industry. This gave them their first large account, a natural gas company. Soon they branched out to railroads, chemical companies, and other businesses where there were gaps in coverage or no coverage available from most underwriters. They were dedicated innovators driven by an obsession to provide service to their clients. A&A tried to do things for clients that other brokers could not or would not do.

Shriver stated A&A was not the largest broker (close to 2,000 employees then, almost 20,000 today), but it wanted to be the very best and it would become the very best by bringing the highest level of service and coverage to its clientele that money would allow. He was dead set against selling services on the basis of price since he felt stability and fidelity were much more important. Innovation was its strength. He asserted that a broker who based decisions on the commission scale (using a particular underwriting company because it paid a higher commission) was not professional. "Don't do it. It's a dangerous trap," he cautioned. He encouraged me to go slowly and look to the client's needs above all else. His parting admonition was "Never let the commission dollar signs cloud your professional judgment. Try to be inventive."

He was asking me to subordinate my own selfish interests to those of the insurance buying client. I felt kindred to Shriver's beliefs. I thought, "How lucky can I be to be working with a company that is really dedicated to a professional approach." I never lost my admiration for Shriver, and he continued to support my sales effort (even at its most unusual) until he retired.

Our manager, Jack Okell, pointed out that the company preferred to work on large risks, such as Fortune 500 accounts, since these risks had more challenging coverage requirements. A&A had done an admirable job of developing some of the country's largest corporations as clients. Things looked good.

Besides Jack Okell, there were two other executive officers, John E. Hanson and John Metcalf. John Hanson was operations manager and later branch manager. He was undoubtedly one of the hardest working guys alive. There was no way you could beat him into the office in the morning, and he was always there after everyone else had left. John Metcalf was production manager and a top-notch property insurance expert to boot. I reported to John Metcalf.

Since they pretty well let me conduct my own affairs, I started calling on contractors and allied risks. One of the first contacts I made was a large dredging contractor. I thought, "If combining coverages works for Mississippi River contractors, why not here?" Boy, was I wrong. San Francisco Bay dredging, Sacramento River work, and Pacific Ocean rip-rap, seawall, and breakwater construction have nothing in common with Mississippi River construction. Oh, they had employers' liability problems that were challenging, but most of it fell in the Jones Act arena. That was outside of my area of expertise, particularly because, except for our New York office, we did not have good marine insurance market connections.

The dredging company's losses were horrendous and the manager was right when he said, "You can make a proposal on our coverages if you want to, but you're not going to find any underwriters interested in them. Trying to predict what the Pacific Ocean will do is a waste of time. Just when you think it will be calm, a storm will come up. You think it will be stormy, and it will fall into the doldrums. Trying to make money on anything that depends on a calm ocean is a loser." He must have been psychic because nine months later a Pacific storm drowned one of their crane barges, and they lost three men. I had not been able to find an underwriter even slightly interested in their risk—a lucky thing. Brokerage people have a deep-seated, all abiding aversion to putting risks on an insurance company's books that cause losses. If they do, the sense of guilt is devastating.

I discovered another feature about selling in the San Francisco area that created problems for me and for all salespeople—the geography. In St. Louis the city was the hub of a circle of municipalities. Some 92 towns were clustered tightly around the city itself. You could travel to any point in St. Louis County and its environs in 45 to 50 minutes. Not so in the San Francisco area. The area was broken up into long, thin strips by the bay, the Sacramento River, the coast range, and the East Bay hills. Travel became a major consumer of productive sales time. Salespeople could literally spend hours on the freeways just to make a few widely spaced calls on potential clients. It was frustrating because insurance sales carries with it a compulsion to bring in orders. "Having a nice day" is getting a client signed up. Wasting time traveling felt burdensome, so I felt that I had to start working on something other than construction risks.

After awhile I was able to pick up a few medium-size accounts. The first was an olive packer with severe workers compensation loss problems. Claims came from migrant harvesters who had broken limbs or received internal injuries from falling off ladders during harvest. We talked them into a "buddy system" in which one person picked while the other remained at the base of the ladder to steady it or break the fall of the picker if he or she fell. Borrowing from the home builders in St. Louis, we also had them "foot" their ladders with plywood squares. This kept the ladders from differentially sinking into the soil and spilling the climbers.

Our safety measures reduced the severity and frequency of claims dramatically. They also slowed down productivity—a bad thing in the olive business. We had the account for only one year. But learning about the olive industry was kind of fun. First we learned that the green olives were soaked in a lye solution. Then they were washed in water several times and put into brine for fermentation. How long they fermented determined whether they were ripe or green. Many were then pitted and stuffed by machines.

The products liability claims the olive packers experienced were almost all the result of pits that were not completely removed by the automatic pitters. "Your olive chipped my tooth!" was the claimants' chant. It was hard to refute. We recommended label warnings, but the insured feared buyer resistance. They had fierce foreign competition and didn't want anything to impede sales. The foreign olive producers were not posting warnings; how could the domestic producers do so and still make sales? They also had an extremely tight profit margin that made every saved expense dollar important. A reduction in sales due to a negative warning was not in the cards. Settling "chipped tooth" claims became part of the expense of doing business for an olive processor.

In St. Louis I had sold a large steel erection company on our new loss prevention approach to workers compensation. It was still working well for them, so I called on San Jose Steel Company in the city of the same name. After a few false starts I was able to get in to see the president, Mr. Honore. He was very polite as he said, "Mister, you're wasting your time. I don't care how good you are or how much money you might save me. You see, we have a professional insurance broker. I mean professional! I'll tell you. He doesn't give diddley about the size of the commission. He's taken care of our needs for years. He has stuck by us in tough times and seen to it that the best interpretation is given the policy in tricky claims situations. I can call him on the weekend, no sweat. I get the best from him, I give loyalty in return. Besides, he's a CPCU (Chartered Property and Casualty Underwriter) and knows all the answers right away! Not after he's had to check with someone else."

"Gosh, Mr. Honore," I replied, "I'm really impressed. Do you mind telling me who your broker is?"

"No, not at all. He's Nigel Renton of Dealey, Renton and Kelly.* Look him up. You'll see what I mean."

I did, and I was impressed.

I tried working with a few paint manufacturers but couldn't make a sale. Markets were just too tight on such volatile materials. Underwriters were very wary about paint manufacturers since there had been too many catastrophic losses: Explosions, fires, and product liability claims.

After signing up a large tractor dealer I called on other tractor dealerships. I had a story to tell about how I had saved the first dealership thousands of dollars on their fire and casualty insurance with a "package" (they were brand new at the time). One tractor dealer I called on gave me the line that all insurance people titter at: "Hey, I don't need any fire insurance on my stock and building. Sure I have a few million dollars tied up in stock, and the building's worth $500,000, but it would be crazy to insure them. See, they're all steel; there's nothing that can burn!" I tried pleading with him but he was adamant.

A year later a fire destroyed his building and stock. I went back to see him and found him operating out of a trailer. He was still in shock. The "fireproof" steel building had sagged into nothingness from the hot internal fire. The girders were twisted and warped, and the stock of steel parts lay contorted, fused, and crystalized on the floor. Later, our fire engineer, Chuck Cross, told me of dozens of cases where the internal combustible load (wooden desks, carpeting, files, chairs, wastepaper, etc.) had been enough to destroy major steel and concrete structures. The owners thought they were fireproof. "They spray the steel with asbestos," Chuck explained, "but when a fire is confined in an area that is not vented to let the superheated air out, the temperature gets so extreme that the steel softens and collapses, notwithstanding the asbestos. It may seem strange, but timber buildings seem to hold up better structurally in fires than steel buildings

---

* Now, Dealey, Renton and Associates.

do." I was able to use that valuable lesson repeatedly in the future. As I had learned at Employers Mutuals, "Knowledge is earning power."

Sales personnel refer to large accounts as "elephants." Some salespeople would hunt (try to sell to) only elephants. That didn't seem like good strategy to me since, once you got them, there was a chance you could lose them, and such a loss could place you in serious fiscal trouble. You could also spend months trying to sell one and never, ever, get the order signed. I tried for a mix of business—large, medium, and small—to balance the portfolio. Nevertheless, I did go after one giant construction company. After calling on it for several months, I developed a good relationship with the chief financial officer, Hal Smith. He gave me to understand that there was no way I could take over its insurance. He informed me, "We have the best possible coverage at the lowest available price. I know all about A&A. They are a fine firm, but you could not touch our costs. I know our coverages are perfect, I designed them myself.

"Besides, young man," he went on, "I get a little tired of salespeople always telling me how much they are going to save me. You see, I have this drafty old house built in 1924. A man came around one day and said, 'Hey, mister, I can save you half of your heating bill if you'll let me put in a forced draft, natural gas furnace. See, your old worn-out furnace uses oil, and the heat is distributed by convection. You lose all the heat up the flue. Oil only partly combusts and that makes it expensive. It also creates carbon monoxide, and that's dangerous. Not good, at all. Cost you only $2,500. Earn it back in three years.' So I gave him the go ahead.

"My fuel bills didn't go down that much. Then another guy came around and he said, 'It wasn't your furnace. You need insulation. I can cut your fuel bills in half if you'll just let me insulate your attic and floor. Only cost you $1.25 per square foot. Will pay for itself in two years.' So I gave him the order and he insulated the place. Did my fuel bills go down? Only a little. I figure I should be getting my heating almost free, if you can believe what the sales guys say. Now you want me to let you do a survey on our corporate insurance so you can save us money and give us better coverage. A likely story!"

After a bit, he agreed to let me do a survey. "Time is money" and it took almost two weeks to gather all of the data. We analyzed the coverages in-house at A&A then tried to figure out how we were going to tell the man that he'd left numerous coverage gaps. I took the survey to an underwriter at Employers Mutuals, Bob Olson. After more time, we concocted a plan—an unusual plan at that time, but one that would save them enormous amounts of money if their loss ratios remained where they had been.

The proposal we put together would save our elephant over $150,000 per year and give them better coverage too. Our proposal didn't make his coverage inadequacies obvious, but we did fill the voids. I felt sure that I had a winner, so I phoned to make an appointment to see Hal. During our phone conversation I asked him, "If I can save you over $100,000 a year, will you give me your account?"

"Hell, yes," he responded, "but there's no way you could do that! Our arrangement is too good."

The day arrived and with a pounding heart I went to his office. We had coffee and minor chitchat and then got down to cases. He was a CPCU and loved to talk insurance theory. That was why our offering should have had special appeal for him. At that time the plan was unique. What we proposed was a self-retention plan; in essence they would self-insure the first $50,000 of any loss, be it workers compensation, comprehensive general liability, fleet, or equipment floater* (the coverage that protected their dozers, cranes, dump trucks, etc. on an "all-risk" basis). The underwriter would charge a fee for claims adjusting costs and the insured would pay a deposit premium upon which taxes would be paid. Then the underwriter would provide insurance excess of $50,000 for any one loss, and an aggregate excess policy that would stop all losses at $2 million. We would adjust the premium for the retained layer and coverage excess of $50,000 retrospectively based upon losses. This would be computed every three years. Matching it up with their loss history over the previous three years showed that the savings would have been over $150,000 per year! We would improve their coverages by adding earthquake and flood, as their current coverage did not include earthquake and flood, in addition to the equipment floater; we changed their comprehensive general liability from "accident" coverage to "occurrence";† and we added several other coverages they did not have, such as personal injury protecting against claims of libel, slander, false arrest, defamation of character, and the like. The workers compensation would automatically include Longshoremen's and Harbor Workers coverage (they did some marine work and had been adding the needed coverage on a case-by-case basis). I was elated when I left. "Hot dog!" I thought, "I've bagged an elephant for sure!"

Time seem to drag on, and by the end of a week I couldn't stand it any longer, so I called him. "Hey, Hal, how's it going? Do you want me to get the binders ready? You're up for renewal in a week."

"No," he responded, "I need to see you about your proposal. Can you make it down in the next few days?"

"Sure, I can be down there tomorrow morning, if that's okay?" He told me that would be fine. I thought, "Gee, I hope he just doesn't understand something minor about our proposal, I want this account!"

The next morning I left at 7:00 in order to be there by 9:00. When I got there he looked very serious. After offering me coffee and a donut he started out by pointing accusingly at the proposal lying on his desk.

"Listen, Ed, there was something I didn't know. The big guy (the

---

* A property coverage that covers items that may be transportable.

† An injurious exposure that results in either bodily injury or property damage that is neither expected nor intended, like the silting of a river during construction due to uncontained run-off, as opposed to "accident," a sudden and unusual happening that results in damages.

chairman and major stockholder of the company) says there's no way we can give you the account. I know what I said, but I can't live up to my word. He says it's a 'political thing' that makes the money insignificant. I can't tell you what it is. I'm really sorry, but that's the way it is. When I give my word on something, I usually follow through. This time I can't. Honestly, I simply did not believe that you could do it. I mean I was certain!"

I knew what a party balloon felt like as the air wheezed out in its rapid descent to the floor. All that work. It was a really good plan, and the price was right. But he'd said it was "a political thing," whatever that meant. My dad, who had been in sales most of his life, told me, "When you don't get the order, remember to leave them happy because you may want to try again in a year or two." So I said to Hal, "I am disappointed, but I also recognize that there may be decisions that are entirely beyond your control. Thanks for giving me a shot at your business. I hope if the 'political thing' changes, you'll give me a call and see if I can do business with you."

Hal looked relieved and apologized all the way to the door, thanking me for taking it "so graciously." I knew he was crushed by the decision his chairman had made. He didn't know that inside I was torn apart. I went home with my tail between my legs, having to face an underwriter who had produced but had to be disappointed, just as I was, and a management who, hopefully, would understand. Not a pleasant chore.

What's a Consulting Engineer?

In June 1962, Bob Olson, the underwriter with Employers Mutuals, called me with an opportunity. "Ed, I live next door to a transplanted Englishman, Bill Jones. He's with a soil and foundation engineering firm, Gribaldo, Jacobs, and Jones. They do subsurface soil investigation for developers, architects, and contractors. He just returned from Washington, D.C., where he attended a meeting of the National Society of Professional Engineers. At the meeting they announced that soil and foundation engineers are losing their professional liability insurance market. You know, Employers Mutuals can't write a line like that. We don't have the reinsurance for it. I thought maybe you knew of a market or could arrange some kind of deal. How about if you give Bill a call. Reference me, and see if you can do anything for them."

So I did. Bill Jones said that the major carrier of consulting engineers professional liability insurance was giving up on soil and foundation engineers and raising the rates on all others. He wondered if there was anything that A&A might be able to do. "Well," I replied, "if there's a group that we could work with, we might be able to get an underwriter interested. But it will take a pretty good size group."

"Oh, I say," Bill answered in his distinctively British way, "that's jolly good. I know just the group, the Consulting Engineers Association of California [CEAC]. You call Bud Kelly, their executive secretary, and tell him I told you to call. Tell him our insurance situation is getting desperate, and maybe you can do something about it."

Before calling Bud Kelly, I called A&A's New York office and chatted with Bob Shipman, one of the marketing gurus who would know about potential markets for soil and foundation engineers or would be able to find out about any in a hurry. His first report was negative. Bob then did a Herculean job, contacting underwriters on a worldwide basis, including the Taisho Fire & Marine of Tokyo, Japan. Everything led back to the one or two carriers willing to work with this exposure, including those who gave up on soil and foundation engineers during the previous year.

I then went to the Mills Tower Law Library in San Francisco and researched consulting engineers professional liability claims. There weren't many claims reported, but this exercise revealed a few claims that seemed to show judges and juries were devoid of understanding when it came to consulting engineers. On the face of the reported decisions, there often seemed to be a wide gap between the consulting engineer's conduct and the damage.

In law school we had a professor, Richard V. Campbell, who taught Torts. He spent a good deal of time hammering away at the problem of *proximate relationship* and the necessity to prove it if liability were to be found against a tortfeasor (one who commits a tort). His proposition was somewhat bewildering because he introduced X factors that were supposed to signify the gray area existing between a tortfeasor's actions and their connection with the injury or property damage and ultimate civil liability. He assigned cases to exemplify the problem, such as a railway crew burning brush beside a railroad track, sparks blowing to an adjoining field, burning the wheat crop, "Clearly a case of liability," he said. "The crew could reasonably foresee that negligence in their activity would lead to such a loss. However, if the sparks blew three miles and set a gasoline tank farm on fire, would there be liability?" He thought not.

It came down to the proposition that liability might be found "if it could be reasonably inferred that the tortfeasor knew or should have known that his or her action would result in the damage that ensued." Does that sound like a cop-out? Maybe so, because what the tortfeasor knew or should have known would always be a question of fact for the jury, and maybe the jury simply would not be equipped to make such a judgment because their education, background, or reasoning ability would not be adequate to make an equitable syllogistic judgment—particularly when they might be considering highly esoteric professional matters.

Charles Debes' professional acts in the Laukkanen case (see Chapter 1) were, in my estimation, wholly unrelated to the injury of Mrs. Laukkanen.

Is this, then, a flaw in the legal fabric of our nation? Are we finding pronouncements of liability that are governed purely by the whim and caprice of juries who, for one reason or another, are incapable of making logical legal judgments? With all due respect to Professor Campbell and his X factors, I think so.

The cases I located in the law library did not on first review show me any patterns of frequency that might be relied upon for analysis as to why claims against consulting engineers were mounting. Allegations of wrongdoing by design professionals claimed damages for several reasons: breach of warranty (failure to deliver the services either designated by contract or by breach of implied warranty); failure in estimating final construction costs of designed elements; errors in the design, errors or omissions in the performance of construction review (observing the work to see if it complied, in general, with the intent of the design); breach of agency (not carrying out the wishes of the owner-client); and claims for damages related to the design.[1]

Risk analysis is a mathematical exercise using multiple regression analysis, which in turn depends on similar quantifiable events occurring at specific points in time. Applying probabilities and chronological analysis to workers compensation risks was fairly easy since the losses are quantifiable. Most losses were physical, explicable, occurred at a fixed point in time, had common attributes, and could be computed by a schedule (a finger loss paid so much, a broken arm so much, etc.). The unknowns were fraud, mistake, or misinterpretation. Plotting workers compensation claims chronologically by type for a particular risk usually gave a basis for analysis that could be turned into a loss prevention or claims remedy.

With consulting engineers professional liability claims, it was not so simple. First, you had to know what the insured consulting engineers did and why. Next, you needed to know what motivated the claimants. Third, it was important to understand whether there had been efficient contributory intervening forces that may have affected a loss (e. g., wind in the Debes case). Sometimes this was difficult to discern. Most of all you had to know what the financial interests of the claimants were. Thus, quantification of these claims was very difficult since no schedule existed, damages varied widely, and it often was hard to visualize the proximate relationship between the design professional's act and the alleged loss. For example, in the Laukkanen case is it possible that the proximate cause of loss was the contributory intervening wind of nearly 100 miles per hour? It seemed that analyzing consulting engineers' professional liability claims was like algebra. I wasn't making much headway.

Following the pattern used in workers compensation risks, I began listing the factors found in the reported design professionals' liability claims in the law library. This list included type of work, nature of loss, discipline involved, claimant's allegation, claimant's profile, geographical location, complaint of error, and so on. Claims patterns were not quick to emerge. With workers compensation losses the loss facts were readily apparent because a statement of what happened made by the claimant served as a basis for adjustment, for example, "I dropped a steel casting on my toe and broke it." Pretty easy to see cause and effect.

Trying to get the loss (causative) facts about consulting engineers' professional liability claims from law book reports was a formidable task because a legal proceeding *cooks* the elements to put them into legal terminology that litigators can work with. The whys, wheres, and whos get pushed and punished into fitting the procedure, rather than being left in the simple form found in workers compensation losses. Charles Debes, the defendant in the Laukkanen case, told me, "It was amazing. In the courtroom, when they started talking about what I'd done, I didn't even realize they were talking about me or my professional duty. The 'facts' were incredibly skewed from what I perceived had happened." It seemed to me that an analysis of consulting engineers' professional liability claims would have to be made from a different perspective.

Without an end in view, I felt it was time to call Bud Kelly, executive secretary of the Consulting Engineers Association of California. I referenced Bill Jones and made an appointment to see him. Since the meeting was some days hence, I went to the Stanford University Library to look for material on loss prevention. No matter where I sought what others had done with professional liability loss prevention or medical malpractice, there didn't seem to be anything written on the subject, not even postgraduate theses. It seemed odd. There were mountains of material on engineered loss prevention techniques such as saw guards, punch press safety devices, eye protectors, welding safety equipment, marine safeguards, fire protection systems, construction safety measures, dual braking systems, and aviation safety plans, but nothing that would aid a consulting engineer in private practice who wished to avoid professional liability claims.

At the meeting with Bud Kelly, he introduced me to the immediate past president of CEAC, Thomas R. Simonson, a top-notch mechanical engineer, and Robert M. Kennedy, president-elect of the CEAC and a principal in a highly reputed civil engineering firm, Kennedy Engineers. John Q. Jewett, president of CEAC, was out of town.

Tom Simonson was a tall, resolute man with a keen analytical mind, quick to see the rationale that I proposed; that maybe, just maybe, it would be possible to develop some loss prevention techniques that would obviate professional liability claims. Bob Kennedy took a show-me attitude; he wanted to know what specifically I might be able to suggest as a remedy. To exemplify my intent, because I had found at least one claim in which an allegation of breach of implied warranty was part of the plaintiff's case, I suggested that perhaps a nonwarranty clause might be used by consulting engineers. In other words, their contract of hire might stipulate, in part, "The engineer will perform to the best of his ability and in accordance with engineering standards within his community, but he makes no other warranty, either express or implied." Bob liked it, and along with Tom he became a supporter of what was a new concept, professional liability loss prevention.

This meeting took place in October of 1962, an exciting time. The electronics industry was spreading wing, John Glenn orbited the earth, and President John F. Kennedy called Khrushchev's bluff on the Soviet missiles in Cuba, ordering a blockade of that nation. The threat of *the bomb* was never more real.

Tom and Bob asked what the next steps were while Bud Kelly took notes. What we proposed was that a survey of CEAC members be conducted to ask specific questions about claims history, causes, type of work, and such. We also proposed to ask the members of CEAC whether they would be willing to participate in an education program aimed at reducing professional liability (at that time called *errors and omissions*) claims frequency and severity. The survey was sent out and a whopping 78% of the CEAC membership returned the questionnaire fully completed.

Although it was too early to discuss insurance, the members were eager to learn whether, in my estimation, a professional liability loss prevention effort might possibly enable them to change directions as far as their professional liability insurance was concerned. I said, "Gee, I hope so," but I was plagued by the response from A&A's New York office that "there is no market for this type of risk other than that which is currently available to them."

Immediately, Bud Kelly arranged for me to do stand-up-and-tells at CEAC's chapter meetings in San Francisco, Los Angeles, San Diego, Fresno, and Sacramento. Each of these meetings gave me an opportunity to discuss claims with the consulting engineer risks. In short order at least one common denominator appeared—unreasonable rancor between the parties on the construction site. It may seem obvious that this should be the case, but it wasn't. Conventional wisdom still decried that errors and omissions are the causes of these claims. Fights would erupt on the job sites over methods, interpretation of plans and specifications, scheduling, and just about anything else the participants could think of. Instead of negotiating a solution, the parties would turn to litigation almost immediately, sometimes over paltry matters. The age of suing to resolve disputes had arrived. In any event, it appeared that there was an enigma about the origins of these claims, and it was going to take time and insight to bring about solutions that could be helpful.

Learning From Lawyers

One possible solution came from past experience. While I was in Seattle, it had become evident that to be successful with the Employers Mutuals I would have to find some type of employers liability insurance to write. Because the state had a monopoly on workers compensation insurance, it was necessary to look at other forms of employers liability. The most promising were the marine exposures not subject to state monopoly, such as Longshoremen's and Harbor Workers' and Jones Act coverages. Employers was already deeply involved with Longshoremen's and Harbor Workers' coverage, so that left Jones Act. With so many salmon fishermen in my territory, this seemed a good place to start. I talked with the underwriters in Portland, Oregon, who said, "We don't like that exposure at all! Forget it! It's terrible!" When I asked why (something some underwriters don't like to be asked) they said, "We had terrible experience with it some years ago in San Pedro, California, with tuna fishermen. The big problem was fraud. When the season's over, the fishermen get laid off for the winter, an invitation for a sore back."

But nothing could deter me from looking into insuring what I perceived to be clear-pale-blue-eyed, honest Nordic fisherfolks. Why had the underwriters' experience with the tuna fishermen been so bad? Was the same fraud flaw true in the salmon fishing business? I talked with some of the insurance brokers writing that coverage in Seattle. "Yes," they said, "the experience is horrible. No, not much fraud. But, hey, that's dangerous work, just like farming." I called on a former neighbor, a defense attorney named Bill Allen. Bill advised, "Ed, don't get mixed up in it. It's a rotten exposure. You can't make it good with any type of loss prevention technique because these guys all run their own shows. They'll do anything to make a good catch, even fish in a 50-mile-an-hour squall. They can make big money, but sometimes they have to bend the safety rules to do it. So they bend them."

Wow, this sounded like a really bad line. Then an idea struck: Why not approach it from the other side; see what the fishermen and the plaintiffs' attorneys had to say.

The fishermen said, "You're crazy if you write this coverage for anyone but me. I'm a safe risk, but most of the rest are daredevils, bent upon making a fortune in a single seining," or words to that effect.

The plaintiffs' attorneys were another story. They said, "Sure, you can write that line successfully if you improve your claims defense work. The attorneys defending those claims don't even plead limitation of liability! It's a marvelous, ancient doctrine that gives vessel owners protection against inflated claims. The insurance carriers don't even use it as a defense (see Chapter 8). I think the insurance companies pay the lowest dollar for defense counsel. They get what they pay for, and not a cent more!"

A lot of friends my age worked in law firms that took only the defense side. I was curious to find out whether some of the insurance companies writing Jones Act and Longshoremen's and Harbor Workers' coverage were in fact being cheap about the legal defense costs. I took a friend to lunch at Maison Blanche, one of Seattle's finest restaurants, and asked, "Norbert, is it true that some insurers are trying to save a bunch of money when it comes to hiring defense counsel in their more esoteric lines of coverage? Do they actually shop for hourly rates without regard to expertise in a particular line? Are they being irresponsible in the name of economy?"

"Ed," Norbert said confidentially, "since you were admitted to the Wisconsin Bar, I guess you deserve to know some lawyer secrets. Some of the defense attorneys are playing a game. They dress down to get work. They wear rumpled polyester suits, have drab unshined shoes, drive 10-year-old Chevys, Fords, or Plymouths, live in run-down neighborhoods, and buy beat-up furniture for their offices. They hire drab people who look poor, and their ashtrays are never emptied to make it look like they're being austere. Their published rates for the insurance companies are about half of the going scale. They appeal to the insurance companies that are *looking for the cheapest service.* They take the company adjusters to lunch at greasy spoons and laugh all the way to the bank. That's because an hourly rate doesn't mean diddley since it's the number of hours they apply to the bill that counts."

Norbert continued, "They can run up a lot of hours, and how are you going to check on them to see if they have done an honest hour's work? Then, too, they train their associates on tough lines and bill for the time the associates spend in the library. The insurance companies end up paying just as much as they would with a firm like ours that has skilled specialists, but they think they're getting a bargain. No way, because those low-rated firms frequently don't have the knowledge to take on Jones Act, Longshoremen's and Harbor Workers', construction liability, aircraft liability, product liability—you name it—claims and win. That's what we're after, right? To win? If you lose or settle high, where's the bargain? In today's legal defense world, you have to be a specialist; we are, and we won't take a case outside of our specialty. Not so with the rate cutters. They'll take anything and plead that they 'know it all.' The few insurance companies that hire counsel by rate are getting just what they paid for, a cheap job," Norbert gloated with a huge Cheshire Cat grin.

"Cheez, Ed, if you want to be successful in the insurance business, you might as well know about the flip side of the game. That's the huge, glitzy firms who have associates coming out their kazoos, high-tech furnishings, fashion-plate employees, and high rates. Their bills always come out in even amounts, like $10,000, $15,000 or $20,000, even though they're supposed to be on time and expenses! How do they get away with that? I'll tell you. They treat the company adjusters like oriental potentates. They take them to Alaska for fishing or to Palm Springs for golf and buy them beef Wellington dinners with all the trimmings. Who's going to give up something like that to save a few bucks or to get the best expertise in a highly technical legal area. I say, about fishing as a risk for your company, stick with something you know, like construction. Don't get drawn into a line that can have runaway defense costs."

I returned to the plaintiffs' attorneys with a different point of view. These attorneys all loved to tell war stories about how they'd won cases due to the inadequacy of defense counsel. Stories like, "My client was the widow of a deckhand on the *Mary B*, out of Ballard. They were fishing near Ketchikan with the wind gusting to 35. The sea was kind of sloppy, with a wave or two topping the bow every once in awhile. The hold was so full that sometimes the waves rose above the scuppers. My client's husband was mending a brail aft that had been torn on the hatch cover. Next thing you know, he just wasn't there; didn't yell for help, just disappeared. It took the crew half an hour to realize he was gone. They thought he might have gone to the john or below to rest. Now, get this, the insurance company guy is denying liability, contending he committed suicide! Can you beat that, suicide. Can you imagine suicide in 40° water? No jury's going to buy that. Brrrr. We're pleading wrongful death and have five good witnesses who say that the deceased was cheerful just before he disappeared. That insurance company counsel doesn't stand a prayer. He works for peanuts. But he'll make himself a career defending this one. They'll depose, depose, and depose, then send interrogatories, make motions, and, on trial day, pay. I can almost guarantee it." He was right. They did.

The plaintiffs' attorneys convinced me that the salmon fishing industry might be too uncertain to underwrite successfully. The law wasn't settled, and the nature of the losses was too indefinable to make it a good risk for insurance. There simply were not the probabilities to set rate nor any good way of setting up a loss prevention program that would work.

I called the underwriter for Employers Mutuals in Portland and admitted, "You were right about fishing, it's probably a loser."

"I know," he said, "what do you think I am, stupid?"

In spite of his comment, one positive thing came out of the exploration. The realization that in baffling claims situations the "enemy" frequently knew where the claims were coming from and why. They also knew why the underwriters were not making profits on a particular type of risk. Asking the plaintiffs and their attorneys to give a perspective was valuable in analyzing any difficult claims situation. They seemed eager to cooperate.

I took this experience with me when I called on several plaintiffs' attorneys who had successfully sued consulting engineers for professional liability. These attorneys opened a whole new vista to the professional liability problem—one that promised "something could be done."

Will Loss Prevention Work for Professional Liability?

Three months of researching, talking, examining claims, and personally interviewing consulting engineers yielded some 30 potential loss prevention measures for use in private practice (see Chapter 10). With these in hand, I called the president of CEAC, John Jewett, and told him what I had in mind. He suggested another meeting, so I met with the CEAC group and presented some of the loss prevention ideas. It was obvious that they had a great fear of antagonizing their clients with these "new" contract clauses, shop drawing stamps, limits on arbitration, changing personnel practices, and even adopting better telephone techniques. They gulped, swallowed their concerns and said, "Let's go for it."

We also discussed some of their jargon. It quickly became evident that they were mostly unaware of an immense communications gulf that existed between themselves, their clients, contractors, and the public. For example, they called the field work they did (that is, observing the progress of the construction to see that it conformed, in general, with the intent of the plans and specifications) *supervision*. This troublesome word was written into their contracts (if, in fact, a written contract existed at all) and it meant something very different to them than it did to clients, contractors, and members of the public. We advised them, "Get rid of the word *supervision* and use a more descriptive term for that portion of the work." They came up with better, safer terms such as *construction review, observation,* and *progress review.*

The consulting engineers' misunderstanding of the meaning of certain words on the application for insurance impeded underwriting practices then in effect. For example, one frequently asked question on their insurance applications was, "Do you do boundary surveying?" Many of them would answer "No," then be upset when the underwriter would deny liability for a claim involving "surveying." When queried about this the consulting engineers would say, "Hell, I don't do boundary surveying, but I do construction staking, layout staking, grade setting, topographic mapping, some photogrammetry, and level setting, just not *boundary surveying.* Why don't they ask what we do, if they want to know?"

The same problem occurred with the application question relating to subsurface soil investigating. When asked if they did that type of work, many engineers would answer, "No." As a result, the insurance policy exclusion for that type work would not be removed nor amended,* leaving many engineers without coverage for subsurface soil investigating. When claims were then presented and denied because of a soil failure, the consulting engineers would not understand why the insurance company refused to provide coverage. They would complain, "Well, I never do

---

* Exclusions in a policy limit coverage; may make coverage restrictive as to certain types of work or activities; sometimes the coverage can be "bought back" if the underwriter is apprised of the exposure and agrees to delete the exclusion.

subsurface investigations. Sure, I make an eyeball judgment about the soil's bearing capacity, or I rely on what I see on the adjoining site, but that's not making a subsurface investigation. Is it?"

Part of the consulting engineers' professional liability insurance problem lay with these major miscommunications between risks and underwriters. I became convinced that a specialist thoroughly indoctrinated in the duties, responsibilities, and communications foibles of consulting engineers was needed to make this kind of underwriting profitable.

It may be true of most people, but the business naïveté of some of these engineers was startling. They supposed that they started a business relationship with others on even ground. They tended to be honest and straightforward in their business dealings, so they figured everyone was. It was inconceivable to them that some businesspeople operate as if ethics are for fools and exploit others as much as the law will allow. Yet, in the claims situations that they related to me, it was obvious that many times they were simply serving as prey for the self-serving intentions of others.

With these findings as a backdrop, the nature of the professional liability loss prevention recommendations we developed, in the main, addressed not their technical proficiency but their business and personal deportment. Exemplifying this deportment was the way they handled slow payment of their billings. The amount of money they were owed, particularly the mechanical and electrical engineers, was sobering. It was hard to see how they could remain in business. One of the reasons they let their accounts get so old, they confessed, was that if they pushed for payment, clients would bring professional liability claims—something the engineers could ill afford to have happen. It was an area that needed creative thinking to obviate the threat.

We learned of one way of handling this problem from a mechanical consulting engineer, Fred Weir* of Bayha, Weir & Finato. Fred was interested in all aspects of our professional liability loss prevention effort. I found out later that his interest was probably stimulated by one of his employees, Joseph A. McQuillan, who was going to law school at night and who, at a later date, was going to loom important in our overall professional liability loss prevention effort. Fred related that his practice with slow-paying clients was to get a document from them stating that they had been satisfied with their work before putting on the heat for payment. This idea became part of our defensive program.

Another loss prevention idea came to us from a plaintiffs' attorney who had been very successful in winning claims against consulting engineers. Robert O. Wilhelm was a good attorney of spotless reputation who had graduated from Georgia Tech in civil engineering before going to law school. He agreed to help define areas of potential risk. He said, with his

---

* Great grandnephew (very possibly) of Capt. Thomas Weir of Custer battlefield fame, and father of Robert Weir, lead guitarist of the rock group, the Grateful Dead.

Georgia drawl, "Why in the name of heaven do they use a shop drawing stamp* that says APPROVED on it? When I have a case involving a dispute between a consulting engineer and one of my contractor clients over the way a particular piece of work was done, I zero in on that APPROVED. 'Ladies and gentlemen of the jury,' I say, 'this college educated man *approved* the work my client performed. Now he's trying to contend that he's not responsible for the failure that ensued. Can we believe that?' See, what I mean? Tell them to get rid of that odious word." (You may recall that the word *approved* played a part in the Vasa tragedy related in Chapter 1.)

Sometime later we were able to get Wilhelm to tell the members of CEAC about his concerns at a regular monthly meeting at the Palace Hotel in San Francisco. He hammered home the fact that engineers in private practice were saying things in time-worn words that meant something to them but had different meanings for the uninitiated laity, that is, potential jurors. They were words that lawyers could easily twist—a bad point of exposure in a litigious environment.

Raymond Hill of Leeds, Hill and Jewett suggested replacing APPROVED with NO EXCEPTIONS TAKEN. Many a claim has been won by design professionals who have reduced the ambiguity of APPROVED with a more appropriate word or phrase. Certainly, this change alone would have an impact on engineers' vulnerability to claims when things went wrong on construction projects and a contention was made that their "approval" was at fault.

New York, the Insurance Mecca

By the fall of 1962, we at A&A had developed some 30 changes in practice procedure that we believed would reduce claims frequency and severity for consulting engineers in private practice. The CEAC volunteered to spend time and effort getting the recommendations disseminated to their membership. At the same time, we continued to look for an insurance underwriter willing to take on the consulting engineers risk, altered by an untried technique—professional liability loss prevention. It was decided that I should go to New York to meet with A&A's top marketing people to explain the idea of professional liability loss prevention to them.

The marketing guys at A&A turned out to be wonderful. Besides Bob Shipman I met Lou Bonar, Bill Hulbert, Connie Giles, Joe Barr, and they all listened to my story, but it did not arouse much interest; my clients were not in the same league they were used to dealing in. Individually, they were experts in their own fields (i.e., railroads, department stores, airlines), but the consulting engineers bewildered them.

---

* A rubber stamp used by architects and consulting engineers to demonstrate that they have reviewed drawings and specifications prepared by a contractor to show how he intends to build a portion of a structure, and that they either will not permit his methods, will permit them, or will permit them if certain changes are made.

A&A's New York office placed me in touch with the vice president in charge of professional liability insurance at one of the few underwriters still writing this type of coverage. He visited our San Francisco office, and we put together what I felt was a solid presentation for professional liability loss prevention as a tool to improve a *marginal line* (their term not mine). He fidgeted in his chair, and I could see that he was not buying the concept. Finally, he could stand it no more and burst out with, "You can't stand at their elbows and keep them from making mistakes! They commit errors and omissions! Lots of them! To say they don't is just wrong! You can't change the way things are done with a few fancy phrases? Forget it! It's not going to work. It's professional negligence pure and simple. You are barking up the wrong tree." He left with a scowl on his face and a firm conviction that what we proposed was ludicrous. Some of the A&A people were sure he was right. I even had a moment or two of doubt about the course I had taken.

Life is funny. Sometimes, when you least expect it, it seems that miracles happen. That was to be the case in this situation.

I received a call from David Farmer, a special agent for the Kemper San Francisco office, saying he would like to introduce me to one of their home office people. I said, "Fine," and he brought Ron Seaver, a young special risks man from Kemper's home office, to our office. Both men were bright-eyed, well-dressed, and looked every inch the insurance professional (although there are those who argue that there is no such thing). I thought to myself, "These guys are like something out of *Dress for Success.*"

"We're looking for interesting risks that other underwriters may shun. The type that, if we do a little work with them, will turn into good risks," Ron started off. He and Dave looked very serious, kind of like they were pulling a gag. I thought, "Where'd they find out about my consulting engineers? Are they just having fun? It must've been the guys in New York trying to get a chuckle." So I decided to play along with their joke.

"Are you just giving me a line of BS, or what?," I asked with my widest, sheep-killing-dog grin.

They both continued to look serious, but now shocked at my resort to the vernacular, and Ron said, "One thing I do not do is kid about a thing like this. Our company is in an exploratory mood, and we will look at large risks and anything you've got outside of automobile fleet exposures."

"Well, if this isn't a joke, have I got a line for you!" I then proceeded to describe a plan for professional liability insurance for consulting engineers in private practice.

As had been agreed with the CEAC, we offered, besides professional liability insurance, all other lines of the consulting engineers' insurance, comprehensive general liability, auto, floater policies,* workers compensation, and so forth. The other lines were to bolster the premium volume to

---

* Coverage on an "all risk" basis for equipment such as transits, lab equipment, office fixtures, and other personal property.

make a program economically feasible from the underwriter's point of view. With the insurance plan outlined we discussed professional liability loss prevention and Ron began to show a keen interest in the concept. He explained how Lumbermens Mutual Insurance Company (Kemper's founding company) had been formed by lumber dealers, much as Employers Mutuals had been formed by timber, pulp, and paper manufacturers. Like Employers Mutuals, Lumbermens Mutual keystone to success had been mandatory loss prevention. He asked intelligent questions and made notes from our CEAC claims and insurance surveys. We tried to give him copious amounts of information so that he could make an intelligent judgment.

Ron and Dave left, promising to get back in touch with us soon with a tentative answer. They needed to talk with the head of their unit, Hiram L. Kennicott, Jr. and Robert L. Moore, a loss prevention expert, and get their concurrence before taking on what they billed as an "experimental venture." A month later Dave left Kemper and was replaced by David B. Mathis,* an extremely bright and enthusiastic addition to the Kemper San Francisco office. He assured me that our proposal was receiving "the very highest consideration, and you'll be hearing from us soon."

---

* Soon to be chairman and CEO of the Kemper Corporation, Long Grove, Illinios.

Chapter 5

How to Build an Insurance Company

In this world there are only two tragedies. One is not getting what one wants, and the other is getting it.

—Oscar Wilde, 1854–1900

In November 1962, Dick Alexander, vice president, West Coast regional manager, and son of one of the founders of A&A, told me that I should drop the consulting engineers and begin working on Fortune 500 type risks. I was devastated and considered seeking alternative employment. Luckily Sam Shriver, chairman of A&A, came to visit our San Francisco office and asked how the program was going. "Gee, Mr. Shriver, haven't you heard? Dick Alexander wants me to drop it and work on large accounts."

"Tell you what, Ed, just keep on working on it. I'll make it okay with Dick and Hugo [Hugo Standing, manager of West Coast sales]. I think an association plan might be a good thing for our organization." I was overjoyed that things had worked out, and I looked forward to 1963.

The year was born without any word from Kemper as to whether they would commit to a program of professional liability insurance for the members of the CEAC. This made me nervous. An awful lot of effort had gone into trying to get a scheme of professional liability insurance started for their members. That effort would be gone, wasted, if something didn't happen soon. Although my employer, A&A, hadn't said anything, I could count, and I knew that the debits outweighed the credits on what some termed "a pipe dream." The clock was ticking, and we still didn't have anything that would indicate future success.

In early January, Dick Alexander and Phil Ness came to San Francisco. As A & A's vice chairman, Phil Ness was in charge of the production department and was very serious about his job. He had an extremely impressive list of his own accounts that demonstrated his capability. One of these was the McDonnell (now McDonnell-Douglas) Corporation in St. Louis. Their affinity for their insurance broker, Phil Ness, was so strong that, in 1959 when I tried, I couldn't even get in the door. Phil and Dick called me into the conference room with stern seriousness and asked what I was doing. Their interrogation included a lot of phrases like, "Is it true that . . . ?" and "How do you hope to . . . ?" I must have waxed great with enthusiasm because after awhile they said "Thanks" and excused me.

A few years later (in fact, December of 1966) Phil Ness told me with a hearty laugh, "Ho, ho, ho! You know, in that meeting we had actually come to fire you for what Dick Alexander viewed as 'gross insubordination'. You see, Sam Shriver forgot to make things right with Dick and Hugo. They thought you were being defiant. Sam didn't explain to them what he'd told you until I got back to New York after our trip to see you. Isn't that hilarious? Ho, ho, ho! But you sold us, by golly."

Phil Ness turned out to be an extraordinary guy, highly perceptive about people, sensitive and concerned about doing things fairly and properly. He is, without question, the best boss I ever had.

Shortly after their visit, about January 15, I got a call from the president of the CEAC, John Jewett, asking that I participate in their annual convention at the Santa Barbara Biltmore the first week of April. "We'd like you to prepare a two-hour presentation—10:00 A.M. until noon—to cover this professional liability loss prevention thing and be prepared to answer questions about insurance. They will all be interested in that."

I'm reasonably certain that he didn't hear me gulp before I accepted the assignment, but I did. I thought that without Kemper's answer it might be tough to carry out. So I began forming in my mind what I would say if Kemper decided they didn't want any part of it. I also had to wonder about job opportunities for a failed insurance salesman for the same reason.

On January 23 the phone rang and the deep, relaxed voice of Ron Seaver said, "I can't promise you anything, but we'd like to talk to you some more about your professional liability loss prevention plan. Several people are involved, so could you come to Chicago? If so, how soon?"

"Gee, yes," I answered, "tomorrow, or the next day. Whatever fits your schedule."

Ron considered the options. "Well, Bob Moore, our loss prevention expert isn't due back for a week. He's critical in our evaluation. How about the first week of February? And, oh, Ed, you might put together an exhibit on rates and forms, that is, the professional liability. We have them on the other lines."

So I called the Los Angeles office of A&A and they, not sure if I knew how to negotiate a deal, called A&A's New York office to break the news. They decided that someone should go with me, I guess to keep me from putting my foot in my mouth. This was fine with me since I'd been known to put my foot in my mouth before. I'd had virtually no experience in developing rates for professional liability insurance on consulting engineers. Neither did I know all that much about forms, even though I'd studied Lloyd's of

London forms, and the domestic insurance companies', and I didn't like them. The contract language just didn't seem to fill the bill.

At that time, professional liability insurance rates for design professionals in private practice were figured by body count. That is, the number of technical personnel working in the firm, the number of others, each times flat rates, times a credit for years of experience, times a debit for type of work (for example, 20% for sewage disposal design or 75% for soil testing). It wasn't a very good measure for exposure, but it was the one being used in the insurance industry, so we thought we would have to follow suit.

The consulting engineers had asked, "What happens to the work I did before the company that you arrange insures me?" This meant that we had to give full retroactive coverage for all work done prior to the binding date of our coverage. It also meant that we had to get full disclosure of any existing situation that might reasonably be expected to give rise to a claim. This area of underwriting rose to haunt us in the future. You see, the consulting engineers considered many of their conflicts meritless, therefore, not likely to give rise to a claim. In reality, of course, even the slightest hint of displeasure should have been reported to the underwriters so they could make up their minds whether a situation might "reasonably be expected to give rise to a claim."

Getting to Know Kemper Corporation

Going to Chicago in February, on purpose, isn't the smartest thing to do. My plane was late, the weather was abominable, and freezing rain impaired the visibility from my taxi as we crept toward the motel that the Kemper people recommended as "close to the home office." Close it may have been, but as my taxi pulled up to drop me off, the motel rose toward me like a Dickensian specter—its dark, dingy windows stained from neglect and its general state of disrepair lent it an almost abandoned look. The neighborhood itself was grimy, run-down, and coated with the gray snow that is the hallmark of winter on Chicago's North Side. My misgivings increased as I checked in with the motel clerk, who gave the impression that people generally stayed in the place only an hour or two.

The negotiator that A&A sent from New York, ebullient, affable Connie Giles, didn't arrive until about 1:00 A.M., so we weren't able to discuss forms, rates, or other particulars of the intended program. But we got up early so that we could talk during breakfast. As we might have expected, there was no place to have breakfast at the motel (and I'm not sure we would have wanted to eat there anyway). We decided to check out and go to a restaurant in the Kemper neighborhood.

Connie and I took a cab to 4750 Sheridan Road, the Kemper home-office building. There was no restaurant in sight, so we went into the building. It was old, dark, stained brick, with no architecturally redeeming features, probably built in the early twenties as a factory and warehouse. But it was perfect for a mutual insurance company where every penny was preserved for the benefit of the policyholders. We were met by Ron Seaver who took us first to their cafeteria to quiet our hunger pangs. Then we met his boss, Hiram L. (Hi) Kennicott, Jr. who gave us a brief history about the founding of the Kemper organization and its philosophy. Since it is important to the theme of this book, here's Hi's narrative the way I remember it:

"James S. Kemper was raised in Van Wert, Ohio. His father was an attorney who hoped that young James would follow in his footsteps or, lacking that, become a Presbyterian minister. Upon graduating from high school at age nineteen, James had a strong mind of his own and decided against either choice. College was out. A close friend of the family, Mrs. M. L. Purmont, suggested that he go to work for the Purmont insurance company, The Central Manufacturers Mutual, which he did. He showed remarkable sales ability and was soon transferred to Chicago to service The Central Manufacturers Mutual's agents and investigate the rising number of fires of the lumbermen policyholders. He performed this duty in such an outstanding fashion that the lumbermen looked upon him as an insurance wizard.

"In 1912, Illinois passed a workers compensation act that quadrupled the rate they had been paying for employer's liability insurance coverage. The lumbermen, sensing in young James S. Kemper a man they could trust, asked him what they should do. He replied, "Form a mutual insurance company, reduce your exposures with loss prevention techniques, and hire me to run it." They took his advice. They borrowed $20,000 as capital, and started the Lumbermens Mutual Casualty Company on November 18, 1912. James hired his brothers, Mark and Hathaway, to help run operations. Then he hired Hiram L. Kennicott, Sr., the husband of his wife's dearest friend, to perform public relations and safety committee work. James S. Kemper, Sr. continued to act in a sales capacity, making calls in the daytime and writing up policies on the kitchen table in the evening.

"They formed several other companies in the years to come, always adhering to the philosophy that blessed them with success with the Lumbermens Mutual Casualty Company. Their keystones were dedicated loss prevention engineering and absolute honesty in their dealings."

Hi went on to explain that James S. Kemper's philosophy was rooted in his culture, and this philosophy was clearly enunciated to all of the people who went to work with Kemper. While it was an eight-point program, the essence of Kemper's philosophy was to give the best coverage possible at the best price, and to always deal fairly with people. The philosophy must have taken hold since in over 25 years of working with Kemper people, I must say that they've inevitably dealt with me and my clientele in a thoroughly fair and honorable way. They were always faithful, loyal, and, above all, dedicated to the James S. Kemper credo. That is hard to say about most companies.

Hi is a giant of a man. His knowledge of insurance is prodigious and his creative mind was fired by our proposal. We found that he and I had many common interests—lapidary, ham radio, and astronomy among them. He called in his team, Art Webster, Joe Luecke, Bob Moore, and Ron Seaver.

Art Webster was (and is) without a doubt one of America's most knowledgeable insurance technicians. Bouncy, exuberant Joe Luecke would reign as the CEO of the Kemper Corporation from 1979 until 1992.* Joe was Ron Seaver's counterpart for the United States east of the Mississippi River, a recent transfer from Philadelphia where he had been in Kemper's audit department. He was very quick-minded—one explanation was enough to give Joe a good grasp of the picture. R. L. (Bob) Moore was the loss prevention superintendent. Bob had a more positive attitude about professional liability loss prevention than almost anyone to whom we had explained the concept. To boot, he was an expert in the overall subject of loss prevention (i.e., fire, industrial, burglary, vehicular) and was a thoroughly can-do type of person when it came to our proposal. Ron Seaver, initially our primary contact, was then very young, but wise beyond his years. He knew casualty and property insurance forward and backward and had a good grasp of social amenities. He was also one of those conscience-driven people who felt "If it's not right, don't do it."

For several hours we discussed the concept of trying to underwrite consulting engineers, the Kemper team expressing some doubt that we would know how to make a proper assessment. One idea that the consulting engineers had suggested caught their fancy. "It takes one to know one" might be a good description of the technique. In other words, we would draw on the consulting engineers' knowledge about their fellow engineers in order to make an underwriting judgment. Actually, this technique had been used by the underwriters at Lloyd's of London in the early days of insurance (circa 1769). Ships' captains were asked their opinions about other captains whose ships were undergoing underwriting scrutiny. These seafaring men could spot dangers instantly that might spell doom for the underwriters if a particular ship and crew were not seaworthy. They would seek out rumors of drunkenness, failure to follow fire saftey rules, neglect about long lines fore and aft without properly weighted anchors, and other risk factors. Many other industry-owned insurance companies had followed a similar underwriting procedure. We felt that the "ask their peers" underwriting technique might be valid with consulting engineers. As it turned out, it was.

Another point that tickled the Kemper team's fancy was the comprehensive, 22-page application form that we had developed with the help of the consulting engineers. They felt, as did we, that if you are going to be

---

* When Joe Luecke retired in February 1992 he was asked what he would like to be remembered for in the years to come, and he responded, "That I was successful in reinforcing the philosophies that have been in existence at Kemper since its founding, and that we treated everybody fairly and created a positive work environment."

writing professional liability insurance, you would be acting not only as an indemnitor but almost as a guarantor of the professionals' technical proficiency. Thus, you had to know a good deal more about them than just, "Have you graduated from school?" We delved into their financial status, contract practices, personnel policies, really all of their business abilities that we believed might be related to the claims brought against them. After hearing Hi's story about the founding of the Lumbermens Mutual Casualty Company and the other Kemper companies that followed, I could see why they felt a kindred spirit with the approach I was suggesting. After all, it coincided with their business philosophy.

The Kemper team agreed that they were ready to proceed, but on an experimental basis. Many features about the process would be new and radically different from anything they'd ever done. Not the least of these was their agreement to give our A&A office exclusive agency to provide the coverage; not a popular thing in a company strongly oriented toward an open-agency system.

Art Webster looked at our recommended professional liability form, and then edited, tweaked, deleted, and added several astute provisions. They agreed to having the professional liability coverage written as an endorsement to the comprehensive general liability policy to fill a void in coverage between the two types of exposures. That is, consulting engineers and architects perform many duties in connection with their practices that do not call for professional training. These duties are not professional acts; they are simply operational acts, not intended to be insured in a professional liability policy of insurance. If someone were to trip in their office anteroom, for example, their comprehensive general liability insurance would come into play for any injury, not their professional liability insurance.

We'd learned that one professional liability insurer sent out reservation of rights letters* on over 20% of the claims presented to them by design professionals because of this ambiguity. This was not a good situation for the insured since it might place him or her in an insurance coverage limbo with neither the comprehensive general liability insurance company nor the professional liability insurer accepting the insured's claim for indemnity. We thought it would vastly improve coverage to have both types in a single policy, with one company, so there would be no question about their being insured.

By 2:30 P.M. we had the details of the rates, form, and communications channels worked out. The insurance policy issuing company would be AMICO. Hi Kennicott agreed that Ron Seaver would be our primary contact and that he could accompany me to Santa Barbara to make a presentation to the CEAC convention. Our business concluded, Connie Giles and I left for

---

* A letter from the insurer saying that they would defend the claim, but reserve the right to deny liability if discovered facts, later, showed that their coverage was not proper for the alleged damages.

the airport. In the taxi Connie asked me with some amusement, "Why'd I come here?"

The Consulting Engineers Association of California

"Holy Toledo!" I thought on the flight back to San Francisco, "How am I going to get all of the work done? Over 150 members of the CEAC, the convention presentation, form letters, and most of all, who's going to do the fieldwork in southern California?"

The next day I called Dick Alexander to explain my predicament. He asked that I come down as soon as possible to discuss the logistics of an association program (one which he had been very much against). The following Monday I flew to Los Angeles, checked into the Chapman Park Hotel (a charming old hotel with Hollywood-type gardens and gracious early-California architecture) and went to see Alexander in his tastefully darkened office at 3440 Wilshire Boulevard. He explained that they were short-handed but that he had a man with whom I could work "if you won't take more than a third of his time and if you will do all of the necessary training. We need for him to develop his own client base of substantial-size corporations. These engineers really aren't the type of clients that we at A&A are looking for. You understand?" He then arched his eyebrows and gave me a look that conveyed disapproval. He rang for Peter B. Hawes, who was going to be my salesperson in southern California. Peter impressed me with his youth and, even so, his good grasp of insurance parlance. (His father was with the large insurance brokerage firm of R. B. Jones in Kansas City, Missouri.) Peter agreed to give our effort his best shot; he seemed to grasp the rationale of professional liability loss prevention right away.

Peter and I went to a conference room to look over the materials that we had developed in San Francisco and to study the rates and forms that Kemper wanted to use. Peter explained that he had graduated from Dartmouth, served in the Marine Corps, gone through a training program with A&A in New York, and was working on his CPCU.

"Look," he said, "your program seems just swell, but I don't know how long I'm going to be here. I'd hate to have you spend a lot of time with me, then leave you in a lurch when I have to go. I'll do my best, but I don't know if I can hang on very long." It seemed he was feeling the frustration that most starting producers in the insurance business feel, that there just isn't anything to sell. Sometimes this frustration becomes monumental, leading producers to think, "It has to be better at some other brokerage house." Peter said that he'd even been talking to other potential employers.

"Listen, Peter, just give me two months. Go with me to the CEAC convention during the first week in April. Then we'll make calls for a month, and if you still don't like the job, then change. You can wait two months, can't you?" I pleaded.

He agreed, but without much enthusiasm. I think A&A had given him an almost impossible task, asking a 26-year-old guy to call on major corporations, run by 60-year-old CEOs, and convince them that *he* was the answer to their insurance problems. Job frustration had to be the result. He did not really have anything to sell except the A&A name. Although the name was good, it wasn't always good enough to tip the decision scales in the salesperson's favor. Most young insurance producers usually quit after a year or so due to the frustration, and they take jobs where the work-reward lag time is not so long.

The Convention

Santa Barbara is a lovely place to be in April. The sun is bright, the palm trees lend it an aura of elegance, and the cool Pacific Ocean breeze keeps the ambience luxurious. The Santa Barbara Biltmore, the site of the 1963 CEAC convention, had been built to accommodate the 1932 Summer Olympics. It had been thoroughly refurbished in an attractive early-California architectural style. Across the road from the main building, overlooking an ocean so blue it looks unreal, is the Olympic-size swimming pool. Ron Seaver, Peter Hawes, and I arrived in time for the CEAC welcoming happy hour and banquet. We were struck by the conservative nature of the engineers' automobiles—all American-made, not flashy, and not the top of the line. At the happy hour, as Spanish guitarists strolled among us, we noted the engineers' restrained drinking demeanor, not like contractors or insurance guys. Their wives were conservatively dressed and were the same age as their husbands. These characteristics told us something. It convinced us that we might have difficulty jarring these guys loose from their current insurance arrangements; they'd take the most conservative route—do nothing. That is, unless we could convince them that they could control their professional liability fate.

The following morning the meeting started with various reports on CEAC's affairs by CEAC President Bud Kelly and its officers. I won't say it was boring, but it certainly wasn't like sitting through a three-ring circus. At 10:00 A.M., John Jewett introduced Ron, Peter, and me and said that we would propose a plan to reduce the professional liability problem. I started by giving them the history of the Lumbermens Mutual Casualty Company, Employers Mutuals of Wausau, the Hartford Insurance Company (merchants that practiced fire-reduction techniques), the Fireman's Fund (I told about whalers and how they cut their insurance losses by having their ships south of St. Paul's Island by September 15th at the insurance company's request), and then suggested that this same approach—loss prevention—would probably work with the professional liability exposures of consulting engineers in private practice.

Ron explained that our insurance plan would be "experimental" and that it called for them to sustain the underwriter with virtually all of their lines of insurance in order to mitigate their expected losses from the professional liability exposure. The three of us revealed the need for them to change their practice procedures so they would be less of a target for claims. We introduced the idea that the claims against them might not be the result of errors and omissions in their designs but, rather, the direct consequence of their inattentiveness to business and legal details in their practice. We tried to show that they were vulnerable because of a host of unmodified business practices in a claims-raging business environment.

Peter Hawes gave them a synopsis of A&A's history and a list of their California clients, which was impressive to me, but resulted in glassy-eyed stares from the consulting engineers that said, "So what?"

Following a coffee break we had a question-and-answer period that we hoped would create a positive, participative atmosphere. It far exceeded our expectations. One young, dark-haired guy, wearing glasses, who had been twisting in his chair the entire morning, raised his hand and said, "I'm Jim Stratta, Simpson, Stratta and Associates, structural engineers in San Francisco. Just who in the hell are you guys, anyway? I know my insurance agent, I've known him for 12 years, and now you want me to dump him and give my insurance to you guys on the speculation that you are going to cut down on claims! What the hell? I've never had a professional liability claim, and I don't expect to have one, so what are you going to do for me?"

"Well, sir," I countered, "while it may be true that you've never had a claim, we all know that professional liability claims frequency is rising at a startling rate. You've probably never had smallpox either, but I'll bet that hasn't kept you from getting a vaccination. We are proposing that you seek protection now from a scourge that, statistically, could visit one in three of you this year. Don't wait until it's too late! What has your 12-years-of-service agent done about this problem except collect premiums? Please give this a chance. You may be glad you did."

This didn't seem to mollify Mr. Stratta.

Questions continued for the balance of the morning. Most questions were about things like, "How come the company issuing the policies will be the American Motorists Insurance Company? Isn't that a company that writes automobile insurance?" We explained how one of the Kemper Companies was best suited to provide this coverage since it wrote all lines of insurance and was a participating stock insurance company. This was to their advantage, we further explained, because it meant that at some point we might begin paying policyholder dividends if the loss experience justified it. That's what participating stock insurance companies do.

"What happens when I retire?" "What about the work I've done in the past?" "Who will handle the claims, and do they know anything about our work?" "Will it cost as much as my current coverage?" "What will you do about our outstanding certificates of professional and general liability insurance?" We answered these questions and others until it was time to adjourn.

The applause was mild as the meeting broke up. Some of the older guys came up to me and said, "Don't let that Jim Stratta bother you. He's somewhat of an upstart. He'll come around." Fortunately for us, he did.

I guess our presentation was not like a three-ring circus either.

As with most meetings of this kind, the real communications come after the formal presentation. Ron, Peter, and I were kept busy running from caucus to caucus answering all of the consulting engineers' special questions. The southern California engineers wanted to make certain that we had sufficient staff to meet their special needs. Many had insurance expiration dates coming up that they were concerned about. They wanted to make certain that we'd visit them first, so we set up meetings with nearly 30 firms to be visited in the month of April.

We had a meeting with the principals of Woodward, Clyde and Sherrard (now Woodward-Clyde Consultants) to talk about their special needs. Richard J. Woodward, CEO of the firm, and Eugene B. Waggoner, manager of their Denver office, both attended the meeting. Both men were important in our future. Ray Lundgren, Arne Ollitt, George Hervert, and Stan Gizienski were also in attendance asking about our attitude on soil and foundation engineers (now called *geotechnical consultants*). We said, "As long as you only do a minor amount of soil and foundation work with residential subdivisions, we may be interested in insuring you."

The unanimous response was something like, "Hey, are you crazy? A majority of our work is in that area. We couldn't quit that type of work. We have a sacred duty to provide those services. Society needs well-qualified firms to perform services on residential property. You are just way off base with that suggestion."

I wanted to say something biblical in response, but all that came out was, "Yeah, but how about all the losses?" That was not the answer they wanted. We parted friends, but the residential subdivision problem kept us from doing business with them for at least fifteen years.

Another engineer who was inquisitive about our program was Thelo Perrot, a Stanford graduate in civil engineering from Palo Alto and an amazing guy. Thelo had passed the bar because he said he wanted to be able to deal with attorneys. He also trained himself and took the test to become an actuary since he didn't trust them. He thought their art was arcane, maybe even a sham. Who could argue with him on that score?

Thelo had just come from the annual convention of the California Council of Civil Engineers and Land Surveyors (CCCE&LS) in Palm Springs. "Hey," he said, "you ought to deal with those guys. They work harder on loss prevention than these wimps. They are principals of the design function, not like most of these guys who work mostly for architects." His lip gave a slight curl when he said "architects." I gathered he didn't like them much.

"Well, gee, thanks, Thelo, but we have our plate pretty full now. Tell your friends in CCCE&LS what we're up to and maybe in another six months or a year we can talk to them," I countered. But Thelo, in his typical bulldog fashion, wasn't going to be put off. He wanted a meeting "next week," and I agreed to one in two months.

Thelo and I became fast friends. He was a person of faultless character and impeccable principles. He was a strong adherent and proponent of the loss prevention concept until the time of his death.

Ron, Peter, and I decided that we liked consulting engineers. They were gregarious, straight talking, inquisitive, mostly honest (the exceptions were shocking because they were so uncharacteristic), and they tended to recognize the extreme importance of loyalty, an attribute I have always felt is paramount in business dealings. As a group, they were knowledgeable about many things besides engineering; they showed their intelligence at every turn, even when talking about politics.

We were still not certain how they would vote on our request for a broker of record letter* the following day. We were pleasantly surprised. They voted almost unanimously to appoint A&A their broker of record for an insurance program. I was tickled to see Jim Stratta raise his hand in our favor. He was on his way toward becoming one of our staunch supporters in the years to come.

Two guys sitting in the first row during our presentation had been scribbling just as fast as they could write. When I asked Bud Kelly about them he said, "Oh, the younger one is Jack McMinn of *Engineering News Record* and the other one is Ralph Torgerson of *Consulting Engineer* magazine."

My, they were interested.

Field Underwriting and Selling

The first month following the CEAC's Santa Barbara meeting, a great clamor for proposals arose from the consulting engineers. Peter and I ran ourselves ragged trying to meet their demands. Because of the length of the application form and the wide geographical area we served, we could not make more than three or four calls per day. Our agreement with AMICO stated that we would go onto the premises of the consulting engineers in order to make a visual evaluation that would be included in our submission. We were also to make inquiry from the peers of the policy applicant to make certain that there were no hidden problems about which we should have been aware. We found many.

In keeping with our professional liability loss prevention analysis, we were most interested in the applicants' business practices, leaving their technical proficiency to their peers. We needed to know if they would be inviting claims by their failure to take rudimentary protective steps against the inevitable failures that seem to be a part of new construction. We had a whole

---

* A letter from a policyholder giving an agent or broker the authority to represent him or her in the insurance marketplace.

list of questions and requests that other underwriters had not been interested in requiring. Each of these questions was aimed at an area of professional liability claims frequency, and although the consulting engineers objected to what they felt was nit-picking, they relented and became cooperative once the reasons were explained for the needed detail.

In very short order we began writing a bunch of insurance; the numbers of policies far exceeded our expectations. Much of the work we did with Ron Seaver and his colleagues was handled by telephone since the rush for coverage was so great.

Holy Toledo!

Ron Seaver had returned to Chicago from Santa Barbara and immersed himself in the files that had piled up on his desk. About a week after his return, on a Monday morning, he heard a great commotion coming from the office of Norris C. Flanigan, Kemper's chairman. Ron's desk may have been a hundred yards from Mr. Flanigan's office, but the roar was certain, "Ron Seaver! Seaver! Get in here! Right now!"

Ron felt like having a heart attack or some other severe illness to give him an excuse for leaving the premises; he was certain Mr. Flanigan was going to do him great bodily harm. Some years later I learned firsthand about how Norrie Flanigan could fly into a rage. He could charm the moon out of the sky when he wanted to, but when his Irish was up, look out! Nonetheless, Ron hurried to the chairman's door and presented himself, "Did you want me sir?"

"Want you? Want you? You're damn right I want you! Look at this! Just look at this!" Mr. Flanigan held up a copy of *Engineering News Record* with a headline blazoned across the cover proclaiming, "Kemper to Start Professional Liability Insurance Program for Consulting Engineers in California." So that's why Jack McMinn had been writing so fast.

"This magazine article mentions you and A&A and says you're going to write professional liability insurance. Is that about right? How in the name of holy hell did you get us involved in something as idiotic, moronic, and stupid as that? Do you realize what you've done? You have made me look like a fool, a lying fool, a laughingstock, that's what you've done! While you were in Santa Barbara, I was in Palm Springs at the Kemper Key Executives' meeting. I told them that there was no way in hell that we would write professional liability insurance of any kind after our disaster with medical malpractice! Now look what you've done. How do I explain this away? Get out! Send in Lansman* and Kennicott. I want to get to the bottom of this!" Flanigan roared.

---

* Manager of underwriting at that time.

What went on at the subsequent meeting has not been revealed, except for the understated comment by Hi Kennicott that "Norrie wasn't pleased."

To Flanigan's credit, he stuck by Ron's commitment in true Kemper form, but he never did get over his dislike for this "long-tail"* business. He was not from the underwriting side of the insurance business and, like so many people who aren't involved in underwriting, he had a fixation about malpractice insurance business of any kind. If it were professional liability business, he thought it had to be "bad, bad, bad!"

Ron recovered from his shock, but he can still give a vivid account of his memorable meeting with Norrie Flanigan, so intense was the perceived threat to his person.

Consulting Engineers' Community

Peter Hawes and I involved ourselves in the consulting engineer community. We attended their luncheon meetings, and if we weren't part of the program, we listened and learned. Before long we began to pick up the parlance and subtle nuances of engineering life, for example, the history of their organizations, why the CEAC had been formed, and by whom.

H. J. Brunnier, a world-renowned structural engineer, told me how when they had feared unionization in San Francisco, the principals of the various firms in San Francisco, including Matt Simonson (Tom Simonson's dad), Clyde Bentley (Bentley Engineers, mechanical engineers), H. Hammil, and others got together and decided they should form an organization to resist unionization. The potential founders met in the Pied Piper Room at the Palace Hotel, where every drink sold is a double. Mr. Brunnier told me about their first meeting at which he remonstrated when the acting president called the meeting to order to start business. Mr. Brunnier said to them, "Hell, we can't start to do business yet. We need to get to know each other first. Until we can call each other S.O.B.s without someone getting mad, we aren't ready to conduct business. I say let's have another drink, then some lunch, and defer business until we're better acquainted. It may take awhile, but we've lived this long without an organization, so let's wait a little longer." And they did.

In selling our program we ran into a fair share of resistance. Most of the consulting engineers were very much in favor of the professional liability loss prevention program, but they had fierce loyalties to their insurance agents and brokers that they were reluctant to breach. I used to go to Los Angeles about once a month to give Peter what aid I could muster with these tough sales situations.

---

* Liability insurance in which the settlement of a claim may come years after the first notice of claim; it makes it difficult to determine whether the line is profitable or not.

Peter Hawes set up appointments for me with those firms showing the greatest reluctance to join our effort (we had promised a person-to-person sales effort). In October 1963 he arranged for us to visit the financial manager of Leroy Crandall & Associates, Leopold Hirschfeldt. We had our proposal in hand and felt confident that we would show an outstanding money savings over their current insurance arrangements. Hirschfeldt spoke with a decided German accent (I learned later that he and his family had fled Nazi Germany to Sweden where they'd lived during World War II) and was strictly business in his demeanor, pleasant but not enthusiastic.

We laid out our figures and explained several coverage advantages, none of which seemed to impress him. He finally said, "I appreciate what you're trying to do, and we want to participate in the professional liability loss prevention effort; however, our insurance agent has been working with us for 10 years. He has performed well, and we have had no instance of his ever failing to deliver what he promised to deliver. We appreciate that. He even told us to sign up with your program. We will not abandon him because of a money savings, no matter how large. The coverage improvements would be nice, but they are not governing. What is controlling is his loyalty to us and our loyalty to him. Loyalty breeds loyalty. So thanks, but put us down as supportive, but not participative."

"Mr. Hirschfeldt," I asked, "do you mind telling me who your agent is?"

"Not at all," he replied, "Richard L. Narver."

When Peter and I got outside, Peter said, "You know, I like that guy. There aren't many people around who show that kind of character. I think Mr. Hirschfeldt is a rare treasure." I agreed.

Some years later, when it really counted, Leo Hirschfeldt showed us the same kind of loyalty. I will always remember him as a rare individual in a money-driven business world.

Another firm we called on was Converse-Davis Consultants in Pasadena. We met with Bob Davis, an extremely pleasant gentleman for whom the term *laid back* must have been invented. He said, "Our agent told us to buy your deal. Fred Converse and I like your proposal, but we just can't leave our agent. You see, he has stepped into several situations for us and given us extraordinary help when we needed it. A major portion of his business is for consulting engineers, and we appreciate his dedication and knowledge. We can't leave a guy like that. Can we?"

"Well, that's your choice," we replied. "May we ask who your agent is?"

"Oh, that's Dick Narver. You know, he's the son of Lee Narver, one of the "dirty dozen" guys who started the Los Angeles chapter of CEAC, and he's a principal in Holmes & Narver, Engineers."

Peter Hawes and I were impressed with the unusual forthrightness of this insurance agent in his dealings with our two potential clients. He had told them to buy from us because he really thought we had better coverage and a better price than he could supply. To do such a thing is almost unheard-of in the insurance business. We got to know him later and he always exhibited the same regard for honesty in his dealings with us that he had with his clientele.

By the middle of 1963 we knew that consulting engineers were an exceptional class of people. Perhaps insurance people become jaded by the people they deal with; the shady stunts we had seen pulled in order to save a few bucks, or to get something for nothing, were rife. Consulting engineers were different; they were what you hear midwestern farmers call "good people."

Consulting engineers had not been treated well by the insurance industry. Our applications proved time and again that the wrong messages were going to the various underwriters of professional liability, general liability, property, and workers compensation. This failure had created disputes about rates, coverage, and good faith. For example, consulting engineers were not aware that they needed special coverage for any joint venture they entered. If they joined other consulting engineers to do a job for a city, for instance, they were unaware that special coverages were needed for the newly formed partnership that is legally created by the formation of a joint venture. They would require separate workers compensation, professional liability, comprehensive general liability, and property coverages (for any property owned by the joint venture). Out of this lack of awareness, disputes arose with their carriers when claims were presented. Understandably, the consulting engineers thought the underwriters were trying to dodge their responsibility. Underwriters thought the consulting engineers were trying to avoid premium payments. Lawsuits and recriminations were the result of these disputes.

Another point of contention that came to light several times was the exposures engineers had with their valuable papers, that is, plans and specifications in progress. For these valuable papers, they needed a special valuable papers floater policy with the value of the documents scheduled and reported monthly. This coverage insured, on an "all-risk" basis, the value of the work they might have put into a set of tracings or documents at the time of the loss (from fire, burglary, vandalism, etc.) on an "all-risk" basis. Most consulting engineers seemed to be unaware of this need. As a consequence, they did not understand why an insurance carrier would pay for the cost of the paper (under an ordinary fire policy), but not the value of the professional work product (i. e., the engineering drawings and computations) committed to that paper when a loss occurred. They thought the insurance underwriters were exhibiting bad faith, when actually the underwriters were simply adhering to the correct procedure. They had not been advised of the special value exposure and could not provide coverage after the loss for a document of speculative value.

We discussed these findings with Ron Seaver, Art Webster, Hi Kennicott, and Bob Moore of AMICO, pointing out the need for a total risks approach with the consulting engineers' exposures. Anything less opened the door to uncovered hazards and disputes with the insureds. This also meant that an agent or broker who took an application had to be specialized in their type of risk in order to do the job right.

By the middle of 1963, Bob Moore thought it was time to produce a professional liability loss prevention manual for consulting engineers in private practice. I was assigned the job of writing it, and AMICO said they would arrange for its layout, illustrations, and printing. We had it ready for publication in November 1963. It was titled *Blue Print for Professional Liability Loss Prevention*, and it may have been the first professional liability loss prevention manual ever produced. It received accolades from the consulting engineers (but, of course, they had nothing with which to compare it). We thought it was great too. But, what did we know?

In September 1963, I traveled to Chicago to work with Bob Moore on the professional liability loss prevention manual. I was asked by A&A's New York office to call on the newly merged Chicago office, A&A-Bartholomay & Clarkson. I did so and told them about our program. They showed immediate interest and committed two of their salespeople, Bob Tivanan, with Dave Shyne as backup, to work with us if Kemper would agree. Before long, we were issuing policies in Illinois.

We continued working doggedly through the fall of 1963 trying to keep up with the growing demand for AMICO's coverage. Applications that I brought in each morning were processed and proposals were ready to be taken out the same evening. We hand-delivered all proposals and went over them with the consulting engineers. We believed that we could not do the job right without a constant one-on-one relationship with our consulting-engineer clients.

Peter Hawes was just as busy in southern California; he no longer seemed interested in a career change.

In early December 1964, I received a call from Hi Kennicott. "Hi, Ed. I just had a meeting with Harry Lansman, our vice president in charge of underwriting. He's been in Seattle. There's a firm up there, Hurley, Atkins & Stewart, that the Seattle office of Kemper would like to do more business with. Harry told them about your program and they are extremely interested. They have a number of consulting engineers as clients, and their business is heavily oriented toward construction. Harry wondered if you would be willing to talk with them about some kind of subagency arrangement. It's up to you, but I thought you might be willing to talk."

"Well, sure, Hi, I'll talk, but most insurance guys won't be willing to do the work. I mean, all transactions on a face-to-face basis, a 22-page application to be completed by the agent on the risk's premises, learning the professional liability loss prevention information, getting involved in the consulting engineers' community, and getting information from the risk's peers. You know, a lot of the consulting engineers' offices are quite small. Traveling for three hours to fill out an application and getting a minimum premium for all that work even has our management questioning this program. But this is an association effort; we have to serve large and small. Have them call me. If this doesn't discourage them, nothing will," I replied.

A day later I got a call. "Hello, Mr. Howell, my name is Jim Hurley. I think Harry Lansman may have spoken to you about our interest in your consulting engineers' program. We think it sounds really swell. We'd like to talk to you about representing you here in the Northwest. My firm, Hurley, Atkins & Stewart, is well suited to do the fieldwork on special construction industry programs. How about if my partner, Jim Atkins, and I come to see you on Friday?"

It was close to Christmas, and we were getting revved up for the holidays, so a meeting didn't seem like a good idea, but then . . . "You can come if you want to," I told him. "I'll be glad to talk, but you may be discouraged by the amount of work it will require. Still, we'll see you on Friday at 10:00 A.M."

The two Jims, both lanky Northwesterners, showed up on time and explained their interest. Their firm was heavily involved in construction. Gus Stewart, the other partner, did bond work* while the two Jims provided the property and casualty coverages for contractors, architects, and consulting engineers. They seemed to have a familiarity with consulting engineers, and they were undismayed by the prodigious amount of fieldwork involved. Jim Hurley was a former Kemper employee and seemed comfortable with them as the underwriter.

In making an assessment of a potential agent or an employee, I always look for four attributes before getting really serious about doing business with them. First, is the initial impression a favorable one? Do they make good eye contact, smile, and say something that shows social skills? Second, does their history show they have exercised self-discipline in a major way; for instance, have they learned to play the piano, pursued a hobby requiring practice and learning, studied a foreign language on their own, earned a major degree, or done something else demanding commitment. Third, have they been involved in some effort that shows a strong strain of selflessness, such as being involved in aid for the blind, the Salvation Army, Planned Parenthood, the United Way, or some other group requiring assistance where payment in return is neither given nor expected. Fourth, is their personal life in order, the thought being that if they can't take care of their own affairs, they won't be able to help you with yours.

The two Jims passed these tests in spades. They were both friendly, self-confident, well dressed without being flashy, and gave a good first impression. Both had exceeded the self-discipline measure. Both were good family men, well liked in their community and admired by their competitors (I asked). So they looked good.

I explained to them that the first thing we needed was a meeting with the two associations involved, the Consulting Engineers Council of Washington (CECW) and the Consulting Engineers Council of Oregon (CECO).

---

* Performance bonds, payment bonds, indemnity bonds, and others used in the construction business.

This would enable us to start a professional liability loss prevention program and secure broker of record letters so we could represent the associations' interests with AMICO. They left, promising to have the meetings set up soon after the first of the year.

Not once did they ask about the commission arrangement. I took this as a good sign since they seemed concerned most about doing the job right. Then too, they knew that the collateral lines premium volume would be as much or more than the professional liability's, so they knew this gave them the chance to make out well financially. They did.

The meetings were scheduled, first with the CECO at the Multnomah Club in Portland, where I spoke to them about the loss prevention concept. The consulting engineers seemed to be receptive to the idea of a mutual effort to reduce claims and dodge the legal system. The president of the CECO, Rowland Rose´, made a short speech about how it was time to "pull together on this problem." He said he had not had claims, but knew this could not last forever. Several members recounted war stories about how they had had claims made against them that were completely meritless. It was a common theme.

I was impressed with the consulting engineers' high regard for the two Jims. They seemed to trust them implicitly; something I learned to do myself as the future unfolded.

We went from Portland to Seattle, where I repeated the speech. The CECW members were equally enthusiastic, and it appeared we had the beginning of a viable program of professional liability loss prevention and multiple lines insurance for the states of Washington and Oregon.

The next step was field training. This was easy since Hurley and Atkins worked as a team, the two of them calling on prospects together. We spent a week calling on the consulting engineers in Washington and a week in Oregon. The importance of field underwriting was stressed. We had the duty of trying to separate the wheat from the chaff: Those consulting engineers who were most likely to have claims due to their laxity in business matters were the chaff; those who were good business practitioners were the wheat.

They also learned how to make discreet inquiry about an engineer's technical proficiency. It was (is) not uncommon for the question to be answered by, "Well, I don't like the S.O.B., but he's a good engineer." I have never been aware of an instance where I thought the information we received was in any way vindictive. The consulting engineers, although fiercely competitive, seemed to recognize the importance of absolute truth when discussing their colleagues' technical capabilities.

Hurley and Atkins decided, as Peter Hawes and I had, that they liked consulting engineers. While we ran into some really colorful individuals, most were dedicated and goal-oriented, that is, really incensed at the way the legal system was dealing them a body blow, from their vantage point, without provocation. Their goal was to fight back. Our professional liability loss prevention concepts seemed to them to be one promising method.

Jim Hurley was, on all accounts, one of the most remarkable men I ever knew. His dedication to his clientele was awesome. He looked for ways to aid them in their insurance needs, and he went out of his way to show them how things might be made better for them by making simple changes. He was a man for whom the word integrity may have been invented. Jim Atkins's technical knowledge was an excellent complement to Hurley's missionary zeal.

The underwriting crew in Chicago were soon trusting the two Jims as much as we did in the San Francisco A&A office. They would take their word on underwriting recommendations, and their faith in them did not falter when they bound coverage* for Rowland Rose´ (president of CECO) on June 21, 1965, and he reported a claim the next day. That sort of thing happens frequently in the insurance business.† They had acted in good faith, and so had Rose´.

The two Jims did a good job so that by the end of 1965 we had a successful program going in Washington and Oregon, despite the fact that their other partner, Gus Stewart, thought they were nuts. "Stick with contractors!" he advised.

More Jurisdictions

In short order we had programs going in Colorado, Maryland–Washington, D.C., Texas, Minnesota, Illinios, Massachusettes, and Connecticut.

In March 1965, I received a call from the chairman of the insurance committee of the Consulting Engineers Council (CEC), which is now the American Consulting Engineers Council (ACEC). "Hey, Ed, this is Sigmund Roos. We'd like to meet with you at our spring CEC convention in St. Louis to talk about your professional liability loss prevention and insurance program. The insurance committee thinks it might be time to be thinking about a national program. Is that a possibility?"

"Maybe," was the best answer I could give. Kemper had said that they were short of insurance capacity and did not want to expand further, but if we wanted to set up a facility they would help. This led to the idea of an industry-owned insurance company, owned mostly by design professionals in private practice, to be called Design Professional Insurance Company (DPIC). "Gosh!" was my first thought, "how do you build an insurance company?"

---

* Issue a memorandum of coverage prior to the time that the policy is issued. Binding coverage is usually done with a written document, but may be done verbally in some instances; however it is done, it is always subject to the terms and conditions of the policy.

† In the mid-sixties, A&A had an account for whom coverage was bound on some underground tunnels (thought to be safe from fire) at noon. At 2:30 P.M. some boys started a fire in one of the tunnels, completely destroying it. It makes you wonder.

Chapter 6

Insuring the Insurance Company

It's time to bake bread.

—Howell family proverb

When the going gets really tough in our family we say, "It's time to bake bread." We said it in 1929 when, during the depths of the depression (the depression visited Butte prior to the rest of the nation) my parents were forced to move from Butte, Montana, to Seattle in order to make a living and feed five hungry kids. We said it in 1942–43 when all the older Howell boys went off to war (and miraculously all came back). I said it when I was charged with the challenging task of making an insurance company go.

My maternal great-great-grandfather, Joseph D. Yeoman, and his wife, Sarah Nowels Yeoman, pitched a tent in 1834 next to the rapids of the Iroquois River in the Indiana Territory (about 60 miles south of Chicago) at the very center of what was to become Rensselaer, Indiana. They were the first Caucasians to homestead in that area, the nearest neighbor being five miles to the southeast. As quickly as possible they began constructing a log house to fend off the subzero weather that winter might bring. They were not able to complete their dwelling before the snows came and spent the winter with a pile of burning logs in the center of the cabin for warmth. The smoke escaped through two empty shingle courses of the roof. While prepared food was scarce, hunting was bountiful, and they survived to plant their first crop the following spring.

In 1837 their first of five children was born. Thomas Jefferson Yeoman was the first non-Native American child born in what was to become Jasper County, Indiana. My great-grandfather, David Huffman Yeoman, was born September 26, 1841. The following spring, Joseph Yeoman had to leave his small family to go down to the Wabash River to buy building supplies. Sarah felt apprehensive but urged him, "Godspeed. We'll be just fine."

In the middle of the second night after Joseph's departure, Sarah was awakened by horrible screams and yells. The walls and ceiling of the cabin showed eerie lights, dancing and dodging in a fantastic display of grotesque shapes. She leaped from her bed, looked out the window, and her blood froze. There, not 100 feet away, were about 50 Native Americans stripped to the waist, standing in the rapids of the river, with torches hoisted in one hand while the other wielded a paddle to fling fish out of the rushing water up onto the bank. She wondered, "Do they know I'm here? Alone?"

Sarah was rigid with fear but climbed back in her bed to contemplate what her next move should be. She prayed. The macabre yells and ghastly howls continued, causing her to shudder fearfully even as her two boys slept peacefully. Finally she resolved, "It's time to bake bread."

She arose, lit a precious candle, dressed, and had three loaves baking by daylight. At sun-up, the Native Americans approached the cabin with strings of fish which they motioned could be exchanged for the sweet smelling bread.

In Great-Grandfather Yeoman's obituary, published by the Rensselaer Republican on July 22, 1921, it was reported: "The savages were very docile and offered her no discourtesy, though it may be imagined that the solitude was preferable to the presence of such visitors, too much cannot be said of her courage in facing the dangers of pioneering life." ('Atta-girl, Great-Great-Grandmother Sarah!)

Reflecting upon her experience, I thought, "Starting an insurance company can't be such a big deal."

Insurance Company Capital

Raising insurance company capital in the early 1970s was a trick best left to magicians. At the time, insurance companies were having severe profit pangs and were not something in which a reasonably prudent investor sought gain. Investment advisors would tell their clients, "An insurance company? With no track record, no management, writing [errors and omissions] insurance? You've got to be kidding." To further delay money raising, we had several regulatory governmental agencies with whom we had to deal—not only the Department of Insurance, but also the Department of Corporations, the Securities and Exchange Commission and the Internal Revenue Service.

To start dealing with these folks in October of 1969 we had to find a good attorney, one with whom there was no conflict of interest and who would not have to be schooled on the "let's build an insurance company" procedure. George Blackstone, who had helped us on other matters (see Chapter 9), felt he was in potential conflict, so he recommended Walter Olson of Orrick, Herrington, Rowley & Sutcliffe, one of San Francisco's "large" law firms. DPIC's executive committee liked Walter. He was cool, knowledgeable, friendly, and had vast experience. We hired him to help us work with the Department of Insurance, and other agencies, and to prepare a public offering to be used in as many states as we could gain admittance. Very soon, Walter turned our file over to a subordinate, Paul Weber. After running up gigantic legal bills, the prospectus was completed, printed, and sent to about two-thirds of the members of CEC. (The other third had state laws, called Blue Sky Laws, that kept us from soliciting their investment. Some of the insurance commissioners were dead set against us. In Wyoming, the insurance commissioner said, "What? Another claims made form? Not in my state, by God!")

The DPIC board was charged with the task of publicizing the company's formation, the issuance of the prospectus, and the urgent need for investment by the consulting engineers' community. Although there was an initial burst of investment, by the fall of 1970 investments in the fledgling company began to lag. We needed $1 million or we were in deep trouble. Many of the management people of A&A were loath to be involved in anything that might fail. A&A had become a publicly traded company and anything that might affect its price adversely on the New York Stock Exchange was given a jaundiced eye. Joe Barr, A&A's vice president of marketing, in particular, began urging us to drop the effort.

Don Buzzell, executive director of CEC, and the executive committee of CEC, pitched in to help as much as they could. They arranged for speaking engagements at their annual convention in Salt Lake City, for Richard Woodward, Chuck Blair, and me. In addition, we traveled the country, meeting with the grassroots members of CEC, pointing out how this was a unique opportunity for them to capture their professional liability insurance future. One thing was hard to overcome—consulting engineers just don't have a great deal of extra cash to invest in anything. Making payroll was tough enough, but to take money out of current cash flow would put a serious crimp in their operations.

The California Council of Civil Engineers and Land Surveyors

From April 1963, Thelo Perrott had been extremely persistent that we work with the CCCE&LS in a program of professional and general liability insurance. CCCE&LS was also interested in group health and accident insurance and group sliding scale workers compensation* plans similar to the ones we had devised for CEAC. There is a good Aristotelian axiom to remember in situations like this: "Man is by nature a political animal." It was

---

* A plan that combines the experience of an entire group into a single retrospectively rated plan; if their experience is good they may get a policyholders dividend; conversely, if their overall experience is poor, they may be called upon to pay additional premium.

not surprising then that the CEAC, through the process of political logic, objected to the civil engineers and land surveyors in *their* insurance programs. This was a point upon which they were adamant.

So in 1965 hoping to use the American Home Insurance Company of New York City as the underwriter we decided to start a second professional and general liability insurance program. One of AMICO's San Francisco underwriters, Lynn Borchert, had gone with American Home in San Francisco and was familiar with both our program and the underwriting process. Lynn said the approval to start the program would have to come from the home office in New York, and he set up an audience for me with the proper party.

The insurance marketing pundits at A&A in New York told me, "American Home plays hardball. So have all of your ducks in order, or they will throw you out the front door." Luck has much to do with the fortunes of life. In this case, luck was on my side.

The American Home Insurance Company is a subsidiary of the American International Group (AIG). They have a fascinating history, starting with their founding in Shanghai, China, by a man named C. V. Starr. In 1965, American Home's president was Maurice R. Greenberg, a man with a knack for making a profit in the insurance business when all around him are crying their woes. The A&A people told me he would never allow our professional liability plan because, "He's just too tough."

I went into their unpretentious, even austere, offices on John Street in lower Manhattan with a mixture of misgivings and high hopes to see Mr. Brewer (not his real name), the vice president of casualty special risks underwriting. He turned out to be a nice, easygoing Canadian—easy to talk to, perceptive, and loaded with questions. Lynn Borchert had sent him a package of materials about our program. He had done his homework, was primed as a steel trap, and like most underwriters, he sought to find the flaws in our offering.

"Tell me, Mr. Howell, this retroactive coverage, is that like the supersedeas clause* in a fidelity bond? I mean does it cover only up to the point that prior coverage was provided or does it cover to the full extent of our much broader coverage so long as claim is made or suit is brought during the policy period?"

I took a deep breath before responding. "Well, it provides coverage retroactively for past errors, omissions, or damaging professional acts to the full extent of the terms and conditions of the succeeding policy. So, from that point of view it's similar to the supersedeas clause of a fidelity bond. It's designed to make certain that there is not a gap in the coverage that could lead to a denial of liability and subsequent lawsuit."

---

* A clause or an endorsement that provides coverage for a loss that took place during the currency of a prior fidelity bond, if it had been insured in the prior bond, but the coverage is subject to the terms of the new bond even if they differ from the bond they replaced.

"How can you be sure that this underwriting method you are suggesting will work?" he countered. "The idea that they survey their peers leads to the possibility of dishonesty, doesn't it? Really, how do you know you can trust these engineers to tell the truth about their colleagues?"

"Mr. Brewer, these guys are engineers. They're different. For the most part, they don't think about being devious or underhanded. They are really different from other professionals. Integrity is part of their discipline. They don't know how to be deceitful. Without this regard for integrity they would be out of business. I have staked my reputation on the fact that they can be trusted. They've exhibited only the utmost good faith and honesty," I answered.

Brewer flushed slightly. "You know, Ed—may I call you Ed?—I'm a licensed civil engineer who left the field to go into insurance, but I do think you have hit it on the head. Engineers are different. I wish I'd stuck with engineering, but a wife and four kids meant making more money. Not easy in civil engineering just after the war."

Unbelievable! Now, was that what you'd call luck? I would.

In slightly over two hours Brewer was ready to proceed. We met with his boss who said, "I hope you know what you're doing." They left the details of rates, form, and procedure up to Lynn Borchert and me.

Hoping to have a little fun with the marketing guys, I went back to the New York A&A office. I entered with a downcast, hang-dog look on my face that they interpreted as an admission of defeat. "See," one of the marketing guys said, "they're too tough for you way-out-west guys. You should have let us handle it. Man, you have to have finesse in New York."

"Oh, yeah?" I responded. "They just gave me more than I asked for. Full $250,000 primary limit and excess as we need it," I answered with a crocodile grin.

Within a month and a half we commenced issuing policies to the civil engineers and land surveyors.

The members of the CCCE&LS were a different breed from the consulting engineers. For one thing, almost all of them were the prime design professional on the job. That meant they did not work for architects, as a majority of the members of the CEAC did, and their firms, overall, tended to be larger than the consulting engineers' firms. The fact that they did not work for architects made them an "easier sale" for certain professional liability loss prevention measures, and their larger size resulted in greater average premium per insured. These two facts resulted in excellent underwriting results for the first two years.

Their group medical and disability insurance program was also highly successful, with a majority of the members becoming participants during the first year.

A large measure of the success of these programs could be attributed not only to Thelo Perrott but to Bill White, their executive director, and Vincent R. Fisher, a smart, wonderful guy who was manager of services for CCCE&LS. White and Fisher were highly pragmatic about these insurance plans. They knew that anything that was good for their constituents was good for the organization and for them. They took a guarded position initially, but when things began going right, really right, they fell full square behind our effort to expand the participation. They saw to it that the professional liability loss prevention messages we developed were communicated to their members in a forceful way. They put the full weight of their governmental affairs committee and their paid legislative advocate, Ad Long, behind our effort to reduce exposures through legislation. I think you'd call the relationship between A&A, American Home Insurance Company, and CCCE&LS "symbiotic."

Many of the civil engineers' claims were the result of residential subdivision failures, such as slope collapses, soil problems, drainage failures—the same as for the soils and foundation engineers. But we couldn't say, "Don't do that type of work" since much of their income depended on designing those spectacularly huge, American-dream subdivisions with names like Sutter Mill Knolls, Avocado Highlands, Quail Acres, or Orange Grove Estates.

It became obvious that if we were going to provide professional liability insurance for civil engineers who designed these suburban enclaves, we would have to live with the high frequency of claims that came from drainage problems, settlement, expansive soil, adobe creep,* and differential settlement. While most losses were not large, if an attorney were involved the claimed damages could be enormous because emotional appeals to sympathetic, home-owning juries often worked. After all, what jury could resist giving loads of money to attorneys' clients who "haven't been able to sleep since they noticed that horrid, unsightly crack in their laundry room floor. The door to their most treasured possession, their house, sticks, and it's difficult to open when they have guests. They want restitution for all of these damages, plus sums for their soul-shattering pain and suffering."

We needed special professional liability loss prevention remedies for the civil engineers' unique claims.

Most of the civil engineers did some surveying—construction staking,† boundary surveying, layout—but there were those professionals who did this work exclusively, the land surveyors. My experience with land surveyors made me conclude that they were a special kind of person. Conventional wisdom would have us believe that they operate scientifically, but I learned

---

* Some soil in the California hills creeps inexorably down at a rate that is governed by the moisture content. It may be only 1 or 2 millimeters per year or as much as 6 millimeters. It slowly twists a house's foundation causing cracking, spalling, and distortions that make doors stick and windows bind. The damage is slow, but unsightly and a nuisance. It frequently is not noticed until the subdivision developer has long gone, leaving the civil engineer vulnerable to claims.

† Setting stakes to show the contractor where various components should go, such as the foundation, walkways, plumbing, and electrical facilities.

that they, like soil and foundations engineers, relied on an arcane art. Their field notes, often passed down from father to son, made it possible for them to keep order in an area of potential chaos. Field notes, frequently kept with a stub pencil, might say, "From the big live oak tree, go 250 yards east to the thalweg [deepest channel] of Bancroft Creek, thence north to the red clay sewer pipe that comes under Iris Canyon Road . . ." Not scientific at all, but it works. Would it shock you to learn that it's worked in places like downtown San Francisco? It seemed unbelievably loose to me when I first learned that surveying was more an art than a science.

Land surveyors' work, similar to that of civil engineers, was subject to claims that, for the most part, were not serious. Buildings would be misplaced,* fences would encroach on neighbors' property, boundary disputes would erupt, but most controversies could be settled amicably—if there were no attorneys involved.† If there were, it would be the same as with the civil engineers, "My client can't sleep, . . ." We needed special professional liability loss prevention methods for the land surveyors. We were able to develop these with the land surveyors' help.

We found in our CCCE&LS clients that an unexpected number of the civil engineers were canny businessmen. They were risk-takers who didn't shrink from betting on long shots. That may have been a major source of their professional liability claims frequency. At least one of them thought so. He was Sydney B. Mitchell, a highly regarded, venerable practitioner with an office in Sunnyvale, California. I visited him to take an application for various coverages in the fall of 1965. I got to the part where I'd ask about claims and he answered, "I've never had a professional liability claim in all of the years of my practice."

"To what do you attribute that good fortune, Mr. Mitchell?" I queried.

"Well, you see, I have worked for the same developers for years. They don't shop around for lower prices and I won't work for developers that do. Many subdivision developers want to squeeze every inch of space out of a subdivision, and they place dwellings where there's bound to be trouble. My plans won't allow that. Drainage patterns sometimes dictate that particular parcels will receive greater than average runoff. These should be reserved as greenbelt, or parks, so someone doesn't wake up some night with 4 inches of

---

* While most surveying claims were subject to low-cost settlement, we heard of some that were not. One of these was the misplacement of an oil well that struck it rich, and then was discovered to be on a neighbor's land. How much do you think that might have been worth in damages?

† One that was not involved a property-line dispute between a doctor and his next-door neighbors. The doctor had a house in Sausalito, California, overlooking Richardsons Bay. He did not care for the sexual proclivities of his next-door neighbors and sought to make them uncomfortable by bringing suit to force the relocation of the common fence. The land surveyor who had set the boundary line was joined as a defendant. The surveying to set the boundary had been done in 1913. Suit was brought against the surveyor in 1963! It cost the land surveyor almost $10,000 to gain dismissal. Pretty tough on an eighty-year-old retired surveyor.

water in their bedroom. Developers who shop for low-price civil engineering will want minimum-sized brow ditches* that may work four out of five years, but on that fifth year they'll run over and cause failures. I don't take that kind of risk. I don't have claims. I just keep working for the same developers. They know I'm not the cheapest engineer in town, but they also know they haven't been sued a dozen times," Mr. Mitchell replied.

Mr. Mitchell taught me a lot. We added a question to our professional liability insurance application aimed at determining what the hiring fidelity level of developers had been with the civil engineer applicants.

Civil engineers also do sewer and water project designs. This means that they work for governmental agencies that let their construction work through a bidding process. Any licensed contractor with the required bonding capacity may bid on the work. Sometimes contractors get hungry and bid much too low. When they do this and find that they are losing money—lots of money—they may look around to see who might aid them in their time of trial.

Hal [contractor]: Hello, Henry, this is Hal. You know we bid that Cypress County sewer job. We were $160,000 low. I thought we could make it up with extras,† but the civil engineer isn't allowing them. He's a nit-picker. Says the plans are clear and that we just goofed. Well, frankly, I can't afford to turn it over to the bonding company. That could ruin me for good. Do you have any ideas? I'm desperate.

Henry: Hal, as your attorney I can only advise you about your legal rights. I don't know construction, but you need to think about putting the civil engineer and the county on the defensive. You know, like we did on that Butte County job. Remember, we found out that there were lots of cobbles‡ in the area to be trenched that didn't show up in the plans and specifications. Oh, don't forget the civil engineer on that job did approve that clay pipe with his shop drawing stamp. You had substituted the clay pipe for the reinforced concrete since it saved a bundle. When it failed, we pointed out to him that he had approved it, and he backed down. Also, have your estimator go over the plans looking for errors. I can almost guarantee he'll find a bunch. There are always the soil problems. Claim that there are "changed conditions." Tell them you didn't count on them. Point these out to the county administrator and ask for extras. He'll lay them at the feet of the civil engineer. Finally, deny, deny, deny! Tell the civil engineer that the plans and specifica-

---

* Ditches dug along the brow of a hillside terrace designed to catch rainwater that would otherwise run down the terrace face causing erosion or even land sliding.
† Sums of money granted to a contractor for work performed that is not clearly called for in the bid documents. Extras are allowed or disallowed according to the architect's or engineer's judgment. It can create a point of contention between the parties, and may result in litigation. Some dishonest contractors make use of minor inadequacies in the plans and specifications and thereby claim extras in order to make more money.
‡ Large, randomly spaced, stones.

tions were ambiguous, equivocal, muddled, garbled, and erroneous to a fault, and we've got four witnesses to prove it. Tell him that we'll see him and the county in court. See, you have to make them think you have the upper hand. You don't want to go broke, do you?

For that type of scenario, we needed a very special professional liability loss prevention approach.

The members of the CCCE&LS took on their professional liability problem as if it were an engineering challenge—"Okay, here's the problem, and here's the solution." So we had a team approach to doing something about the runaway costs of professional liability claims defense and indemnity. We at A&A tried to identify the problem areas, devise professional liability loss prevention remedies, and the CCCE&LS members had to implement these remedies in their day-to-day practice. They pitched in, and we began to make real headway. By the end of 1967 we had a good program going, with an acceptable loss ratio, growing premium volume, and happy policyholders.

Robert Burns (*To a Mouse*, 1785) wrote, "The best laid schemes o' mice and men Gang aft a-gley" (often go awry). It would seem he was right with respect to our complacency with what we viewed as a well-established program of insurance. We were at the height of an insurance capacity crunch, and the insurance companies were scrambling to increase their ability to improve profits. This led to what one employee at the American Home Insurance Company's San Francisco office billed as a "bloodbath." The manager of the office and some others were discharged. Lynn Borchert eventually left, and went with the Department of Insurance, leaving American Home without an underwriter skilled in our area of professional liability insurance for civil engineers and surveyors. As mentioned earlier, Greenberg was known for his ability to show a profit when others in the property and casualty business were foundering. For whatever reason, the San Francisco office of the American Home Insurance company went into a retrenchment, part of which was their reevaluating the casualty insurance business that was being written. They didn't like long-tail business, which meant they didn't like our program. This is when you want to scream, "Tilt!"

In 1967, the CEAC hired a new executive director, John Beebe. John is an amazing guy. A skilled writer, creative and innovative. Above all he has keen political skills. He needed them. The person he replaced was Ralph Wescott, a mechanical engineer from Pasadena, with a flamboyant gift for gab and a strict protectionist of CEAC rights. Ralph was highly protective of the CEAC's insurance program. He was a great guy and fun to be with since he had a bottomless pit of anecdotes from which he would extract clever stories to regale all who listened. For example, he said about Joseph Sheffet, a structural engineer and a nondrinker, "I really feel sorry for Joe as a teetotaler. When he wakes up in the morning with a slight headache, he doesn't get to say to himself, 'This will be gone by noon.'" With John as the new executive director, we thought it might be timely to combine the two associations, CEAC and CCCE&LS in one insurance program with AMICO.

Our AMICO team at that time, Art Webster and a new man, John Roscich,* took a look at the loss ratio,† particularly the workers compensation, which was 13% for the previous year, and said that would be fine with them. CEAC's insurance committee met, and when we explained the advantages of combining the programs, such as further spread of risk, and greater volume, etc., they agreed to the unification.

RAR

In 1968, the personality of our programs was running counter to the culture of A&A. Then, too, there was some worry about professional liability. So A&A set up a subsidiary company, Risk Analysis and Research Corporation (RAR), making me president, to do our type of consulting work. We moved our operation to One Maritime Plaza, San Francisco.

When it came time to raise capital for the insurance company that was going to be DPIC, the CCCE&LS and its members made an investment that far exceeded what was expected from them. The organization made a hefty investment in its own name and the members rose to the challenge as individual investors as well.

By the late fall of 1970, things had become desperate. We had raised about $600,000, but further investments had slowed to a trickle. Many of our board members despaired of our ever being able to meet the deadline of April 1, 1971, set by the Department of Insurance. Dick Woodward and Chuck Blair remained stalwart, but others on our board of directors were convinced we would fail. Many of the A&A management people believed that my project was doomed; something they wanted desperately to avoid for financial reasons. Somehow, I just couldn't believe that things wouldn't work out—they always had. I had faith that all of our work would bear fruit of some kind. It is impossible to predict the future, but good things had happened and I expected they would again.

Phil Ness retired on January 1, 1971 and was replaced by K. W. S. Soubry, a more traditional-thinking man who really didn't think we should venture outside our own brokers-place-insurance-with-existing-insurance-companies arena. Maybe he was right.

Joseph R. Barr, one of the vice presidents of marketing in the A&A office in New York, placed a conference call to the West Coast regional vice president of sales, Hugo Standing, in the A&A office in Los Angeles and patched in my office in San Francisco, "Let's face it," he said, "you're never going to get that company off the ground. I'm going to renew the market search for a 'real' insurance company."

---

* Born and raised way up north in Athabasca, Alberta, John had a keen mind and vast knowledge about workers compensation and casualty insurance.
† Developed by dividing the gross premium earned by the losses paid and incurred.

"I don't think you should without getting the CEC's approval," I cautioned. "They are the client. What they want goes. Give us until March 1, then we'll make an evaluation."

This was followed up on February 12, 1971 by a letter from Joe Barr to Hugo Standing, with a carbon copy to me and Peter Hawes saying, in part, "We cannot ignore that our wholly owned subsidiary (RAR) is vitally involved in an unsuccessful venture, and we must insist that not later than March 1st, the prospectus be withdrawn, even at the risk of losing a client." The day I got my copy of that letter is the day I baked bread; that is, we formed a team and called every executive director of the CEC chapters in the United States and told them it was time to put-up or shut-up.

Toward the end of February, I was beginning to sweat. The investment still was a long way from complete, and the A&A deadline of March 1 was just ahead and the Department of Insurance's critical date of April 1st was near at hand. The Department of Insurance called a time or two to make sure that we understood our date for investments was April l, 1971. We did. Dick Woodward and I continued to visit the local chapters of CEC pleading for further investment. March 1st arrived, and since I did not hear from Joe Barr, we continued in our endeavor with white-hot zeal. On March 15, 1971, something almost biblical happened. Further investments began to pour in, so much so that by March 20, we were oversubscribed and had to plan on sending back thousands of dollars. By April 1, 1971, we were oversubscribed by over $250,000, all of which we were forced to return. This seeming miracle reinforced our resolve to make DPIC Different by Design and the very best insurance company operating in our field. We were sure we could do it. We did.

During the protracted capital-raising effort our reinsurance slips had become stale and it became necessary to seek new reinsurers to participate with us. I called Hi Kennicott at Kemper to see if he had any ideas. "Well, I can't promise you anything, but we are just starting a reinsurance division, Kemper Reinsurance Company. I can introduce you to them if you like. Also, I know some people at Guy Carpenter,* who might be able to help."

"Gee, Hi, that's great," I responded happily. Two days later I sent a package of material off to obdurate, unflappable, inscrutable Frank Aldrich, president of the new Kemper Reinsurance Company. He called and suggested that we meet the first week of May 1971. When I got there it was obvious that they were just barely starting their operation. They were housed in an old building about two blocks from Kemper's home office, on the same street as the elevated train, above a Chinese restaurant. Their offices reeked of onions frying in coconut oil, and the el rumbled by about every ten minutes with an earsplitting roar that caused all conversation to go on hold. They were literally crammed into their space with no room for any

---

* A subsidiary of Marsh & McLennan, and one of the largest reinsurance intermediaries in the world.

amenities. Even the reception area was piled high with boxes of files and supplies.

Frank's secretary met me and led me back toward his office. Indicating that I should sit and wait, she said that he was on the phone but would be with me in a moment. She pulled up a straight-backed chair and placed it just outside his door. Frank had his back to me so he hadn't seen me come up, and he was talking loud enough to overcome the ambient noise created by fans, the el, typewriters, and copy machines. What he said went something like this, "Yes, he's due some time this morning. A $250,000 limit. No, he says he can arrange the excess. Continental* says they are not breaking even. I know, I know. Yes, Hi Kennicott. Well, he's got something he calls 'limitation of liability.' No, 'limitation of liability.' George Tinker, our counsel, says it sounds crazy to him." Then Frank spun around and, seeing me, said, "I'll have to call you back."

Frank called in one of his vice presidents, Henry Tyas, who could be aptly described by the term *old pro*. Not that he was particularly old, but he certainly did know his reinsurance. I explained to them that we were hoping we could get our insureds to adopt a business policy of using limitation of liability clauses in their contracts of hire that would limit their potential liability to a stated amount. I had to admit that it was going to be a slow grind, but thought that it would eventually catch on and reduce losses dramatically.

We broke up our meeting at noon and went downstairs to the Chinese restaurant and had a sumptuous lunch of onions fried in coconut oil, boiled rice with just a hint of pork rind served on stainless steel pipe and plastic tables. As the el shook and shuddered by, Henry looked at Frank, and Frank looked at Henry, and they didn't say a word—just looked. Reinsurance people seem to communicate that way. I guess you could call it the "language of silence." Maybe it's part of being inscrutable, but whatever it was, I had no clue as to whether Frank would buy our deal or not. If I were to bet on it, I probably would have said, "No way."

About the time they were bringing the twisted cookie with the messages in them that say things like, "Boy are you in for a surprise," or "Do not faint from your good fortune," Frank cleared his throat and said, "Well, yes. I think we can do that—but with conditions. First, we will go quota share† at 50% of 80% of gross loss and loss expense only if you can get an-

---

* Continental National American Company (now CNA), the largest writer of design professionals' insurance at that time.

† Reinsurance is usually configured in one of two different ways. Think of the reinsurance as being books on a shelf; if they are stacked one upon another they are called *layered*; Reinsurance can be sold in that form with the reinsurer taking one of the layers above the primary layer (like the bottom book). This type is sometimes called *excess of loss reinsurance*. It can also be sold like books that are stood on end one next to the other, with the thickness of each book determining its share. Frequently sold this way reinsurance is called *quota share* or *shared-loss* reinsurance. In *quota share*, if the reinsurer takes a 75% share, it would be equivalent to a thick book, conversely if the reinsurer took a 10% share, it would be equivalent to a thin book.

other Best's rated A+ AAA* company to pick up the other 50%. That will leave DPIC with a $50,000 share of the first $250,000 of loss. You must pay us 84% of gross premiums written. You will have to arrange all excess insurance above the $250,000. We will pay you a ceding commission of actual expenses plus 12.5% for management that will be performed by RAR. The deal is good for 6 months, if you can get a quota share partner for us, which may be difficult." At which time Frank lost his inscrutable look and actually smiled a big friendly smile.

I agreed with Frank's plan, although the numbers were still spinning in my head: 50% of 80%, 84% of gross premiums written, 12.5% for management. "For Lord's sake, what does it all add up to?" I asked myself. I wondered all the way to O'Hare whether Frank thought I would find it impossible to find another participant. Then I wondered all the way to San Francisco whether I could.

The manager of the American Re-Insurance Company's San Francisco office was tall, good-looking Jim Koehnen.† We had put together a program of professional liability insurance with American Re-Insurance for soil and foundation engineers that had done well (see Chapter 9). I asked Jim if they would be interested in participating and he said, "Gee, Ed, I don't know. I really don't think we should be involved in any more professional liability. True, we got involved in that strange soil and foundation engineers program, but I don't think I'd want to commit to more. Besides, it wouldn't be up to me. It would be a decision made in New York. If you want, I'll set up an appointment. The guy you should see chews nails just for fun, so don't blame me if you draw a blank."

American Re-Insurance Company was located in one of those generic high-rise buildings, a yard wide and a mile high, on John Street in lower Manhattan. I had rehearsed my presentation on the plane and hoped that the head of underwriting, executive vice president John Sellen, who chewed nails for fun, was not as tough as Jim Koehnen had said. But he was. His secretary, who must have forgotten how to smile years before, led me into an office piled high with ragged, dog-eared files and folders of all description. Sellen was on the phone, reaching over to put his cigarette ashes behind the radiator and cussing a blue streak. "I don't give a rat's a - - what he told you. I'm telling you No, N-O, negative, nay. Can you understand? Yes, and you can go straight to hell." Crash! He slammed down the phone on its cradle so hard it sounded like a rifle shot. He turned to me with glaring eyes, and evidently didn't think a handshake was in order, because my hand hung foppishly in midair with no responding grasp.

He roared, "What in hell do you want?"

"Mr. Sellen, I'm Ed Howell. I think Jim Koehnen called you about my visit. I need reinsurance for an insurance company we're starting in Cali-

---

* Now, A+ XV.
† Became president of American Re-Insurance Company in 1973 and retired in 1982.

fornia—Design Professionals Insurance Company. I need about an hour of your time, sir," I answered apologetically.

"Young man, do you think I am out of my goddamn mind? Do you take me for a raving idiot? A lunatic? An insurance moron? Is it that you want me to reinsure a bunch of designers who have designed buildings along the San Andreas fault? Why are you wasting my time? You've got fifteen minutes." With that he took off his watch and, with a dramatic flare, set the alarm for fifteen minutes, laid it in front of himself, and gave me a scowl.

"Well, no sir, I don't think you're an idiot, that is, unless you don't give this new concept a fair hearing. About those earthquakes, the Prince William Sound, Alaska quake[1] of March 27, 1964, with a magnitude of 8.4 on the Richter scale did extensive property damage—some $310 million—killed 115, and injured several thousand. A number of the structures damaged were engineered, that is, they required passing and approval by local authorities for the engineering, such as the Westward Hotel, J C Penney Building, Hillside Manor Apartment, Knik Arms Apartment, and Four Seasons Apartment. Even so, there has been almost no litigation or claim for damages based upon allegations of design failure. This is not because there were no design flaws. There were. There were also construction inadequacies. The building owners and members of the public seemed to take the view that such a giant quake is "an act of God," outside of the reasonable foreseeability of a designer or a contractor. Then, too, the contributing multivariables that would go into a damage assessment preclude any credible claim from being made, on account of design negligence. You know, a person is not liable for damages caused by their tortious act if there is an efficient, intervening cause that may be the actual, effective source of the damage like an earthquake.

"If you can get by the earthquake exposure, Mr. Sellen, then I think I have an exciting concept to tell you about that will make this line of insurance attractive to you. We intend to make our company Different by Design. By that I mean we will be participative with our insureds in an ongoing effort to reduce losses by altering the course of their practice and changing our claims management techniques to obviate claims and claims' costs. We will do the job right! But let me tell you about limitation of liability—a technique whose time has come." Then I started a dissertation on the historical, legal, social, and business uses of limitation of liability.

Mr. Sellen scooped up his watch, held it out in front of me, and snapped the alarm button to "off." Two hours later he picked up his phone and called Donald McKay, president of American Re-Insurance Company, and said, "Don, are you free for lunch? I have this zealot in my office. I'd like you to hear his story."

At lunch John Sellen repeated my presentation, recalling figures, word nuances, anecdotes, and, in general, doing a rerun of what I had said straight from his memory. An awe-inspiring performance. It made me think of those guys who would read a page and then be able to read it again in their minds with total recall. What did they have in their genes to make it possible?

Don McKay gave John Sellen the same silent language. They didn't say a word—just looked. The "Oh, I see what you mean look." They had decided something, but what?

Back in his office, Mr. Sellen said, "We've decided to be a player in your plan. We'll take the 50% of 80% of the first $250,000 of gross loss and loss expense, and, if you like, we'll take 100% of $750,000 excess of the primary limit on the same ceding commission terms. That way you can issue policies of $1 million. But we'll be reinsuring Kemper in all states except California and Texas, where your company is licensed. Is that all right? Now, get the hell out of here. Can't you see I'm busy?" He did shake my hand at this point, asking, "You really believe in this loss prevention stuff, don't you?"

I was on cloud nine (wherever that is*) when I hailed a cab and said, "No argument. Kennedy Airport, by the 59th Street Bridge."

"Hey, mister," the cabbie said, "that's out of your way."

It was, but I didn't care, "Yeah, thanks, but do it anyway."

For some obscure reason, on my trip back to San Francisco, I had ringing in my ears the recount of my Great-Great-Grandmother Sarah Yeoman's frightening night.

Excess Insurance

A great animosity exists among many U. S. insurance companies. You might blame it on competition, but it seems to go beyond that. Even though the U.S. companies have ample financial strength to insure most U.S. risks, they have not been able to unify in an effort to accommodate some of the more difficult risks. As a result, for centuries U.S. insureds have had to turn to mother England and the European continent insurers for many of the more challenging-to-place risks. A whole subindustry exists for the placement of surplus lines risks. At one time *surplus lines company* meant an insurance company that provided insurance when all domestic, licensed insurance companies had run out of capacity to insure a particular risk. Now, it is more broadly interpreted to mean any company that is not licensed by a state to do the insurance business as a domestic insurer within its boundaries. It does business by subscribing to a surplus lines code that governs its mode of doing business. Another term that has become generic to mean surplus lines is *excess lines*.

This explains why the company that was to be Different by Design turned to Lloyd's of London for excess insurance for limits above $1 million.

I had been advised by A&A, in New York, that there was no market

---

* Maybe from the U.S. Weather Bureau typing of clouds with *cloud nine* being the highest cumulonimbus cloud that may shoot up to 40,000 feet. Thus if you're on *cloud nine*, you're way up there.

for excess professional liability insurance for design professionals in London. I wanted to see for myself since I was not convinced that excess underwriters had heard the whole story. So in June of 1971, my wife Jo, daughter Melinda, and I, climbed on a brand new Boeing 747 and flew to London.

I was told by an A&A New York marketing man, Bill Hulbert, to see Alan Parry, director of Sedgwick, Collins & Co. Ltd, Regis House, King William Street. I rubbernecked my way to Regis House, staring at all of the famous sights like Buckingham Palace, Whitehall, and Trafalgar Square, and finally arrived for the appointment. Alan was a very gracious individual who told me he did not have high hopes that any underwriters would be interested in "your scheme."* He introduced me to Bill East who was to take me to the "Room"† and guide me through the process.

We met several underwriters, and my guides explained to me how it was normal for the underwriters to be brokers too. In fact, when you count up the layers of intermediaries in a Lloyd's deal, you wonder how there is enough money left of the premiums to pay the claims. There is the originating agent or broker in the United States. Second, there is an excess lines or surplus lines broker in the United States that has a connection with a United Kingdom broker. Third, the United Kingdom broker (who may also have an underwriter's hat) will take the deal or, as they like to say, "scheme," to the fourth layer, the underwriter. Through each layer, a commission is paid. In spite of this inefficient business method, Lloyd's does considerable business in the United States.

I noticed that there was an air of formality in all dealings. Brokers stood in queues waiting, respectfully, to see the underwriters at their benches. All of the parties' moods precluded being addressed by first name, and social hierarchy prevailed throughout. Interpersonal contact of the players, while not stuffy, was rigid. It was "Mister-so-and-so" at every turn—something foreign for a California boy, where we are usually on a first-name basis at the first meeting. The thing they stressed to me was that, at Lloyd's, they believed in the absolute necessity for trust and honesty in all dealings. "Without that we would not be able to operate," Bill said. Jack Fleisch had given me similar counsel. I felt the same way and thought that was understood in our dealings with Kemper. The guys in London thought U.S. insurance brokers tended to shade their schemes to get the best deal. Is that possible?

---

*The term *scheme* does not have the negative connotation in the United Kingdom that it has in the United States. It means, simply, "strategy" or "plan" and not "conspiracy" or "plot" as it may here.

† A large, cavernous room at Lloyd's filled with "boxes" (high-back desks that could seat several persons on a front bench) from which underwriters conducted their business. The din was substantial; queues were formed for the purpose of negotiating with the underwriters; business was done on three-by-five cards.

We met with Adrian Dodnoble, Robert Hayes, Robin Jackson, and half a dozen others, all known underwriters of professional liability insurance of various sorts. At Lloyd's, everyone is betting the farm on the business that is written. That is, these underwriters had unlimited liability for the overall results of the Lloyd's syndicate. It is possible in a given year for the results to be so bad that they would have to sell or mortgage their homes, take their kids out of college, sell the family jewels, and then the farm, just to try to remain solvent. A sobering, financial burden. One which I don't think I would like. It makes them cautious, but still they are able to write business on risks that would turn a U.S. underwriter's hair white.

I told them about limitation of liability and how we hoped to beat the professional liability disaster facing consulting engineers. One of them, Reginald Postlewaite (not his real name), said: "Oh, I say, Mr. Howell, don't you think you are cutting your own throat with this limitation of liability strategy? I mean, actually, if your losses are all limited to a certain amount, won't your premium volume fall commensurately? Could put you out of business, you know."

"Gee, Mr. Postlewaite, wouldn't that be great? To be the person that so impacted professional liability that he went out of business. On the other hand, that isn't likely, is it? Look at Lloyd's. You've been using limitation of liability since 1601 on all of your marine risks, a major portion of your business, and you're still in business. It kept you from being sunk entirely. I am only following your lead."

"Oh, jolly good! You caught me there. Just wait until I tell Mum about the American who used *argumentum ad hominem* on me! Good show, chap. Sign me up. Oh, I'll go on that Land Stability scheme too," he answered with a toothy grin (see Chapter 9, p. 143).

Even though the others were not sure that limitation of liability was a good idea, because Postlewaite had signed as lead on our slip* they agreed to participate as quota share reinsurers of an admitted (licensed in all states) U.S. underwriter. Now we would be able to issue limits of $5 million of following form† coverage for our policyholders.

Jim Koehnen of American Re-Insurance was able to introduce us to an interested carrier who, for a fee, would be willing to issue excess insurance policy in all states. His word and the magic of the Kemper name made it possible to provide limits of liability that would satisfy even the largest design firm.

Great-Great-Grandmother Sarah would have been proud.

---

* A description of the risk is prepared; it's called the slip. It is submitted to an underwriter knowledgeable in the field. If he signs it, they are the "lead." Others who are interested in the risk "underwrite" their names as participants. The premium is proportioned among them in accordance with the amount of the risk they have agreed to assume—10%, 20%, or whatever.
† A policy of excess insurance that has the same terms and conditions as the primary insurance policy.

Chapter 7

Without Losses There Would Be No Need for Insurance

The remedy is worse than the disease.

—Sir Francis Bacon (1561–1626)

July 6, 1975, was going to be a nice day. Joseph L. Brennan, Sr. and his son, Joseph Jr. (Larry), had looked forward to the christening of their catamaran for some months. They, along with their good friends—Key West Fire Chief Gilbert Gates, Elsie Gates, Gilbert Gates, Jr., and Larry Brennan's girlfriend, Claudia Cooper—spent the day skimming across the water between the Florida Keys. Their shallow-draft vessel was able to glide over the reefs, inches above the coral and its schools of colorful fish. The twin hulls knifed through the water at incredible speed, and the group sang out with joy as the cool spray drenched them on the fabric deck. The colorful blue, red, and gold sail hummed as the westerly winds caught it and pushed them along. It was a day of laughs, foam, and joy at being alive. The thrill of the new vessel promised many days of sun, fun, and camaraderie.

By 2:30 P.M. they headed back to the Big Pine Key Marina. At the shoreline they stopped for more laughs and exclamations about the sunburns they'd all received during their four-hour sail. Their exhilaration was boundless. Mr. Brennan then assumed command and ordered his crew to heave to and help load the cat on the aluminum trailer. It was a light vessel. The six of them could easily lift it and seat it properly on the trailer for the pull back to their house. The sails had been furled and the rudders stowed in their truck. They all pitched in to push the trailer to the awaiting hitch on Brennan's truck.

Joe Brennan, Sr. gave the command, "Okay, you guys, one-two-three, push." Then came an ear-splitting "ZZZZIT," a flash of blinding blue-white light, a bone-searing flame, and all six of them were hurled to the ground as if squashed by some giant hand.

When the ambulance and the emergency fire station rescue crew arrived, Joe Brennan, Sr. and Gilbert Gates, Jr. were declared dead; Larry died in the ambulance. The others were so badly burned they were not expected to make it to the hospital. With tears in his eyes, the assistant fire chief looked at his maimed chief and was quick to see what had happened. The aluminum mast of the catamaran had come in contact with a 13-kilovolt secondary power line that sagged over the marina to a transformer on a residential property. The power had surged through the unsuspecting revelers leaving them dead or painfully injured.

"We did the construction, but we're not sure who did the design. But, hell, it's been 23 years, and we don't know if the engineering firm is still in business. They were from out of state, and they did the design on the primary right-of-way high voltage lines, but we don't know if they did the secondary line to the marina. One thing is for sure; as owners of the project we can expect to be sued. If our insurance is inadequate, we could have a serious financial problem," said the worried local manager of the electric company as he talked with the city counsel about the horrible accident that had decimated the crew of Brennan's catamaran. The accident was a terrible tragedy. It was no help that there were marina rules against towing a vessel with an erected mast. There were going to be claims. Three of the people were dead, and the others were in such grim shape it appeared they might be incapacitated for life.

The first to bring suit was Kathryn N. Brennan as administrator of the estate of Joseph L. Brennan, Sr., and in her own right for loss of consortium. The trial did not last very long. Design Professionals Insurance Company's insured was the civil engineer who had designed the primary high-voltage line in 1952. Although their records did not show that they had anything to do with the secondary line, they were named as a defendant. The defense attorney put up a prodigious fight for the insured civil engineering firm, pointing out that there was no evidence they had designed the secondary line which had caused the accident. No one seemed even slightly interested in that fact. The jury quickly returned a verdict favorable for Kathryn F. Brennan in the amount of $400,000. This did not bode well for the company and its insured, because five claims had yet to be litigated. The injured parties still looked pitiful and had the sympathy of all who saw them.

The defense attorney, Henry Burnett, of Fowler, White, Burnett, Hurley, Banick & Knight of Miami, interviewed one of the jurors after the verdict to see what she had thought about the evidence showing that the civil engineer might not have designed the errant secondary line. She reported, "Oh, we didn't understand all of that technical stuff about there not being a violation of code, or that maybe the design was done by others. We just wanted to make certain that Mrs. Brennan got some money. After all, she's one of us [meaning from Key West] and she deserved to get the money." Mr. Burnett opined that it might not be possible to get a fair trial in a court where the jurors were impaneled from residents of Key West. We in the insurance company were deeply concerned by the fact that the plaintiff need not prove that the damages were the result of our civil engineer's professional negligence, as it should have been. We felt it was time for extraordinary measures; it was time to "bake bread."

One of the most important aspects of insurance company management is how to deal with claims. Consulting engineers had advised us that they were displeased with professional liability claims management in the past, and they wanted to see a change. Part of the problem had been that claims adjusters usually worked on many types of claims, not just professional liability for consulting engineers and architects. Most of their time was spent on automobile claims, fire losses, or product liability demands. Handling a design professional's professional liability claim might be a rarity. This meant that their grasp of the technical matters involved was not clearly honed to the problems at issue. Good claims management dictates that every claim, no matter how spurious, must be treated as a potential threat. In our special kind of claims, we felt a duty to make the technical facts so clear to jury laypeople that they could find with a clear conscience for our insureds, if they had not been professionally negligent. That had not happened in Key West.

I explained our problem about Key West to a friend, Steve Petrakis, who had worked with me at A&A and who ran his own very successful self-insurance service and surplus lines insurance company.

"Steve, we have to find someone who can go the extra measure to find out the facts in this case. Our insured should not be liable to the extent that was found. Some of these professional liability claims come years after the engineering work has been done, and we have to reconstruct what happened. The lawyers don't seem to be able to get the necessary investigative work done to gird us for defense. We're dead if we can't cure that problem. Do you have any thoughts?"

"Well, Ed," Steve responded, "you know the toughest thing about the insurance business is finding good people. For every good person there are dozens who work nine-to-five and really are not interested in the policyholder and the type of service that you espouse. You need someone who doesn't give up when the going gets rough, like in your Key West claim. I know a guy like that, but I don't know if he'd leave his present position. Give him a try. His name is Bernie Engels, and he's with GAB [General Adjustment Bureau, the largest adjusting company in the United States]. He was trained in Seattle by Safeco Insurance Company, joined the GAB, and worked as a claims supervisor for them for a number of years. They transferred him to Hawaii as the manager of that office, then brought him to San Francisco to head up their self-insurance services office for the West Coast. They have a tremendous volume of that type of work, and Bernie is not just good, but supergood at it. I ask for him on my self-insured programs 'cause he delivers. Give him a call and reference me. Tell him it can't hurt to talk."

Bernie Engels was one of those people who smile with their whole face, not just their lips. He positively beamed as he gave you solid eye contact, and said just the right thing for a first-time greeting. He started right out by saying, "Hey, I'm not looking for a job. I'm happy where I am. They've treated me right, and I want to treat them fairly. You said we'd just talk. Please tell me about this different insurance company."

I began. "Think about everything you ever did in the insurance business that you could call 'right' and everything that you could call 'wrong,' and I'll bet there are more wrongs than rights. What we're trying to do at our company is to tip the balance dramatically to the rights. We want to deliver to our policyholders unparalleled service in the form of innovative loss prevention, fair underwriting and pricing, and superior claims management. The latter is where you'd come in. We haven't been able to deliver the superior level of claims management that we have envisioned. We just do not have the magic we were looking for. We have to have people who put their own agendas behind them and serve their customers in such a way that they will say, 'Golly, these people are different!' If you came with us, you would be in charge of some of the most difficult claims in the world to properly defend and manage. We want to be fair to the claimants, but not give away our policyholders' money. You'd be asked to build a department of highly experienced, caring claims people, most of whom will have been on the level of managers of claims offices for prosaic insurers. We want people who have done it all—adjusting, reserve setting, negotiating, acting as intermediaries—and who can take the guff claimants give without getting mad."

I went on. "Right now we are facing a claim in Key West, Florida, in which we do not believe our insured should have been involved as the main culprit. Yet we've lost the first suit and there are more to come from the same accident. The fire chief of Key West who lost part of his right leg will be looking for us to make good for his loss, unless we can ferret out the facts to clear our insured. It has been 23 years since any engineering work was done. We don't know who did it, but we have to find out. A lot of our claims are like that. They require superhuman effort, constant travel, a technically oriented mind, and a good sense of humor to preserve sanity.

"You'd love doing our work. We're helping people—I mean, really helping them. These claims cause psychological meltdown in our insureds. Their self-esteem is destroyed by being told, 'You blew it. You're no good.' That hits them where it hurts. This is where you'd step in and shoulder much of the burden of the claim that they had been professionally remiss. Their attorney is not likely to do that, because he has nothing to lose. You would have something to lose, sometimes millions of dollars, and you would be trying to make sense out of chaos. Finding out who was liable is tough. Many of these claims come straight out of left field. They are maelstroms of facts and perceptions. It is almost impossible to discern how the insured might have been involved since their engineering or design was perfect. Mostly they're involved just because they had once been there where something happened. What a challenge!"

I could see that Bernie was warming to the subject because he leaned forward and said, "You mean I'd run the operation with no second-guessing by you or anyone else? You wouldn't be looking over my shoulder telling me what to do?"

"I mean exactly that," I assured him. "We're guerilla fighters, not ranked troops. We have a management team, and you would be expected to keep it informed about what was going on with any of the more important claims, but we don't wet-nurse our people. They're all in their majority, and they all want this company to stand out like a beacon as the one that wants to do the job right. In my opinion, one of the biggest mistakes insurance companies make in claims management is requiring approval from the executive suite on business claims. People are inherently able to cope with all sorts of threats. They're inventive. Let them use their own techniques and they can win. If they goof, and we all goof, we'll yell, but it will be a yell of encouragement, not recrimination. If you can put the policyholders' welfare ahead of your own, you'll fit. If not, you won't," I told Bernie, and I could see he liked it. I learned later that he had been a sergeant in the Marine Corps and had had his fill of organizations that ran by the book; the idea of individual initiative fired his enthusiasm.

Several other people interviewed Bernie, and they liked him. "Steady" was the word we used to describe him. We called Jim Hurley at Hurley, Atkins & Stewart in Seattle since Bernie said he knew him. "I'll tell you, Ed, he's just top drawer. If you can, get him," Jim advised. Although we didn't do it often, on this hire we decided to have Harry Marcus, a claims manager at Kemper Reinsurance Company, interview our prospect. Harry came back with, "I don't care what you have to pay Bernie, hire him. He's one of the best in experience and knowledge I've run into in 30 years of claims work."

Bernie wanted to talk about our company with his family and, I'm sure, investigate us by talking with Steve Petrakis, A&A, Kemper, American Re-Insurance Co., and others. About a week later he called for another get-together. "Hey, I find you guys are really serious about doing the job right. The Kemper manager, Harry Marcus, says you're 'dedicated people, a one-in-a-million company, running your outfit just like they did in the old days.' Steve thinks highly of you, too. Told me some funny stories about how you two beat the system. I think I might like to join you if you will give me time to make things right with the GAB. They've helped me; I want to help them. I can start in about a month. Depending on how they want to work it."

"Sounds perfect to me," I rejoined. Bernie got up to leave. "Just a minute!" I exclaimed. "Aren't you going to ask about pay, benefits, and vacation?"

"No, if you guys are really going to do things right, you'll pay claims people better than they're used to, and give good benefits. Extended vacations for claims people aren't in the cards since we have to stay on top of our files. If I'm wrong on these counts, I won't be here long. Thanks!" he answered with his famous smile.

Bernie Engels added a new dimension to our company. The claim in Key West was a sword of Damocles hanging over us. He said, "I know just the guy, Jim Havron. He'll get the facts on that case. He's the best investigator I know. I'll give him a call in Atlanta and get him on it."

Havron, a GAB man, interviewed dozens of people. One of the potential witnesses, a former employee of the power company, hearing that Havron was looking for him, moved away one Friday afternoon in just three hours. He left no forwarding address. Why would he do that? We found out later that he had the information we finally uncovered. Havron pulled every trick in the book to get a line on who had been involved in the design and construction of the secondary line. Finally, an old guy told him about the line crew that used to work for the company. He even named names. Havron started calling on them. It took awhile. Finally, one guy said, "Hell, I know who spotted that pole there. He walked along, dug his heel in a spot, and told them to put a pole at the heel mark. Then he told his assistant where the secondary line was to go, and he sketched a map. The design was done after the fact. It's as simple as that."

Since the person named had worked for one of our codefendants, we were largely relieved of liability. Bernie's experience and human network had saved the day. That's the way an organization should operate. The innate human desire to cooperate had won again. Guerilla warfare can be the best way.

A Hyperbolic-Paraboloid Roof

It wasn't a fluke that Bernie's experience had paid off. That same year we had another bell-ringing claim.* This one involved the collapse of the Cheyenne Municipal Airport roof. The roof had been designed by an insured subconsultant to the structural engineer. The failure took place some fifteen years after the design. The roof was a hyperbolic-paraboloid, which is to say that it looked (from above) like a saddle draped over some columns. There were peaks at the north and south ends, the south end being a higher, more pronounced peak, with more supporting columns. The roof was made of reinforced concrete but not prestressed. On July 2, 1975, at 12:20 P.M. the north peak of the roof collapsed with a sickening roar over the bar, snack shop, dining room full of guests for lunch, and the security area for boarding aircraft. There were screams of anguish as human forms littered the collapsed area. Emergency vehicles from the surrounding community arrived with screaming sirens and flashing red lights, and they prepared to remove the injured first, then the bodies. They were naturally concerned about further collapse, so they positioned ladders and beams under the remaining north roof to bolster it against continued downfall.

---

* So called because in the "Room" at Lloyd's of London, whenever there is a major loss they ring a large Lutine bell (taken from a sunken ship, HMS *Lutine*) and proclaim the nature of the loss to the underwriters on the floor.

When the sirens stopped wailing, sixteen people had been taken to the hospital with minor injuries. Miraculously there were no deaths!

This event was tragic, but it could have been worse. It was reported by the people in the terminal that there had been warnings that something was wrong. They indicated that large cracks appeared in the ceiling's concrete, there were noises, and chunks of concrete were actually falling on people. This happened the day of the failure, and it may have been happening for years! The owner of the barbershop said it was a common occurrence, "I told them (the airport managers) over a year ago that something was wrong, but they wouldn't listen."

Cracks had been fixed in 1962, but virtually no maintenance work had been done on the sensitive roof since. It is likely that hairline cracks left unremedied allowed winter rains, ice, and deicing salt to enter the concrete and corrode the reinforcing steel. But the actual cause of failure was going to be difficult to sort out. Was it lack of maintenance by the owner who had been told that the cracks should be sealed and filled annually? Was it the hyperbolic-paraboloid roof design? Was it the structural design, that is, the columns designed to hold up the roof? Was it failure to build in accordance with the plans and specifications? Was it failure to observe construction by a competent structural designer?

Our company made contributions for payment to the injured people without admitting any liability on the part of our insured. The injuries were minor when considering the immensity of the event, and we viewed that as a major plus. We knew that the costs of defending against these bodily injury claims would far exceed the alleged damages. So, with our insured's permission, we made contributions, with the other defendants, of minor amounts.

The Cheyenne Air Terminal, Inc. (manager of the terminal for the city of Cheyenne) had the building insured against the usual perils of fire and extended coverage, which included collapse. They made a claim against their insurer. The insurance company that provided coverage for the building paid the Cheyenne Air Terminal, Inc. for the loss of the building, then brought suit against all parties to the design and construction under their right to subrogate.* They alleged in their suit that there were latent errors in design of the roof for which our insured was legally responsible. We assumed their "latent" language was for the purpose of circumventing the statute of limitations, which ostensibly limited claims to a 10-year-period after the work is done, but this did not start running until the negligence was discovered. Discovery for latent defects occurs when the failure happens.

Confucius said, "Not a single snowflake takes responsibility for an avalanche." So it is with many of the professional liability claims that are

---

* Most property insurance policies contain a clause that gives the insurance company all of the rights of the insured to collect from third parties who may have caused the loss. If a building is destroyed because of a construction flaw, the insurer may have a right of collection from the contractor. It is the same with almost any act of negligence that may have caused all or part of the loss.

brought against design professionals. So many factors impinge on the ultimate loss, it is difficult to say that any one factor is the cause. Our expert on
the Cheyenne Airport failure was Richard Elstner of Wiss, Janney & Elstner
and Associates of Northbrook, Illinois. Elstner's findings were that "the rust-
ing of the reinforcement [rods] caused microfractures in the concrete. This
action was occurring in an area where the reinforcement of the edge of the
beam was spliced. We very definitely have a state-of-the-art situation. So
much so, that I have called a few professional friends to suggest they check
their shells" (meaning hyperbolic-paraboloid roofs). What he implied was
that the design was acceptable for the period in which it was done, but it
might have been done differently, with new state-of-the-art technology, in
1975. What was the cause then?

Construction, with its subtle nuances, is a far more complex enterprise
than most people appreciate. People, including judges and juries, tend to
look at construction failures in a linear way, expecting a failure to be related
to one overriding factor. Actually, Bernie's experience had taught him that
there is turbulence in losses, similar to those in a weather system, that defy
credible analysis. Turbulence, or chaos, makes it impossible to identify "the
cause." He was convinced that our insured's design was not the "snowflake
that caused the avalanche." This being the case, he stepped back from the
allegations, and sought a way for our insured to avoid being tarred and
feathered for something they did not do. While he was shaving one morning
in the spring of 1978, he had an idea. One of the first things Bernie did after
he got to the office was make a phone call to our Cheyenne attorney and
arrange a meeting with Joe Williams, of Guy, Williams & White, one of
Cheyenne's reputable defense attorneys.

At their meeting Bernie started, "Joe, you're the attorney. You tell me.
Do you know anything about subrogation and volunteer payments?"

"What do you mean, Bernie?" Joe asked.

"Well, I mean we're being sued by the property insurer on the
Cheyenne Airport Terminal, right? The building collapsed and they paid
$431,000 to get it repaired or rebuilt. They allege that our insured committed
errors in the design that resulted in latent defects that caused the collapse,
right? But in my experience, standard property policies exclude losses due to
latent defects. They made a voluntary payment that their policy didn't cover,
so how can they subrogate against our insured? I mean the subrogation
clause only gives them the same right to collect from a third party that their
insured might have had because of the loss, right?" Bernie questioned.

Joe went white and his face tightened as he realized the full implication
of Bernie's remarks. Without a word, he jumped up out of his chair and
hissed, "Come on, Bernie, let's get out of here. We've got work to do!"

The case went all the way to the Supreme Court of Wyoming, which
found that Bernie's guess was correct. A subrogee's rights are no greater
than a subrogor's. If an insurance company makes a payment to an insured
for a loss not covered under its policy of insurance, it gains no right to subrogate against third parties since the insured would have no such right. We

were concerned that the Supreme Court of Wyoming might remand the case to try the issues of fact surrounding the cause of the latent defects, but they did not, probably since the plaintiffs had never given evidence or testimony on the probable cause of the collapse. The insurance company that was Different by Design had once more served its insured in an extraordinary way.

Negotiating Skills

There are dozens of books on the subject of negotiation, but it has been our experience that it is not easily taught. There are people who seem to have an innate ability to negotiate. It may be taught by their family culture, or it may be something they picked up on the schoolyard. Whatever it is, it can mean the difference between paying large sums on losses where the insured is minutely involved or staying outside of the inner ring of paying tortfeasors.

A defense attorney told me an interesting story about Bernie Engels and his negotiating skills. It introduces additional elements to a turbulent claim that raised the complexity level of the claims management. The additional elements? Evil and treachery. The story involved an insured who had participated in the design of a marina. The marina was one of those new-fangled projects in which a corporation was formed by a group of folks who sought to build a skimpy development, then "condominiumize" the marina, selling individual slips to boat owners. Instant profit! The buyers would own the slips in tenancy in common with the other slip owners.

Our insured did a good-faith design which was fit and sufficient for the purpose intended. During the course of construction the president of the corporation sought to lessen the cost of the project by reducing the safety features called for in the design. Our insured engineers properly declined to participate in what they viewed as a cheapening of the breakwater (a structure to lessen wave surge) to a dangerous low. Thereupon, the corporation surreptitiously hired away a disgruntled structural engineer who had worked for our insured engineer, and convinced him to make design changes that greatly lessened the cost (and safety) of the project.

In that state, in addition to incessant winter storms, they also have unexpected, unseasonable heavy winds. These surprise winds can be sudden and severe. Coupled with winter storms, they are every boat owner's nightmare. If you own a boat there, you must be prepared to deal with high winter winds almost anytime. This means your moorage should be sheltered and designed to protect against bad weather. Most of all, if you are going to build a marina, the design should be ultraconservative, rock-solid all the way.

In the winter of 1975–76, the winds blew and the rains pelted the new marina, destroying part of the breakwater and damaging several vessels. The president of the owning corporation put the DPIC insured engineer on notice that "your inadequacy of design was the cause of the damage." Even though there was major damage to the breakwater, the corporation continued to sell boat slip-condominiums without revealing the damaged breakwater to the buyers of the slips. In my opinion, this was an *evil act.*

The DPIC-insured engineer learned in late 1976 that the owner of the marina had done no repairs to the breakwater, had not notified the slip owners of the problem, and was continuing to sell slips to the unwary buyers.

In order to protect itself from possible further loss due to upcoming winter storms, the insured engineer notified the slip owners (several of whom were attorneys) of the problem, and put the owner on notice that remedial work should be done immediately. The owner pleaded lack of funds, contending that the engineer's design was the sole cause of the loss and that, therefore, the engineer should pay for the total remedy. Investigation revealed that this was not the case, and that the reduction in design by the ex-employee was probably the sole, intervening cause of the loss. There were, however, some relatively innocent parties involved: the slip owners. Thus, to protect against further damages, something had to be done. The engineer made an offer to the president of the owning corporation to loan them sufficient funds to do the remedial work. This loan was to be secured by a mortgage on the marina. The president of the corporation first accepted, then declined this offer, trying to substitute another piece of property as security, claiming it to be worth $200,000. (It turned out to be worth, at most, $50,000.) Continuing to balk over the terms of the loan, he placed his corporation and the insured engineer at jeopardy. He showed the letter from the insured engineer making the offer of the loan to the slip owners and averred, "See, this is proof that they know they are liable for all of the damage." In my opinion this was an *act of treachery* on his part and making such an offer not very bright of the engineer.

The loss was complicated from a technical point of view. Much of the breakwater was lost in the 1975–76 storms, so determining whether the loss was the sole result of the cheapening done by the disgruntled employee would not be easy. The marina owner and the engineer they hired from our insured both contended they had followed the original design, even though photographs clearly showed this was not the case. Specifically, they had removed an inverted T in the design that the civil engineering laboratory at a university contended would have reduced wave action dramatically. Several material design changes were probably the actual, intervening, proximate causes of the loss, but would a jury believe our testimony? The slip owners were caught in a conflict. They recognized the shortcomings of the marina and the perfidious nature of the owner, but they also were shocked by the potential assessment that might be made against them to rectify the inadequacies in the breakwater and slips.

The slip owners' attorneys filed suit, asking for huge damages. Depositions were taken, but they were limited since there was virtually no evidence that any of the independent subconsulting engineers (soil and foundation, electrical) had done anything wrong. Legal costs climbed on both sides with no conclusion in sight. The claims were of the type that would be better settled than tried since the cost of defense would be enormous. Litigation in a loss of this nature is truly "the remedy worse than the disease." The attorneys all postured, strutted, and preened, but then called a settlement conference. Bernie Engels and the defense counsel he had hired prepared for the meeting. Bernie loaded up his briefcase with all of the experts' files to use as negotiating props as much as for what they contained, hoping to convince the various parties that we had done our homework by having engineering experts take an extensive look at the design. He felt they had not done the same.

The day of the meeting came. Bernie flew to the meeting with his huge volume of files, and he instructed the defense counsel to follow his lead in the meeting. The meeting was held in a lawyer's conference room of immense proportions and was full of uptight people: the president of the marina development corporation, his attorney, attorneys for the boat slip owners, attorneys for the subconsultants (soil and foundation engineers, electrical), the insured's private counsel, and our insurance company's defense attorneys, Barokas and Martin. The plaintiff's counsel started off, "Mr. Engels, we believe that your insured is the primary defendant in this case, and we expect your company to pay for 85% of the remedial work costs plus attorneys' fees in the amount of $34,000 for their errors and omissions in design."

With that, Bernie smiled, rose from his chair and began throwing his files in his briefcase. "Who do you think I am, Santa Claus?" (Actually, he did look a little like him.) "See these files. We have expert opinions that clearly indicate that the design prepared by our insured was in accordance with generally accepted engineering practices in this community, meeting every criteria of sound engineering practices. Your client changed them, and now wants to avoid the responsibility for the changes. We could spend 90 days in court explaining it to the judge and jury. While you're explaining your side of the story, try explaining why your client continued selling slips after the damage was done without revealing the facts to the buyers. I've got a plane to catch. Have a nice day." With that Bernie bounced from his chair, still smiling his cherubic smile, and was out the door before any rejoinder could be offered. He did have solid contrary expert opinion that substantiated his position, but it was something neither judge nor jury was apt to understand, even in 90 days. He was playing a dangerous game called "claims management hardball."

Thirty days went by. Then the plaintiff, without benefit of counsel, wrote a letter to our defense counsel taking a more conciliatory tone, but never admitting to wrongdoing. Evidently, Bernie's brinkmanship worked because a subsequent meeting was called in which he was able to settle the claim at a sum far less than had been originally sought by the plaintiffs. We never felt that our insured had committed any errors in design, but the circumstances of the loss were so very complex that a trial would have been counterproductive and may have led to *jury black out* (the state of turning off their minds and settling the case with their hearts).

The insured and the management of DPIC felt that Bernie's negotiating had been masterful and deserved plaudits. The plaudits showed up in his year-end bonus.

Emotional Elements

Sometimes even the best negotiator will run up against circumstances that defy rational resolution in these complex, turbulent claims. A case in point involved Novoply, a particle boardmill subsidiary of Champion Paper Company in Anderson, California.

During the graveyard shift on March 23, 1976, the protection cage over an electric motor drive shaft became clogged with sawdust. The friction from the shaft caused a fire that was sucked into the number two Rotex machine (a device that shakes the wood particles at high speed causing the smaller particles to settle through various screen gradations). After the Rotex, the particles of wood are sucked into silos for storage. That day two silos were almost empty, but they were filled with combustible dust. The fire reached this dust creating a tremendous explosion, followed seconds later by a greater explosion throughout a large portion of the plant. Fire experts said the first explosion displaced wood particles from rafters, the floor, and stairways and created a dust medium that exploded when ignited by the existing fire, thus forming the second devastating explosion. One witness said it opened the plant, "Just like a giant bullet had been shot through it."

A total of seven workers were killed and eleven were horribly burned. The shocked community of Anderson rose to offer assistance to the injured and families of the dead. A three-member panel was set up as trustees to administer a fund started at a bank for assisting the injured with medical expenses and other monetary needs. Food was collected and doled out to the families of the dead and injured on an as-needed basis. Estimates were up to $20 million for repairs to the mill, and there was talk of closing the mill, one of Shasta County's largest employers.

In 1970 the U.S. government passed the Clean Air Act, to be administered by the Environmental Protection Agency. One provision of this Act made it illegal to spew waste material into the atmosphere. Novoply had complied with that law by installing a series of cyclone precipitators in their plant to cleanse the air used in their process for handling wood chips. Novoply then hired a civil engineer, insured by DPIC, to make periodic tests of the stack ash and vented cyclone air to make certain that the waste air met the standards set by the Clean Air Act. The civil engineer had absolutely nothing to do with the design, construction, or running of any plant equipment or air cleansers. They were responsible for atmospheric testing only.

DPIC felt that its insured should not be involved in any liability since their connection with the explosions was extremely tenuous. However, in cases like these, where there are a number of deaths, there is plenty of potential for emotional judgments, so extreme caution was in order in the claims management. Our claims department hired a fine defense attorney, Ernest Y.

Sevier, of Severson, Werson, Berke & Melchior of San Francisco, who began to review the facts to analyze potential liability. What he discovered was disquieting. He was concerned about an allegation of negligence in the sampling of air that was somehow contributory to the secondary explosion, that is, the testing engineer had made some tests inside the plant. While it seemed clear that the primary explosion was not a proximate result of any negligent act of the testing done by our insured civil engineer, a judge and jury staring at widows and orphans might conclude otherwise. They might reason that the secondary, larger explosion was related to airborne particulates that had escaped the notice of the testing engineer inside the plant. This meant that a trial, which would be a remedy worse than the disease, was a possibility.

Mr. Sevier was also concerned about the comparative negligence and how it might be brought into play to involve our insured.*

Our expert witnesses seemed to think that the cause of the explosions was a direct result of failures in the design and fabricating of the dust controlling equipment. Much of the design and fabrication work had been done by a sheet metal company and a blowpipe company. As the trial date of August 28, 1979 drew closer, the fabricators entered into an agreement with the combined plaintiffs (widows, orphans, and injured employees) in which they agreed, among other things, to guarantee, as settling defendants, no less than $2,350,000 (making no payment at the time of agreement) if they went to trial against the other defendants and recovered less than that amount. If, on the other hand, they collected more than that amount from the other defendants, the fabricators, would pay nothing. This so-called Mary Carter agreement† was entered into on May 3, 1979, with a hearing set for May 15, 1979, to request that the trial court declare the fabricator's agreement in "good faith."

This proved to be a major shock for us and our insured since the trial court, on attorneys' affidavits alone, found that the agreement had been in "good faith." This finding was made even though it appeared that the trial judge was not thoroughly familiar with the intricacies called for in such an agreement, that is, Mary Carter agreements are supposed to have a good-faith monetary payment made by the settling defendants at the time of the agreement. In this case no such payment was made. In spite of any doubts the trial judge may have had, he found for the settling fabricator defendants without making any kind of inquiry into the relationship of the acts of the settling defendants and the explosion and fire. Our defense counsel ap-

---

*In some states, California included, damages may be prorated between or among the parties based upon the percentage of negligence that each contributed to the loss.

† From *Booth v. Mary Carter Paint Co.*, Florida App. 1967, 202 So. 2nd 8, that now is generally used to apply to any agreement between the plaintiff(s) and some, but not all, defendants whereby the parties place a limitation on the financial responsibility of the agreeing defendants, the amount of which is variable and usually in some inverse ratio to the amount of recovery which the plaintiff is able to make against the other defendant(s).

pealed this finding to the Court of Appeals, but appeal was denied. Then our counsel filed a petition and request for a stay with the Supreme Court of the State of California for a hearing, but this too was denied. Things were getting rough.

Besides our insured, one of the Factory Mutuals companies* was a defendant since their fire engineers had made a survey of the plant and found that it was safe from fire and that there was no apparent danger of explosion of airborne particulates. The Factory Mutuals company had turned the defense of the claims over to their comprehensive general liability insurer, Liberty Mutual Insurance Company. They were caught in the same vise as we, with an insured who had performed adequately but was now the target of a claim that was the result of someone else's acts.

Bernie Engels and our attorney, Ernie Sevier, were flabbergasted by the Mary Carter agreement. The situation occasioned an enormous loss of sleep. To make matters worse, Liberty Mutual's claims manager, Elliott Gleason, was adamant in his position that their insured had done no wrong. We argued, pleaded, and moaned, but neither our attorney nor Bernie Engels could get him to budge from his position. "I've never seen such a hard-nosed guy," Bernie complained. Finally, we split a major portion of the claim, 50-50 with Liberty Mutual, and the other defendants paid the balance. The total sum paid was $3,910,000. The plaintiffs' attorneys took $1,191,000 as their fees!

Bernie was crestfallen when I talked with him the next day. He said, "You know, that guy Gleason just out-negotiated me. It makes me mad."

"Yeah," I said, "what are you going to do about it?"

"I think I'll try to hire him," Bernie replied with a big grin. He did.

Elliott Gleason joined us as the manager of the San Francisco claim office in December of 1979 and became overall manager of the claims department in November of 1985; Bernie moved on to become a kind of ombudsman for our insureds and to maintain contacts with professional societies.

Reporting Claims and Its Effect on Rates

For many years ordinary professional liability insurers of design professionals raised the rates of an insured if they reported a *possible* claim. Claims files and claims numbers were set up, which would automatically trigger action in the underwriting department. This was too bad since it conditioned the insureds to wait until they were in deep trouble before reporting a dispute

---

* An affiliation of large insurance companies formed in 1835 for the purpose of insuring very large, well-protected fire risks. Now composed of the Allendale Mutual, Arkwright Mutual Insurance Company, and the Protection Mutual Insurance Company. They are well known for their superior loss prevention fire engineering. The stock insurance companies have a similar affiliation in the Factory Insurance Association.

complication. We decided to cure that situation by having our insureds report to us "loss prevention issues." These would be any circumstance that might arise in connection with jobs upon which they had done work and out of which contention arose. If they reported to us, we promised help in the form of expert technical expertise (like Jim Stratta, the structural engineer who at first did not like our insurance plan), legal aid, or negotiating participation. In exchange the insured's professional liability premium rate would not be debited upon renewal. This has worked well.

This technique became a mainstay for the company and it also embodied a real benefit to the insured in that the deductible was not called into play if the case could be resolved by the claims person.

We called a case in point Watergate West. It involved a condominium complex built on the shore of San Francisco Bay in Emeryville, just across the Oakland Bay Bridge from San Francisco. The complex had originally been built as an apartment house on a landfill that was once a solid-waste disposal site (garbage dump). The spot had been an eyesore, with floating tires, industrial waste, and a site for free-spirited art forms that were constructed out of driftwood.

There was a community spirit at Watergate Apartments since it was an adult community of 1,240 units, with swimming pools, the Clipper room where exercise classes were held, an adjacent Trader Vic's restaurant. The people were loving and gregarious, proud of their little bayside community. When the owners decided to do a condo conversion on the apartment buildings, there was a great public outcry, and tempers flared white-hot. Some of the rental tenants of the apartment complex, the Watergate Apartments, didn't think they could afford to buy the $30,000 to $80,000 condominiums (think of that now!). They liked it just fine the way it was, paying rents of $275 to $750 per month. Overnight this community spirit turned into rancor and unfettered animosity when Canadian developers bought the Watergate Apartments for $31 million with the intent of condominiumizing them and selling them all for about $60 million—a very neat profit.

Some 40% of Emeryville's residents lived at Watergate. It had always been an industrial town until the Watergate Apartments were built. Then suddenly, Emeryville became a chic bedroom community. Two members of the city council were residents at Watergate, and they were all in favor of the condos since they would double Emeryville's tax base. The irate anti-condo tenants were so incensed by the condominiumization they sought a recall election for the two pro-condo city council members. The pro-condo city council members, in turn, brought suit against those who sponsored the recall election. Things were nasty.

The buildings were replete with construction flaws, some predicted in the original design, some not. It was predicted prior to construction by the soil and foundation engineers that the buildings' piles would settle. They also forecast that the garage floors would experience differential settlement of a few inches to over a foot. Not anticipated were many roof leaks that plagued the buildings and kept maintenance people energized for seven years. To them, rain meant trouble. The plumbing was in constant, stopped-up, atrocious shape.

The anticondo group stood up at a town hall meeting and told how they were being ravaged by "the moneyed elite," but they did not win enough support. The city council said it would grant permits as soon as the buildings' shortcomings were rectified. While the biggest problems were in the plumbing, there was enough wrong with the building to keep an army of construction workers employed for months. DPIC's insured, a small civil engineering firm, wandered into this antagonistic milieu. It was hired to do some easement tract maps and to coordinate the paving of the garage floors to make certain that the cracked, subsiding, pitted floors were paved to "a level condition." They did their surveying job and observed the remedial paving. This latter task was accomplished by hiring a retired engineer, who had a transit, and he watched the progress of the work. The paving work was completed and accepted with no complaints. The other repair work was said to have been done, permits were issued, condominiums were sold, and Watergate Community Association, a group of condominium owners, was formed to manage the building complex.

Although the garage paving was performed well, the balance of the remedial work was alleged to be wholly inadequate. When it rained, the structures leaked—a lot. The Watergate Community Association decided that it would sue everyone, or almost everyone, who had anything, no matter how minor, to do with their building complex. The complaint stated, in part,

The Plaintiff homeowners association has inherited from Defendants a complex having extremely serious design and construction defects and deficiencies, including widespread leakage of water through common areas, corrosion throughout the plumbing system that prevents homeowners from obtaining hot water on a timely basis, continuing failures of posttensioned steel tendons, improperly functioning hallway heating and cooling systems, leaking swimming pools, settlement of garage floors, garbage coming up into residents' sinks, and other problems.

Cross complaints were filed by some defendants. Some 88 defendants and cross defendants were named.

This was, without doubt, a classic case of a shotgun suit.* Would you think it time to hire legal counsel even though your insured was not in the direct line of fire? Our San Francisco office claims manager, Elliott Gleason, thought not. Recognizing that the insured's $10,000 deductible would be consumed by legal costs and fees within a month, if not a week, Elliott said, "I'm going to handle this without a lawyer for as long as I can and try to save the insured its deductible. After all, there is no reasonable basis in fact or fiction for the insured to be in this complex lawsuit," he said. Elliott believed that we were a company that sought to reduce, not exaggerate, legal in-

---

*So called for its indiscriminate scattering of summons and complaints to a class of individuals without regard to their involvement in the complained-of loss or injury.

volvement. Maybe the plaintiffs' attorneys would see that our insured was not even remotely involved in the defects alleged in the complaint and would grant dismissal. Thus, Elliott decided to try on his own to get the insured out of this convoluted claim.

Many attorneys have a disease that might be described as *depositionitis*. At least they seem to spend an inordinate amount of time conducting depositions, sometimes to the point of being ludicrous. This disease was to be present in the Watergate West condominium case. With a confirmed open extension to responsively plead on behalf of the insured in hand from the plaintiffs' attorney, Elliott completed the necessary factual investigation regarding the insured's involvement in the project and proceeded to get his name on the twenty-page mailing list of potential defendants. He presented and incessantly repeated his position to plaintiffs' attorney that the insured was without liability with respect to the construction defects enumerated in the complaint; he attended meetings with the insured as well as certain depositions to hear testimony from witnesses who might have had something to say about the insured's services (this, of course, was done with the consent of the attorney noting the deposition and with the understanding that, not being an officer of the court, Elliott would only listen and ask no questions). Elliott produced the insured's contract documents for those who wanted them; corresponded with the Court at its request and, with its permission, answered questions propounded by various parties to the litigation with respect to the insured's services; and attended status and settlement conferences with the Court (again, with the presiding judge's permission), all the while persistently pressing for dismissal of his insured, who had to be befuddled by the legal charade in which they were entangled without logical reasons. Eighteen months later, with files almost 6 feet deep, the cross-complainant admitted that the garage floors had been paved to "a level condition" and stipulated that they would permit dismissal with prejudice* if the plaintiffs' attorney were willing. After several months of harangue, they agreed, and our insured was dismissed with no incurred legal expenses. Elliott could not save all of the insured's deductible—they had to obtain a transcript of one witnesses' depositions at a cost of $133.24 (an "allocated claim expense" and, hence, chargeable to the insured's deductible) to study the testimony in more detail and, thereafter, wave it in the face of plaintiffs' attorney. The insured was most grateful for this demonstration of an insurance company being Different by Design.

Elliott was extremely pleased because he had been able to render a service to his client that, perhaps, no other professional liability insurer would have troubled to give or even attempt. There is a sense of well-being that comes from doing a job for someone, without really having to, that is of major help or consequence to them. Elliott's action saved the insured, not

---

* "With prejudice" means that following the dismissal, the plaintiff may not open the action again even if new evidence is discovered. "Without prejudice" means the action may be dismissed subject to opening again if new and material facts come to light.

only their considerable deductible, but also hours and hours of nonproductive time that they might have been called upon to expend had they been insured with a less accommodating company.[1] This type of service is one of those elusive factors that escapes some buyers of insurance who are perennial price buyers. Insurance service is one of those things that no one needs, until they really need it, then it's nice to have the very best.

A Roar Like an Earthquake

During the lunch hour in Houston, Texas, on August 18, 1981, Terri De-Board, 22 years old, was just returning to park her car in the parking structure adjacent to Greenspoint Plaza II where she worked for Amoco. As her vehicle started up the drive, she paused, feeling something just wasn't right. At that instant, a large section of the third floor collapsed onto the second floor which, in turn, collapsed onto the first floor in front of where she was about to drive. She jammed her car in reverse as a dark cloud loomed over the collapsed structure. "The roar sounded like an earthquake," she said. "The third floor fell like a big domino, which then fell through to the other two floors. It was awful. It still gives me the shakes to think about it."

The fire department had every available rescue unit in the city at the scene within an hour, and firemen began peering (they could not enter due to the continuing threat of further collapse) into the wreckage looking for the dead and injured. Temporary timber props were hastily erected along the edge of the floors abutting the collapse to try to stave off further collapse. An eerie light, probably from an automobile turn signal, kept blinking on the crushed first floor, leading rescuers to believe that an ignition had been on at the time of the collapse, and that some poor soul was crushed in the ruins.

The police cordoned off the wreckage, and the people who still had cars parked in the structure were advised to find other transportation since no one knew whether other sections might fall at any second.

DPIC had an insured who had been involved with the design of certain foundation elements of the failed structure. It was hoped that they would not be involved in any claim. Nonetheless, our message about being notified when *anything* happens had stuck with their management, who got on the phone to our office in Tucker, Georgia, where Bob Jansen was manager. Bob notified an expert in structural design, Chuck Guedelhoefer, of Wiss, Janney & Elstner, Northbrook, Illinois, of the collapse and asked him to meet him at the site as soon as possible. Bob was on a plane and reached the site within two hours. It seemed to him that tell-tale blue and red lights of emergency vehicles were flashing everywhere. "How many dead?" he wondered aloud. Just moments after he arrived, rescuers announced that they had not found any dead or injured! This was good news for Bob since he never wanted to see anyone killed or injured and in addition he knew that dead and injured people introduce an element in losses that makes it difficult for even the blameless to escape.

Our insured was savvy to the existing problem. The first thing next morning, they pulled out the plans and specifications for the structure and gave them to Chuck Guedelhoefer so that he might see what had gone wrong. The above-foundation structure was a precast fabricated garage, designed and cast by a large national corporation. The fabricated building had been trucked to the site and assembled by a contractor. Bob, Chuck, and the insured's risk manager visited the site after the smashed cars and crumpled concrete had been cleared. With very little searching they were able to see that some of the structural steel that had been called for in the design was missing. There should have been a row of re-bars protruding from the third-floor beams where the floor sheared off. It was clear to them that the insured's design of the foundation elements was not involved in the collapse. They returned to the insured's office, made some hurried sketches, and made an appointment to see the owner's representative and the contractor who had assembled the precast building.

Both the owner and the contractor saw instantly that Bob and Chuck made sense, and they agreed to assume all responsibility for the failure. The insured engineer was saved any claims expense because this cause was handled as a professional liability loss prevention matter, not subjecting the insurance policy deductible to expenses, as would have been the case with most other professional liability insurers. The policy of insurance was designed that way.

Never Act Like a Defendant

DPIC was twice blessed with reinsurers (Kemper Reinsurance Company and American Re-Insurance Company) whose claims people became part of our team. Our claims people would keep them informed whenever it was likely that their reinsurance might be subject to claim. Their claims people had amassed years of claims management experience, and they were generous with their expertise. Special help came from Harry Marcus of Kemper Reinsurance and Bob Lempke of American Re. Harry Marcus's shrewdness and sagacity had pulled our chestnuts out of the fire more than once. One case, for example, had us really concerned. It involved a DPIC-insured civil engineer that had been hired to perform design on the special construction facilities of a large sewer-tunnel job in a midwestern state. This was one of those jobs in which a giant drilling shield was pushed along underground by hydraulic jacks in order to bore through stone, hardpan, or glacial till that might be in the path of the tunnel. DPIC's insured designed the concrete sleeve that lined the bore to the rear of the bore shield. They also prepared the specifications for moving concrete forms along the bore so that a retaining wall could be poured as the tunnel progressed. The crew were working like demons since they received bonuses for exceeding the general contractor's projected schedule.

On the 29th day of the tunneling, just before a midmorning shift change, there was a tremendous explosion that turned the $2 million boring machine to junk, left nine men dead and a dozen more with second-degree burns. Removing the injured and dead took nine hours.

Our claims people were notified of this tragedy. Within hours they had an expert geotechnical engineer below ground with a methane gas detector (since tunnel explosions and methane seem to go hand-in-glove) trying to determine what may have gone wrong. Had we been in Lloyd's of London we would have called this tragic event a "bell ringer" because it looked like we might be embroiled in a major cataclysm.

The claims department notified our reinsurers immediately about the potential liability in this calamity. They informed the reinsurers of our theory, which was developed by piecing together the probable cause of the loss. Our geotechnical expert said he thought it had been "a pocket of undetected methane gas caused by some glacial carboniferous material left over from an ancient ice age. See, the bit broke into the pocket and the gas was under tremendous pressure. It swooshed out and was ignited instantly, before any detector could give a warning. Whose fault? Well, if you're in a hurry, and you can't send a probe ahead, you're bound to have methane explosions. Those are the breaks."

In losses such as this one, almost everyone gets sued. The insurance company of the employer of the dead and injured pays workers compensation, but then the survivors of the deceased and the injured bring action against all other parties involved in the project, trying to get more than workers compensation pays. The roster of defendants might look something like this: The manufacturer of the drilling machine, the designer of the drilling machine, the manufacturer of the automatic methane tester (which was supposed to sound an alarm), the metal producer that made the (supposed) spark-free drilling bit, the geotechnical engineer, the prime design professional for the tunnel, the ventilation subcontractor, the spoil removal subcontractor, the workers compensation insurer's safety engineers, the lighting supplier, the generator manufacturer, and maybe two dozen John Does. It looked like it would be a long year.

Time went by. We thought the potential plaintiffs might let the statute of limitations* run, however, as the last week for filing came, 20-odd defendants were named in the action, and service of the summons and complaints commenced. Our insured called when the papers arrived and sent them to our claims manager in his area. We were soundly of the opinion that our insured had not committed any professionally negligent acts for which there could be liability. However, nine dead men and twelve others badly burned, some needing plastic surgery, were sobering reminders that sometimes things did not go in these claims as they should.

---

* A state statute which requires that tort liability action be instituted by a plaintiff within a prescribed time or the right to such action is surrendered in perpetuity.

Interrogatories* began flying, and we helped our insured with the answers. We then asked Harry Marcus for advice on how we should play our hand with this claim.

"Well," he said, "if you act like a defendant, you'll be one. I'd recommend that you play it real cool, like we're sorry about the loss, and we didn't do anything wrong. However, we can explain to you what happened. Be polite, but be adamant about the fact that our engineer had nothing to do with the explosion or the equipment that may have caused it."

We played it cool. When they called for settlement meetings, we had our engineer beg off as being too busy. That can be dangerous because sometimes the other defendants can gang up on you if you're absent, but in this case Harry said, "Take the chance." What he advised worked. The other defendants put together a settlement pot and did not ask our insured for a contribution, probably since they recognized his remoteness from the cause of the loss, or maybe because Harry's "don't act like a defendant" strategy worked.

Why Not Sue the Attorney?

It galls me that some attorneys persist in bringing action against our insureds when they know, or they should know, that there is no proximate relationship between our insureds' professional acts and the claimed injuries. I have thought, and continue to think, that any such attorney should be liable for his negligence in bringing action in such cases. This is a position that neither I nor our claims manager, Bernie Engels, had any success in convincing our various defense counsels to employ. They just did not feel it would be proper to sue their colleagues under any circumstances. Then, in 1976, we hired a young attorney, Charles (Chuck) D. Maurer, Jr., to help on claims matters. Chuck voiced a strong opinion that it might be worth a try to countersue attorneys who utterly disregarded the need for reasonable inquiry into the grounds for suit.

A case came up that we felt would be perfect for testing such a strategy. After making a large losing bet, a disgruntled racetrack bettor, to show his displeasure, picked up a brick and threw it through an Arizona racetrack restaurant window, showering the occupants with shards of glass. Some of the restaurant patrons, superficially cut about the face and head, required medical attention. Suit was brought by these patrons against the restaurant owner and the architect who designed the restaurant. The complaint stated, in part, "The window was ordinary plate glass, easily broken, and it should have been shatterproof tempered glass that would not have shattered causing the injuries to the patrons." While the complaint seemed ridiculous, that was their claim.

---

* Legal documents that ask questions that must be answered by the defendants in writing about their role in a loss.

Some $24,000 was spent on defense. Finally a jury found that it would be unreasonable for an architect to be required to anticipate the throwing of a brick, that he was not negligent, and that the plaintiffs could not collect from him.

With cooperation from the architect, we brought suit against the lawyer who represented the plaintiffs but the trial court gave the defendant attorney a summary judgment.* The trial court found that we had no cause for action. The appeals court upheld its finding. In the end, the Supreme Court of Arizona refused to entertain a hearing, in effect giving the plaintiffs' attorney the right to sue without restriction. We felt that attorneys should be held to the same standard of care as other professionals. If they are negligent in their professional performance and cause damages, they should be liable for them. Why should they have a special status that gives them the right to sue without making reasonable inquiry into the cause of injury? Even judges should be held to the same standard of care as others.

Trying to Do It Better

By the end of 1976, we decided to codify what we had been doing in claims management. It was our attitude that in claims management our methods were some of the best in the industry. Still we thought, "we could do it better." Since our company was growing at a prodigious rate, it seemed only right to provide a heritage that would enable new hires with information on our unique claims management methods. We wanted to preserve claims peoples' individual initiative—the guerilla-band approach to claims management—but we had learned some things that were worth passing along.

Professional liability claims against design professionals tend to be complex, multifaceted, turbulent, and sometimes lacking resolution of what caused the loss, even with the most careful analysis. This meant that every claim presented to our company had to be looked at as totally unique. Unlike burned buildings or automobile collisions, the proximate cause of loss was a whirlwind of technical data, not always traceable.

We hoped that our claims people would fill a different role from most insurance companies, particularly those companies that did not feel the social obligation to treat claimants fairly. When I first started in the insurance business some of the people who had graduated from law school went to work as claims adjusters for large insurance companies. One company taught their young adjusters to say to claimants, "No, we are not liable," no matter what their circumstances. To me that reeked of perfidy. I cannot imagine a more treacherous act than saying "No" to a valid claimant, no matter what the circumstances. We decided we would not resort to that type of deportment, despite the potential savings. Instead we decided to handle

---

* A judgment in favor of the party making a motion, without hearing the facts of the case.

claims more as an intermediary between emotionally overwrought disputants. This meant that our claims people had to guard continually against being swayed to our insured's point of view without hearing the other side of the story. At times this led to emotional outbursts of our insureds who thought we were showing the claimants too much favor, but in the long run it has had a salutary effect on our insureds' psychological well-being.

Harry Marcus had taught us not to act like a defendant lest we become one. That stance was made part of our claims people's manner. Although this had the negative impact of slowing down settlement, it was beneficial in that it gave us more time to study a claim, and more time for hidden factors to emerge. When it was clear that our insured was culpable, it was up to the claims person to make swift, equitable settlement without unjust enrichment for the claimant.* (Very often we would find that a claimant would want the full construction value of rectifying an error instead of the cost of redesign and the remedial work. Even juries are befuddled by this state of the law. They tend to want to pay for all construction associated with an error in design, not just what is necessary to rectify the damages caused by the error.)

One factor in the success of our claims management was treating policyholders as if they were friends, because they were. Uppermost in our claims people's minds was to be caring in claims settlement. Some insurance companies look on this attribute as a weakness. Our claims people seemed to have an affinity for being genuinely concerned about the welfare of their friend, our insured, and their attitude is the same with the claimants.†

Young claims people who came to work for DPIC used to ask, "How do

---

*The case of *Robb v. Urdahl, 78 Atlantic 2d 186 (1951)* succinctly points out that damages for a design error should not be the total cost of the correcting work, but the value of the work as it should have been designed minus the value of the work as designed.

†A law firm in San Francisco was interested in demonstrating to our claims department their superior capability for handling design professionals' professional liability claims. They knew of our aversion to legal fee bills that seemed to be plucked out of the air in even amounts, such as $5,000, $10,000. They were proud of the fact that they could keep track of time to the minute with a computer system, so they called for a meeting to demonstrate their exceptional record-keeping prowess. They invited our claims department and set up projectors and computers to show how well adapted they were to meet our needs. Our entire claims department trooped into their office where they found a sumptuous catered lunch waiting for them and a team of bright young attorneys eager to show off their technology.

It was impressive, so much so that Bernie Engels said, "Wow, this is impressive for a clod-kicking boy from Enumclaw, Washington. I'm really overwhelmed."

Our San Francisco claims manager, Elliott Gleason, looked absolutely shocked, and said, "What? What did you say?"

Bernie reiterated, "I said, this is impressive for a clod-kicking boy from Enumclaw. What's wrong? What did I say wrong?"

Elliott just beamed and said, "I didn't know you were from Enumclaw. I've worked with you for two years and didn't know you were from Enumclaw. Heck, that's my hometown."

Then they hometown talked for two hours, stuff like, "Did you know Elmer Wiggins?" We thought we had a formula: Hire claims people from Enumclaw.

you set reserves?" With workers compensation you have a schedule with dollar amounts for different types of injuries that makes claims reserve setting relatively simple. With automobile liability and other types of liability a company has claims histories of similar claims that give a guide for claims reserve setting. With professional liability bodily injury claims we used the same technique that we used for ordinary comprehensive general liability claims. All of our claims personnel had years of experience in the comprehensive general liability line and were able to set reserves within a few percentage points of the final cost.

It was not the same for professional liability property damage claims because the technical intricacies of engineering and architectural losses were difficult to sort out in any reasonable way. Because of this, we had to rely upon experience, not only our own, but that of the engineering and architectural experts we hired for technical help following a claim. They would look at all of the loss data and then say, "It's going to cost $100,000 to fix all damages. Your insured was probably a little at fault, so you'd better be prepared to pay about $15,000—10% of the property damage, plus $5,000 for legal fees." This would give us our basis for an initial reserve figure, which could be adjusted up or down depending upon events. In the final analysis, reserves were set and adjusted based upon the individual claims manager's experience. We had input from the reinsurers as well, and their depth of experience was a help. Harry Marcus of Kemper Reinsurance or Bob Lempke of American Re-Insurance would take a look at a claims file, and if it didn't match their feelings on the proper reserve, they would discuss it with the claims manager. He could then ignore their suggestion or follow it. It is interesting that our reserves came extremely close to the final settlement figures.

Better Pull Together, If You Don't Want to Get Pulled Apart

Good claims management results when all persons work together and have an interest in the equitable outcome of a particular claim. This would include the insured, investigators, expert witnesses, claims managers, insurance company management, reinsurers, and professional societies. Coordination of these parties is the job of the claims manager, who must be ever alert to the fact that there are people out there, motivated by greed and avarice, who have no real interest in equity or fair dealing. In spite of this, a good claims manager will step into the shoes of the claimant and make certain equity is done. It's a tough job. Too often claims managers will hide from the truth and pay a claim to "get it off my desk." In the company that is Different by Design an alternate attitude prevails, that of looking at each claims action with a critical eye and governed by the question, "Is this right?" A positive response to that question has made it possible for them to earn the respect of the design professionals' community, management, and shareholders.

Chapter 8

But Is It Legal?

Every peasant has a lawyer inside of him, just as every lawyer, no matter how urbane he may be, carries a peasant inside of himself.

—Miguel de Unomuno, 1864-1936

One thing seems certain: Once a person is ensnared in our legal system, he or she is doomed by its intricacy, expense, and its lack of responsive equity. It is just not fair very often. Too many times, persons who are not really culpable are found liable, or they face the huge financial burden of runaway defense costs. The system is especially unfair to persons whose resources are limited, those who cannot afford the draining expense because it forces them to settle rather than bear the cost of litigating a fallacious or spurious claim.

Then, too, there are hidden costs. The loss of productivity can be devastating to a professional's practice. If he or she has to spend days or weeks in depositions, productive cash flow may be ruined. In the case of workers compensation claims, one insurer averred that the hidden costs to all parties for a loss were four times the amount of compensation paid. As an insurer of design professionals, we became painfully aware that professional liability claims created a similar expense burden for the professionals and involved participants in the defense of professional liability claims. In fact, we discovered that four times the damages may be shy of the actual costs.

As a new insurer interested in being Different by Design, how do you deal with the potential predation of your policyholders by this system called "law"? This was a question we had to address early in forming the company. We decided that we would seek methods of mitigating involvement in the legal process in order to save our policyholders from the loss of time, money, and self-esteem associated with litigation.

Avoiding the Legal Tangle

You cannot just drop out of the litigation game with the statement, "We don't like the rules of the legal system. We quit." But that is what we wanted for our design professional insureds. So we began searching for means by which we could avoid involvement in the legal process. A few hours in the library revealed that others, faced with similar legal problems in the past, had developed remedies for them. One remedy in particular seemed worth a try.

One day I got a call from Gus Gendler, a mechanical engineer in Berkeley. "Hey, Ed, you sent back a contract with red marks through the arbitration clause, making it permissive instead of mandatory. My attorney says you're all wrong about arbitration. He recommends it for his clients, and I'm one of them. Why don't you give him a call. I don't like being between two advisors who don't agree. His name is Sam Kagel."

Sam and I arranged a get-together at his office. His son John was to sit in on the meeting. Sam and John had quite a reputation in the labor community for settling labor disputes. They had brought peace and harmony to San Francisco's combative waterfront, which had a history of militant labor unrest dating back into the last century.

Sam was one of those soft-hard guys. He could be charming and soft spoken, but he would rise to the challenge and become tough and boisterous if the circumstances called for it. He started out soft. "Mr. Howell, what is it you don't like about arbitration?"

I explained to him the disadvantages, with particular emphasis on the disparate bargaining power that our small business clients had in disputes with larger, lawyer-staffed entities. I also explained that the rules of procedure that the American Arbitration Association promulgated seemed to favor the fiscally strong.

"No, no, no," Sam said. "You've got it all wrong. There should be no lawyers. The way we do it is with what we call Med/Arb, a contraction of "mediation" and "arbitration." You see, we have a mediation first—no lawyers allowed. Often I serve as the mediator. If for some reason the parties can't agree, then the mediator is empowered to act as arbitrator and arbitrate the dispute; again, no lawyers allowed. The mediator can ask for any and all documents he wants, and may cross-examine any person connected to the dispute. He has absolute power to look into any aspect of the conflict. If anyone balks, he can put on his arbitrator's hat and make a ruling; again, no lawyers allowed. I tell you it works. We've used it with dozens of labor disputes, and they get settled, by God."

Sam went on, "Look, if you have a dispute with someone, and a third party can be called in to settle it—no matter what—you're very apt to settle it yourselves. That's what we find in these labor disputes. The parties don't like the idea of a Med/Arbitrator being called, so they work out the problem. We've saved millions of dollars in legal costs, and the parties are happy too! That's what your engineers, architects, contractors, and owners should do."

I had to admit that Sam and his son John had a point with their suggestion. So we decided to take it a step further. We borrowed their agreements,
had them studied by Joe McQuillan, by now a full-fledged member of the
California State Bar, and decided on a strategy. We had been working with a
group of soil and foundation engineers who were still smarting from the loss
of their insurance market in 1968. We determined that they would be the
most likely group to be interested in Med/Arb. So we prevailed upon Sam
to make a presentation at one of their meetings. The meeting attendees
thought it was a revolutionary idea that might relegate litigation to a back
seat in construction disputes.

Two people in particular became excited about Med/Arb, John
Gnaedinger, the owner of Soil Testing Services, Inc. of Northbrook, Illinois,
and Eugene B. Waggoner, president of Woodward-Clyde Consultants in San
Francisco, and past president of the Consulting Engineers Council (now the
American Consulting Engineers Council). John took on Med/Arb as his personal crusade and made speeches about its use throughout the country.
Gene Waggoner got the significant clout of the CEC behind Med/Arb.
Through John's and Gene's efforts we formed an organization, the Construction Industry's Communication Net. This organization had members
from CEC, the Associated General Contractors, the American Institute of Architects, and many larger owner corporations.

Med/Arb was looked at from every point of view, and its legality was
studied interminably. Finally, everyone agreed that this method of dispute
resolution gave the promise of freeing up the construction industry parties
from the unbearable mantle of courtroom litigation. A vote was taken in
May 1970, in Burlingame, California, and the group decided to adopt
Med/Arb as a standard procedure for the construction industry. We all
thought, "At last we are free of litigation. Hurrah!!!"

Our reverie was interrupted at the next meeting when one of the major
contractors reported, "Well, our company will go along with your
Med/Arb, but with a $200,000 limit. They just can't see turning over the keys
of the company safe to some stranger, when there is $5 million or $50 million
involved."

A disappointed murmur went through the crowd, and a multiple-
project owner rose and said much the same thing. This attitude dashed our
hope for Med/Arb as a total replacement for litigation, but we continued to
foster it and urge it as a solution. Even so, the idea of using mediation as a
dispute resolution method had caught hold, and since the early 1970s the insurance company that is Different by Design has urged its insureds to use
nonbinding mediation as a means of settling professional liability disputes.
This has been done in close to a thousand conflicts—successfully! Of course,
this effort has reduced the amount of litigation and the attendant legal costs.

When the decision was made to form the insurance company that was
going to be Different by Design, we realized that it would be in our interest
to make some type of major step to take our insureds out of the litigation
game. Med/Arb, nonbinding mediation, and other alternative dispute reso-

lution concepts were one possibility, but a grander, broader, major change seemed in order; perhaps an $E = mc^2$-type change—a whole new way of conducting a professional practice. One of the things that struck us was the plaintiff's lawyers' misuse of the weaknesses of the law as a means of gaining their goals. One of the law's shortcomings is the vagueness of determining damages once a tort has been alleged. It never ceased to amaze me how a plaintiff's attorney would exaggerate the damages as a ploy to intimidate a defendant into making a favorable settlement.

Claims against design professionals for piddling actual damages would show up on the summons and complaint in the millions of dollars. This occurrence wasn't rare. Rather, it seemed to be an everyday happening. In fact, some lawyers have been known to recommend this procedure as one that should be de rigueur when suing design professionals (and others). It has a demoralizing effect on any defendant whose minor infraction suddenly becomes a source of major alleged damages. The courts, while empowered to bring things into proper perspective, have been casting a benign eye on this practice, allowing it to flourish unimpaired as though it were proper. It is not.

When questioning the admiralty plaintiff's attorney in Seattle about what the admiralty defense attorneys were doing wrong in the defense of Jones Act claims by fishermen, he said, "The attorneys defending those claims don't even plead limitation of liability!" Evidently, if they had pleaded limitation of liability, the case would be transferred from the state court to the federal court where the claim would have been limited to the value of the hull of the vessel at the time of the loss. The federal courts are also reluctant to allow "kiting" the damages as a bargaining ploy, the practice so common in state courts.

Jack Fleisch, too, had talked about limitation of liability and explained how it had an ancient history, dating back to the seafaring Phoenicians (circa 1100 B.C.). They had found that being liable for the loss of a valuable cargo, including the potential profit therefrom, was so burdensome that they could not afford to take the risk. They had to find an answer or go out of business as merchant seamen. They devised the plan of spreading cargoes among several ships (that is, spreading the risk, just as we do with insurance) so if one vessel sank, the others would preserve most of the cargo. They also limited their liability contractually for the loss of the cargo to the value of the ship (hull) at the time of the loss. This enabled them to continue their near monopoly on the Mediterranean as marine transporters of goods. Their idea of limitation of liability caught on and was in existence with most European mariners, and it was codified by the British Parliament in 1601.

Would this limitation of liability do what we hoped? Would it take the bargaining maneuver away from plaintiff's attorneys who had been asking for damages soaring to the moon? Was it enforceable as a binding, valid, defensible, legitimate contract clause? These were questions for which we had no immediate answers.

I went to the public and law libraries to look into limitation of liability to see if anyone else had thought it might be a good defensive device. What I found was fascinating! Limitation of liability was being used in trade and commerce in a broad spectrum of businesses and professions. While we had heard references to it in connection with marine exposures, it was, in fact, reaching into all sorts of commercial crannies where it was working its good. Many of these were businesses that would have been crushed by the burden of litigation without limitation of liability's beneficial consequences.

I found that interstate truckers were using it on their bills of lading, limiting their liability to $25,000 per load due to their negligence. If the shippers wanted greater protection, they had the option of buying special "all risk"* cargo insurance.

Large construction companies were using contracts of hire that stipulated, in part:

The contractor shall maintain comprehensive general liability insurance with a combined single limit of $1,000,000 per occurrence which shall name the owner and the owner's agents as additional insureds, as their interest may appear. The owner will limit any claim against the contractor to the insurance limit for allegations of negligence or other insured perils, and will require a like limitation from his agents or employees. In the event the owner requires a greater limit, he may purchase coverage from the contractor's insurer at their rates and subject to their terms and conditions.

This very effectively limits the liability of the contractor to the limit of the contractor's comprehensive general liability insurance. Most large turnkey† contractors use a similar clause in their contracts of hire.

Financial advisors also had limitation of liability clauses in their contracts of hire. The clauses stated that they would perform in accordance with the rules governing their profession, but they would not be liable for alleged negligence in their professional service for any sum in excess of their fee.

Patent attorneys, too, have such clauses in their appointment agreements. The unstable nature of patent applications almost made it mandatory that they limit their liability to a sum equivalent to their fee, and not more, if a patent failed to issue due to, or allegedly due to, negligent professional performance.

If you were to look at an international air travel ticket you would see that it contains a limitation of liability clause. Damages are to be "proven damages not to exceed U.S. $75,000 per passenger (death or bodily injury), and that this liability up to such limit shall not be dependent on negligence on the part of the carrier." This limitation was agreed upon by countries that

---

* Does not usually insure to cover all risks; commonly contains exclusions such as earthquake, flood, design errors, and latent defects. Thus the term "all risk" is in quotes.

† Firms that design a project and build it as well are frequently referred to as "turnkey" because they are able to complete a structure, turn the key when finished, and hand it to the owner.

participated in the Warsaw Convention,* and it has been upheld by U.S. courts of competent jurisdiction.

The air carriers also have a baggage liability limitation, unless a higher value is declared. The limitation is $1,250 per passenger between U.S. points and $9.07 per pound on international flights.

The telephone company has a limitation of liability clause in the contracts they sign with users listed in the yellow pages. When the telephone company has goofed and failed to print users' listings, users have frequently claimed horrendous damages. However, the limitation of liability clause, limiting damages to the amount of fee, has been upheld in the courts many times.

Data processing companies (those that process business data such as payroll or group medical insurance) also usually have limitation of liability clauses in their contracts.

"If all those businesses and professions could successfully use limitation of liability, why not design professionals?" I asked myself. The biggest objection I could see was inertia; that is, they had never used it before, so why use it now. Many design professionals would rather go through a Jonestown-type mass self-destruction rather than change the status quo. We had run into this self-immolation attitude with professional liability loss prevention recommendations of other types, such as Robert Wilhelm's admonition, "Change your shop drawing stamp to be more precise about what you mean by using it. Get rid of the word 'approved.' That does not say what you intend." Even professional bodies rose to defend the ritual of using "approved" on shop drawing stamps. They treated Bob's (and our) suggestion as the worst kind of blasphemy, even ridiculing the idea as "unprofessional." "Why, what you are suggesting flies in the face of our tradition!" said they (and their legal counsel). It wasn't until we were successful in defending claims against design professionals who had used our recommended language on their shop drawing stamp (while those who had not were found liable) that the tide began to turn. Today, almost thirty years later, finding a shop drawing stamp that hangs on to the archaic "Approved" is getting difficult.

Our first step toward using limitation of liability was to look into its legality in a design professional's contract of hire. I had researched it in the law library and it appeared to be perfectly legal (although there were no cases of limitation of liability being used by design professionals that had been tried). To be certain, we hired Joe McQuillan, then a full-fledged member of the California State Bar, to research it. In addition, we hired the law firm of Heller, Erhman, White & McCauliffe to do the same. At the Heller firm, we

---

* Made famous by the Jane Froman case. Jane Froman was a famous singer who was badly injured on an international flight. The court held that she was bound by the Warsaw Convention. That convention convened on October 12, 1929, and the United States entered into the agreement, subject to a reservation, on October 29, 1934.

had worked with George Blackstone (really his name) on other matters and knew him to be a top-notch jurist. Joe and George did their research and came up with essentially the same answer: "Limitation of liability was legal and enforceable so long as it was reasonable in amount, and it was not gained through disparate bargaining power.* George Blackstone found a case that held that $25,000 was "a reasonable amount,"[1] so he felt $50,000 (allowing for inflation) would be upheld. George also thought the enforceability would be improved if the person expected to limit his or her claim were given the chance to bargain his or her way out of the limitation by paying a greater fee or buying insurance (such as is done in interstate trucking).

We had studies done in many other jurisdictions, such as New York, Texas, South Carolina, and Alabama. Former Chief Justice of the Illinois Supreme Court, Walter Schaefer, opined its legality and thought it was a good remedy for the runaway torts situation. Many engineering firms had their own attorneys study it and, to my knowledge, all reported the same conclusion—limitation of liability is legal and enforceable.

How do you introduce an unpopular concept to a group of rugged individualists? That was our next challenge. Here we were with a little-known legal remedy that we thought would turn the design professionals' claims situation around. We knew, also, that tampering with traditional ways of doing business could wreak havoc with our other ongoing professional liability loss prevention programs. We didn't want the design professionals to say, "Aw, to hell with them! All of them!"

We sensed that since the soil and foundation engineers had been through the worst professional liability claims travail (that is, they had a high frequency of claims, soaring severity, and had lost their insurance markets twice in less than ten years), they ought to be ripe for a far-reaching concept like limitation of liability.

How ASFE Came To Be

Some time after Kemper insisted that we discontinue providing coverage for soil and foundation engineers, I received a telephone call from Jim Hurley in Seattle. Jim lived by his Catholic convictions: He had a fierce dedication to doing the right thing in his life and business affairs without regard to any monetary reward and an inbred desire to help those less fortunate than himself. "Damn it, Ed," Jim would say, "can't we do something for these soil and foundation engineers. My clients just haven't had that many claims. They are big supporters of the professional liability loss prevention program. They've been loyal to us, and now we're treating them like any other insur-

---

* This means having a far superior power in a bargaining situation that makes it almost impossible for the other party to resist taking a stand that is not in their interest.

ance company would, running when it gets a little tough. I think we have a duty to come up with something. It galls me just to say, 'Tough' to them. How about it? Don't you know of anything we might try?"

"Well, Jim, I agree. We do owe the soil and foundation engineers a try at something. London (Lloyd's) has dried up as a market. Things are rough right now (1968) due to the lack of insurance capacity. But let me work on it. One thing is for sure, they need to form an action body—an association—to do anything effective. I don't know any soil and foundation engineers down here that could get their competitors together. They really hate each other. A lot of them left the larger firms to form their own companies, took business with them, and rancorous feelings are running high. Real high! Do you think Bill Shannon of Shannon & Wilson would be able to get them to go to a central location, say, Chicago, to talk about the problem?"

"Well, I think he'd be willing to try," Jim replied. "We've got to come up with something though. If we fire blanks, we'll never hear the end of it. How about the first week of December?"

Bill Shannon wrote a well-thought-out letter, similar to, "We are all in this professional liability bind together, so we'd all better prepare to do something about it." He sent the letter to about 30 firms, and on December 8, 1968, we met in a smoke-filled room at the O'Hare Inn in Chicago. I had never seen such an incongruous group as those soil and foundation engineers! They were all principals of their firms, and they had some pretty strong opinions about themselves and their peers. Elio D'Appolonia (D'App) started the festivities by saying something like, "I don't know what in hell I'm doing here. I have absolutely nothing in common with you S.O.B.s. We run a *professional* firm, not like most of you. I think I'll leave."

It took us a few minutes to convince him to stay and at least see what we had in mind. He hated John Gnaedinger of Soil Testing Service of Northbrook, Illinois, and John would like to have crucified D'App given the time and place. They loved to snitch on each other. The guys from California wouldn't even speak to one another. They, too, liked to tell about their competitions' indiscretions in engineering and love. Everyone thought the problem of professional liability claims was the result of engineers in other regions, not their own, and they didn't know why our meeting had anything to do with *their* firm.

Bill Shannon is a born leader, never using threat or bluster in his persuasive propositions, and with his quiet eloquence, he led a gentle discussion that may have been like the one the Indians had before the Battle of Little Big Horn, that is, "We'd better get together, bury our animosities, and deal with the common enemy." With this approach, he gained grudging commitment from those present to listen to our proposal. He had an impeccable reputation since their firm was extremely successful, both professionally and fiscally. When he spoke, it was best to listen. His engineering firm had not been involved in some of the bitter, acrimonious battles of territory characterized by the soil and foundation engineers in other geographical areas.

The proposal was a replication of the founding of Employers Mutuals of Wausau, Lumbermens Mutual Casualty Company, and the Hartford. We stressed the importance of reducing losses through intelligent loss prevention activity. We told them that for a professional liability loss prevention program to work, considerable effort would be required on their part; that it would entail twice yearly loss prevention seminars, manuals of practice, reduction of predatory business practices, such as bidding for work (no professional engineer would have knowingly bid for his work, would he?), improved personnel policies (including involving all personnel in professional liability loss prevention), and above all, better communications. After several hours of sometimes bitter haranguing ("You did it, you S.O.B.! You bid that job. I saw your letter!"), they agreed to give it a try. We incorporated a loss prevention association, the Association of Soil and Foundation Engineers (ASFE), with Bill Shannon as president.

RAR accepted the assignment to run ASFE during its formative years. A month before the meeting, I called A&A's Felix Kloman, one of the best insurance brains in the country, who has a compelling sense of social responsibility that makes him constantly aware of the ethical implications of anything he does. His imagination in insurance matters is boundless, and he keeps the ethics pot stirred. He took it upon himself to act as the conscience of the industry by chiding it to reform in various ways. For example, he made a speech before the American Management Association in New York, stating that insurance brokers should not receive commissions, but fees based upon the actual work they perform (much to the consternation of his fellow employees, some of whom turned vermilion as he spoke). He argued that the commission system paid whether or not any work was done by the broker. (If a client bought a new plant and had its value added to their schedule of insured properties, the broker would do little or no work and would still get a commission. On a $100 million plant, that could be quite a lot.)

Felix is what many of his fellow employees called "iconoclastic" since he smashed some of the holiest of insurance idols. He spoke at a Risk and Insurance Managers Society (RIMS) meeting in Miami in 1970 and, to the horror of almost everyone, suggested that the insurance industry was not being responsible in its race policy nor in excluding females from the hallowed, all-male management ranks. He was right. He wrote under a pseudonym (because his employer wouldn't allow him to write under his own name and corporate identification) and was published by one of the insurance business's best publications, Rance Crain's *Business Insurance*. His articles still vibrate with challenging, thought-provoking content. Today he continues to question some of the more archaic practices of the insurance industry, and he usually has well-thought-out logic on his side.

Felix had been acquired by A&A when they purchased Lukens, Savage & Washburn of Philadelphia, a large, well-known insurance brokerage firm. I explained to Felix that we had this group of soil and foundation engineers who really needed help. The word "help" appealed to him since money never was his motivator. I explained how the engineers had high claims frequency from work in residential subdivisions and infrequent severity of claims from commercial and governmental work (large claims being made only about every 5 years). Further, their claims usually resulted in enormous legal expenses, but no indemnity ever being paid.

Felix put his Princeton-trained brain to work on the problem and, faster than a diving hummingbird, told me, "It would be a perfect setup for a high deductible (on the residential work), chronological stabilization insurance plan."

"Hey, wait a minute. A high deductible stable what?" I asked in complete bewilderment.

"You've got frequency in residential work, right? Well, make the deductible for that type of work $50,000 per claim (a high number in those days). Then set up a pool that everyone pays into to take care of the large losses that take place every five years or so. That way you have the firms that work in the residential area paying most of their own losses, but you provide for the low credibility,* high severity losses with "true" insurance. See, you spread the cost of the risk over a chronological period and you have the high frequency guys paying for their own indiscretions with a high deductible," Felix replied with some enthusiasm in his voice.

"Can we do that? How do we do that? Is it legal? Have you ever done it before?" I queried.

"Sure we can. Come to New York. We need an all-states underwriter.† I think it's legal. You're the attorney, you tell me. We do it all the time with things like crop insurance, strike insurance, oil-well fire insurance, all the tough stuff with catastrophe exposure, and no available insurance market. This stabilizes the cost because when you reach a certain reserve you don't charge any more premium until a loss happens. Come on back here. I'll look for a carrier," Felix offered with now, white-hot enthusiasm. He had sold himself.

In New York Felix gave me a lecture on the chronological stabilization insurance plan. "You say these claims go on for five years before they're settled. That makes it perfect. You've got five years to earn investment return to offset the cost of a claim, or five years in which to fund for a loss once the probable cost is known."

"But, Felix," I complained, "Phil Ness,‡ Lou Bonar,§ and I visited Norrie Flanigan at Kemper to try to expand our program to Maryland. Norrie and Lou had a parking-lot type argument, with lots of swearing, glaring, and posturing, about the adequacy of reserves in our program, and when I brought up the high rate of investment return from this type of insurance,

---

* In insurance rating, large losses are considered to be anomalous, having little or no believability, thus low credibility.
† An underwriter licensed to issue policies of insurance in all states of the United States.
‡ Phil Ness was chairman of A&A by this time.
§ Executive vice president of A&A.

Norrie came close to having apoplexy. He said, 'You can't consider investment return in rate making—not under any circumstances!' He looked at me as if I were a 24-karat idiot. I checked the CPCU manual, and he was right. So how can we in this chronological thing?"

"Mister Howell," Felix began, "that's just what makes this perfect for your soil and foundation engineers. They can include most of the investment return in their reserves. Over five years that would mean about 40%. That's a lot to offset any reserve inadequacy. That's what we have to negotiate with the underwriter. I've made an appointment with John McHugh and his boss, Bob Lumm, at American Re-Insurance Company for 10:30 A.M., then lunch. You pay," said my frugal friend.

We actually met with only John McHugh, who, like Felix, was a student of insurance and liked dealing with weird deals, like ours. John's glasses gave him a slightly owlish look, which I translated into elevated brain power. It turned out that way. John worked in the facultative department of American Re-Insurance Company. "Facultative" means that they would deal with a single risk or a well defined group of risks of the same type—usually of a high risk nature. Strictly speaking, they were set up to sell reinsurance, which is insurance sold to primary insurance companies so that the primary insurers need not take the entire exposure of a risk. They almost never sell coverage directly to the risks, as they would be doing in our case. Reinsurance typically is sold through a treaty, which is nothing more than a contract issued by the reinsurer, calling for them to accept a portion (or all) of a risk ceded to them by a primary insurer (one selling insurance to members of the public). If a primary insurer has a one-of-a-kind exposure, like a shot to the moon, an experimental open heart surgery blood pump, or a chance of rain on drying raisins in the San Joaquin Valley, they would apply to the facultative department of a reinsurance company for a specific treaty to cover the risk.

John asked, "Can we begin by calling your ASFE plan a chronological stabilization *reinsurance* plan? You know, internal politics and all."

"Sure, why not?" Felix answered, and that's how we billed it to the ASFE members. We proceeded to negotiate a plan that had a master facultative policy with a single limit ($250,000 all losses), with certificates of insurance running to each insured participant. The participants were to pay a deposit premium that would create a pool of reserves large enough to cover a maximum possible first-year loss (that is, $250,000) and they would pay additional premium to replenish any deposit premium depleted by losses. American Re-Insurance's exposure would thus be credit: If losses depleted the deposit premium and the participants would not, or could not, pay additional premium the reinsurance company would suffer a loss. Since my experience with the soil and foundation engineers showed them to be honorable men in most instances, we thought the risk to American Re-Insurance was small.

The treaty was written to give a credit in the future for investment return, and it called for a policyholders' dividend of all sums remaining of deposit premium at the end of five years. The insureds (participants) were to pay their own state premium taxes. We thought we had worked out a good deal. Felix became my hero, but some at A&A thought our plan for ASFE was a type of Howell-Kloman suicidal folly.

The ASFE members liked the plan, and we put it in effect in mid-1969. We failed to collect the entire $250,000 deposit premium the first year, and we were horrified that a loss might wipe out the premium reserve. But divine providence smiled and blessed us with no claims for the first two years. The second year the ASFE participants came up with plenty of deposit premium. Then, too, the clamor from other soil and foundation engineers to be admitted to the plan burgeoned the deposits and the premium reserve grew.

ASFE prospered. They were the most active group of design professionals in the United States in matters dealing with professional liability loss prevention. ASFE's insurance plan continued to go well, and as it did, its members grew more confident and dedicated in their professional liability loss prevention effort.

Limitation of Liability Revisited

For many reasons we at RAR felt that ASFE would be the best group from whom to gain support for regular use of limitation of liability in contracts of hire. At their fall 1969 meeting in New Orleans, we proposed that they use it in all of their contracts. On January 22, 1922, the Knickerbocker Theater in Washington, D.C., collapsed under a snow load, killing almost 100 people.[2] The screaming, yelling, and chaos must have been close to that occasioned by our limitation of liability proposal to ASFE.

"Of all the hare-brained schemes you've put forth, Howell, this is the worst! I've cut out paper dolls [one facilitator at a seminar, Jack Fordyce, had the ASFE participants form teams to cut out newspaper pictures, pick up floor debris, and use other junk to make a collage that would communicate a concept] and listened to behavioral science kooks, but this takes the cake," D'Appolonia fumed. Others were equally disturbed by what they viewed as an impossible task.

"How do you know until you try," I argued. "You guys aren't out of the woods yet. These claims against you are for millions, and most of them are specious. You are paying defense costs that far exceed the damages. The lawyers and their greedy clients are having you for lunch. You've got to find a way to stop them. This may be it. Other professions and businesses have used limitation of liability successfully. Now it's time you try!" I argued.

Fortunately, good old, loyal Bill Shannon stepped into the fray and came to my rescue, "Wait a minute, guys. His other suggestions have worked. Maybe we should take a closer look at the limitation of liability and not dismiss it out of hand."

So they did. They were eventually satisfied with its legality, but they thought no one would sign a contract that contained such a clause. They were wrong, but they needed reinforcement to help them with their clients.

The howling and negativism were not over. In 1972, Eugene Waggoner chaired a program, sponsored by the Engineering Foundation, at the Asilomar Conference Center in Pacific Grove, California, called "Professional Liability: Who Pays? Who Benefits?" It was a conference cosponsored by the American Institute of Architects (AIA), the American Society of Engineers, the Associated General Contractors of America, the Consulting Engineers Council, and the National Association of Home Builders. The conference attracted dozens of defense and plaintiff attorneys, virtually all of the insurance people interested in design professionals' liability insurance, judges, and a large number of design professionals who had a keen interest in the subject. The soil and foundation engineers were particularly well represented.

Asilomar is a California state-operated conference facility that is a little bit like summer camp. The facilities are meant to be Spartan, but they are not. The food is like army chow (I should know) but the setting is beautiful—nestled in the white sand dunes contiguous with Pebble Beach, next to the radiant Pacific Ocean, under a canopy of Monterey pines.

Gene Waggoner had given most people who attended, and who wanted to, time to tell what they thought should be done about the design professionals' professional liability problem. One architect said, "I think we should do away with insurance. Insurance becomes a target for the attorneys, and if there were none, the problem would go away."

Robert E. Cartwright, a San Francisco attorney who was at that time president of the American Trial Lawyers Association (plaintiff lawyers), answered that idea by saying, "Hell, I don't care if an architect or consulting engineer is insured when I sue him for professional negligence. I figure he or she is good for a judgment of $50,000 or $100,000 even without insurance. They make good money, don't they? What do I care if they're insured?" He also said that the design professionals should thank the plaintiffs' attorneys for policing their profession. "If it weren't for us, the charlatans in your ranks would be fleecing the public. There are designers that really should not be allowed to practice. We're keeping you guys and the money grubbers in your ranks honest. You aren't doing anything to police your profession. Absolutely nothing." There was no argument raised about his statement.

Some good ideas were put forth at this meeting. There were government officials present who hadn't even realized how claims-prone their projects seemed to be. When they found out how much litigation was costing in government construction (about 5% of the project cost), they became quite agitated. Med/Arb was discussed and it became a focal point of interest since everyone, except the attorneys, were appalled by the exorbitant legal costs. An official from HUD (D. Earl Jones) showed keen interest in trying to cut costs with a Med/Arb type approach. This was the era when public housing was a big issue.

Joe McQuillan gave a learned presentation on replacing our current jury system "with persons, many of whom are familiar with normal methods of construction, customary duties and responsibilities of those persons involved in construction and, if required, technically knowledgeable." It seemed to make sense, but no one rose to move for it.

Peter B. Hawes, at this time a vice president of A&A, presented a Dartmouth-type oration on "Professional Liability as a Factor in Inflation." He made it clear that professional liability claims and other construction related claims were at the heart and soul of the run-away costs in construction.

J. Sprigg Duval, president of Victor O. Schinnerer & Co., Inc.,* gave some interesting statistics to the audience. "Origin of Claims: 80% to 90% of claims grow out of engineering rather than architecture. Sources of losses: 65% come from problems related to the original design/specification documents; 25% relate to the construction phase; 10% miscellaneous (sources). In the period 1957–1964, 33% of cases were defended with no loss. 1964–1971, 75% of cases were defended with no loss or only defense costs. An estimate for 1972: 80% of cases defended with no loss or only defense costs. Cost ratio of premiums for 1972: premiums were 1% of the gross fees of the insured design professional. This was about .04% of the cost of the projects designed. Although my statistics professor told us, "Distrust figures (or lawyers fees?) that come out even," Mr. Duval's figures were close to our own; that is, we felt that costs of defense, not indemnity, were the killers. We also concurred in his statement that "local governments and quasi-governmental groups are frequent plaintiffs."

My turn to expound came at 9:00 A.M. of the second day, March 18, 1972. I was the chairman of the session and moderator. Limitation of liability was to be my opening shot, and I knew that it was going to be an uphill battle to get it properly considered. I presented my information about Phoenician seafarers, truckers, patent attorneys, and so forth, and our major insurance competitor got up with a noisy display of disdain and left to play golf. The attorneys had to display their knowledge, so some of them started throwing out opinions about it like, "It's an exculpatory clause and it may be considered an adhesion contract. Clearly, not enforceable," or "While it may be practical for mere tradesmen, it has no place in the professions," or "No owner in his right mind, having legal advice from a well-trained attorney like me, would ever agree to sign a document containing such a clause."

When you buy something, no matter how inferior, when someone criticizes it, you tend to defend it vehemently. "I tell you my 1970 Chevy is the best car ever built," or "No matter what *Consumer Reports* says, my Minolta is tops." That same phenomenon, pride of ownership, burst forth at this meeting. The soil and foundation engineers, who felt that limitation of liability was *theirs*, roared to the defense of this experimental concept, and roundly criticized the negative-sounding attorneys for their greed and pro-

---

* Victor O. Schinnerer & Co. manages an AIA-commended insurance program with CNA as underwriter.

fessional avarice. The discussion became quite heated, with the preponderance of those present saying, "It won't work."

In his quiet way, Bill Shannon once more rose to defend limitation of liability by saying, "I don't believe everyone here is aware of all that is being done regarding loss prevention education. CEC has issued a loss prevention manual and has an ongoing program. ASFE has probably the most active loss prevention program with annual expenditures of over $10,000. DPIC allocates 3% of its gross premium toward professional liability loss prevention. These three groups together with the American Council of Independent Laboratories, the California Council of the AIA, and the California Council of Civil Engineers and Land Surveyors, have raised over $30,000 for a public relations campaign to promote the concept of limitation of liability. Limitation of liability has been used by soil and foundation engineers and will be used more and more. My firm has had an excellent acceptance of limitation of liability and so have other members of ASFE. We intend to use it habitually." Bill received mild applause.

During the happy hour, Dick Yedziniak, executive director of the Connecticut Consulting Engineers in Private Practice, had introduced me to their attorney, Peter G. Kelly, Esq., of Updike, Kelly & Spellacy, Hartford, Connecticut. Peter is a big man, 6 feet, 7 inches tall, 300 plus pounds of Irish-Danish-Scottish mix, and a combative, spirited man. In addition to his size, another positive attribute is his quick, analytical mind that leaves most people in the dust, saying to themselves, "What happened?" Above all, he is a persuasive speaker who lilts his words like an accomplished singer (which he is). This is all backed by an outstanding education (Georgetown University, B.S. in political science, magna cum laude; Yale Law School, with honors, and the *Yale Law Journal*).

Peter listened intently to the rabid condemnation of limitation of liability at Asilomar, raised his hand to speak, and finally rose to say, "I've listened to these proceedings wondering what some of you are trying to accomplish. It is puzzling because, so far, there has been a general condemnation of the legal system and all of its trappings, but, until this recent suggestion—limitation of liability—no one has suggested that there is anything positive to do about this odious professional liability situation, except to opine that we can expect more of the same. We can't change the legal system, can we? Wouldn't it be far better to grasp this potential lifesaver? Your professional ship seems to be sinking, and you now seem to be saying, 'Let's not try this simple concept which might save our professional lives.'"

Peter went on, "Look at the system we have: You know insurance isn't the answer. You think it too expensive and it may be exploitive of your unfortunate plight. You feel the legal profession is not filling your needs, and it, too, seems to you to be manipulative. Last, in American business, the moneymaker is the admired person. Most people strive to make money (some without regard for the consequences), so maybe your profession's preoccupation with profit is contributing to the problem in some small way.

"History has dumped on your lap a tried, proven methodology for mitigating your exposure. From my vector, your arms should be thrown wide in a welcoming gesture toward this limitation of liability, not reacting like someone dragged in a dead and putrid cat. Franklin Delano Roosevelt once said: 'The country needs, and unless I mistake its temper, demands bold, persistent experimentation. It is common sense to take a method and try it. If it fails, admit it frankly and try another. But above all, try something.'

"I hope his thoughts and words will influence your thinking on the subject we are here to explore," Peter propounded.

He then cast a smile around the room and sat down. The audience was silent for a few moments, then burst into resounding applause for his lucid eloquence.

In spite of Peter's persuasive words, his remarks fell on the deaf ears of our insurance competitors, their attorneys, and the leadership of certain national professional societies. They continued to belittle limitation of liability with vilification and denunciation for almost 20 years. There has now been a change in attitude. Those who were militantly against limitation of liability now find it acceptable, and even surreptitiously recommend its use.

Following the Asilomar meeting, Peter continued his unstinting support of this concept by making speeches before design professional groups, argued with less enlightened attorneys, and performed negotiations long after lesser men would have abandoned it as a lost cause. Now it looks as if it is here to stay as an offspring of the insurance company that is Different by Design.

Hi Kennicott attended the Asilomar meeting to give insight into the problem from the insurance industry's point of view. His greatest contribution may have come after the meeting when he called me and said, "Ed, on the plane back to Chicago, I got to thinking. What the CEC needs most is some kind of source of funds so they can make a major expenditure on professional liability loss prevention without having their dues structure torn apart. How about a nationwide workers compensation dividend program, that would pay 25% of the dividend to CEC, to be expended on professional liability loss prevention?"

"Gee, Hi, that sounds great. Let me talk to Gene Waggoner and I'll get back to you," I replied with enthusiasm.

At Hi Kennicott's suggestion we started the workers compensation plan with AMICO as the underwriter and DPIC agents selling the coverage. The second year the dividends started flowing, returning 42% the first year and more from then on. Don Buzzell* saw to it that the sums were wisely spent.

While employed by the Employers of Wausau, I witnessed an interesting strategy. Instead of hiring outside counsel to represent their interests and those of their policyholders, the Employers of Wausau had an in-house attorney, Carlotta Beale, who performed some of the necessary legal duties on

---

* Executive director of CEC and ACEC from about 1963 to 1978—a very accomplished administrator who was able to work well with an organization of individuals of highly diverse ideas. He was a participant at the Asilomar conference.

workers compensation cases. She was wonderful. She won almost every case she took before the Missouri State Industrial Accident Commission. She won because she knew her subject matter better than her adversaries, and maybe even better than the commissioners. During the time that we worked with AMICO, we had Joe McQuillan to oversee the performance of the AMICO attorneys to ascertain whether they were performing well. Too often, they were not.

The good results from the efforts of Carlotta Beale and Joe McQuillan, when we formed DPIC we thought, "It might make good sense to have in-house attorneys to handle all claims. That way we can circumvent the cost of counsel and thus mitigate the enormous legal costs that professional liability claims seem to generate. Maybe we will get superior results since the in-house attorneys will be working in an area where they can develop special expertise."

From the very first, we hired young, eager, highly motivated attorneys to handle our claims. It should have worked, but it didn't. First of all, they fell back into the habit of hiring local counsel in jurisdictions where they were not admitted to the bar. In addition, after a few years they would notice with envy how well the outside attorneys were doing financially, and they would wonder, "Why can't that be me?"

Has there really been much change in attorneys between my grandfather's day and now? In the company that is Different by Design, we think not. Attorneys seem to reflect a cross section of society. There are greedy, manipulative, entrepreneurial, stupid, honest, courageous, aggressive, ethical, and devious people. The same is true in the legal profession. Yet there are those who stress service to society and their profession like my grandfather, Edward Beach Howell, and Peter G. Kelly, Joseph A. McQuillan, Sam Kagel, Walter Schaefer, James C. Moore (Rochester), Jamie Frankel (New York), Landon Morris (Los Angeles, deceased), Chuck Maurer (San Diego), Robert Gogick (New York), Sam Muir (Pasadena), Ernie Sevier (San Francisco), Byrom Lee and Bill Knapp (Denver), David Hatem (Boston), Steph Marcus (Chicago), and many, many others. These men eschew the pecuniary nexus in the interest of serving. If you can believe it is not the individuals who have created the morass of legal pitfalls that plague our society, then perhaps you will believe, as I do, that the social/legal systems are at fault. Since the late 1800s and early 1900s there have been extreme, dramatic, sweeping, revolutionary legal and social changes that have so impinged upon the legal system that it would not be recognized by those lawyers who practiced in the late 1800s and early 1900s. I must confess, the changes, just since my graduation from law school (1950), leave me awestruck.

The company that is Different by Design recognizes these far-reaching changes and seeks to reconcile its operations so as to serve successfully in a rapidly changing social and legal environment. We salute those attorneys who work with us in an effort to serve the design profession's insurance and legal needs. Nonetheless, we will continue to avoid the legal process when possible.

Chapter 9

The Business of Forming a Business

Elan is a quality of personality—a way of doing things with spirit and impetuosity and always with enthusiasm.

—*Morris Dictionary of Word Origins*

Risk Analysis and Research Corporation's 1968 formation was perfectly timed. Tired of the offhand treatment or lack of any coverage, businesses started a movement to do something about it. Their exasperation took the form of innovative, sometimes quasi-legal, self-insurance plans. "Captives" was the word most uttered by corporate risk managers, but mutuals, industry-owned insurance companies, and risk funding were also coming into being. RAR was positioned to be in the midst of the innovative insurance company fray. Its activities in the formation of these ancillary companies had great impact on the company that had been formed to be Different by Design.

The Offshore Insurance Company

ASFE Insurance Ltd. had piled up so much in loss reserves in their Chronological Stabilization Reinsurance plan, that American Re-Insurance Company wanted to place those reserves with a more traditional insurance company. This was 1971 when it was just becoming voguish to set up insurance companies in Bermuda, and other offshore jurisdictions where the regulations were not so strict and tax advantages might accrue. Most of these insurance companies were captives, which meant that they were wholly, or almost wholly, owned by the entity for whom they provided insurance, groups of businesses who, for one reason or another, were unable to purchase coverage from the regular insurance markets. Noncaptive companies were also being formed in Bermuda and the other localities. Typifying these would be companies formed by the asbestos industry, scaffold erectors, athletic equipment manufacturers (football helmets, trampolines, etc.), marine transportation companies, the petroleum industry, drug manufacturers, chemical processors, newspapers (to write strike insurance), and a host of others.

I sought out Felix Kloman, for advice on forming an offshore company. Felix had left A&A on October 1, 1970, to form Risk Planning Group (RPG).* Felix felt he could not be a consultant to us because of the conflict of interest question (having left A&A), but he was very generous with his information anyway. "Make sure that you have more than 10 owners with no one of them owning more than 9.5% of the stock. That way the company will not be construed by the IRS to be a controlled foreign corporation. Insist that the potential insureds write a letter to your manager in Bermuda asking to buy the insurance. You would be breaking the law if you solicited the insureds to buy the insurance in their home states. Each of the insured firms should pay the department of insurance the surplus lines tax owed in their company's state of domicile. Also," he advised, "talk with Bob Ainslie at A&A. He has a good grasp on the offshore insurance company situation and can show you the ropes."

I called serious-minded, tennis-loving Bob Ainslie immediately and he said, "Yes, I can introduce you to our counsel, and the Bermuda Fire & Marine Management Co. (BF&M), who could act as your manager in Bermuda. You have to have a Bermuda company as a manager. I'm going over there in about a week. If you want to tag along, be my guest. We can spend the first week of November there. Do you play tennis?"

Ainslie was kind enough to introduce me to the law firm of Conyers, Dill, and Pearman (CDP) and their partners, Charles T. M. Collis and John A. Ellison. There was one other large law firm on the island, but A&A had used CDP so we didn't even call on the potential alternative firm. CDP explained that, to form an insurance company, we had to get a certificate of deposit from the Registrar of Companies office. It would show a deposit of capital of (minimum) U.S. $120,000 and additional surplus (unassigned funds) of U.S. $130,000 for an authorized capital and surplus of $250,000 for our new insurance company, ASFE Insurance Co., Ltd. (ASFE, Ltd.). Our Memorandum of Association showed that on November 3, 1971 ASFE was empowered under Bermuda's laws to:

Engage in and carry on outside these Islands from a principal place of business in these Islands the business of insurance, reinsurance, coinsurance and counterinsur-

---

* Now part of Tillinghast, a Towers Perrin company, Management Consultants and actuaries, Stamford, Connecticut.

ance of all kinds and guarantee and indemnity business of all kinds and in particular, without prejudice to the generality of the foregoing words, to engage in and carry on errors and omissions, professional liability, life, accident, sickness, hospital, health, fire, marine, surety, automobile, aviation, ship, steam boiler, plate glass, windstorm, hailstorm, earthquake, flood, war risk, insurrection, riot, civil commotion, strike, employers' liability, workmen's compensation, disease, survivorship, failure of issue, bonding and indemnity, burglary and robbery, theft, fidelity, transit and other casualty insurance, including loss from the interruption of business due to any of the foregoing;

"Wow!" I thought, "Are we going to do all of that? Never mind, it will work out."

Bob then introduced me to David Lines, an accountant (later merged with Coopers & Lybrand to form Coopers & Lines) whose great interest in life was fishing. This interest did not deter him from doing a good job of accounting, but his eyes kept wandering to the window to see what the sea was doing. "Could he go out to fish?" was the question that seemed to be on his mind. This avocational proclivity gave us a common ground for communication since I viewed myself a fisherman of sorts. He was hired on the spot. Next was Mr. William Thomson, an American, with The Bank of Bermuda Limited. The Bank would hold ASFE Ltd.'s assets as custodian and make its investments.

Initially, we hired BF&M Management, with Cyril Rance as president, to manage the company, paying them a flat fee of $5,000 per year, which on an hourly basis would have made our stateside $200-per-hour lawyers look like poor, penniless paupers. In "managing" there was not much to do except bank the premiums monthly and set up a balance sheet.

A meeting was scheduled for the board of directors of ASFE Insurance Co., Ltd. for January 20, 1972. The Board of Directors of ASFE Ltd. was composed of three Bermudians and five soil and foundation engineers, Bill Shannon, Charles Bragg, Elio D'Appolonia, Leo Hirschfeldt, and Robert D. Sayre. CDP had volunteered their office for the formation meeting. We arrived at the law offices of CDP at the appointed time and were ushered into a large conference room graced with a polished Honduras mahogany table and red leather conference room chairs. We waited, and waited, and waited. Finally, Charles T. M. Collis, Esq. came in, greeted us all, trying to remember names, seated himself, steepled his hands and said in his clipped English accent, "Oh, I say, there is a small problem. I'm certain we can sort it out, straight away, but you see, it seems, well, we seem to have misplaced your file. Dreadfully sorry, but could you come back this afternoon?"

That one event so typifies our experience dealing in Bermuda that it might be called a "Bermuda Classic." We stateside types were so uptight about everything going right in business that running into a commonplace thing like misplacing a file seemed beyond our realm of experience, but there it was. In the afternoon, the file had been retrieved (from typing) and the documents were signed, making the ASFE Insurance Co., Ltd. a viable entity. Doing business in Bermuda calls for a laid-back mien. We grew to like it.

We changed the name of ASFE Insurance Co., Ltd. in August 1972 to Terra Insurance Ltd. Bill Shannon of Shannon and Wilson, Seattle, continued as president of Terra with Leo Hirschfeldt of Leroy Crandall and Associates, Los Angeles, as vice president, becoming president in 1973 (Leo had refused our AMICO coverage in 1963, but later became one of our staunchest supporters). The purpose of the change in name was to simplify the separation of the ASFE from the professional liability insurance offered through Terra. A large percentage of the members of ASFE were not acceptable risks for Terra, or they had insurance plans of their own which they did not choose to disturb. They did want to participate in the professional liability loss prevention effort, however, and being members of ASFE gave them that opportunity.

Scott McKown was in charge of Terra's internal affairs, including underwriting, accounting, and coordination of activities. We sought outside financial counsel for Terra's investments. In December of 1974 we hired Towneley Capital Management Corporation of New York to make all investment decisions. That company was owned and run by Dr. Wesley G. McCain. McCain had been assistant professor of finance at the Columbia University Business School, earned his M.A. and Ph.D. at Stanford, and a B.B.A. from the University of Michigan. Appointing McCain as financial consultant was one of the best moves the Terra board ever made (we duplicated the appointment and made him a member of our DPIC board some years later). He quickly turned our paltry returns into a gusher of capital growth and income, mostly in government securities. In insurance it is axiomatic to place the preservation of capital uppermost in investment strategy. McCain did that for us.

In June 1978, Hiram L. Kennicott, my mentor from Kemper, was made manager of Kemper International's office in Bermuda. We quickly made them the manager of Terra in Bermuda and they did an excellent job. His colleague, Ted Hoeh, handled our day-to-day affairs and did such a good job that Scott McKown and I wanted to hire him—but that wouldn't have been a nice thing to do to Kemper.

Terra grew and exists today as a risk retention group domiciled in Vermont (a federal law permits groups of like businesses to join in a group to write their own insurance; much like our chronological stabilization reinsurance plan).

Land Stability Insurance Company

Following World War II California's land development businesses burgeoned. Construction was awesome, with subdivisions moving further and further from the urban hubs, and freeways to service them never quite keeping up with the enormous traffic flow. As more and more houses were constructed, the competition to sell them became keen; some developers boasted that they were lucky to make a profit of $500 per house. This meant that they took shortcuts in the design and construction of these hastily erected buildings. California's winter weather is unpredictable. One year it will rain torrentially, then be dry for three following years, or vice versa. This lack of predictability led some mercenary developers into taking risks on their civil engineering and soil and foundation work. Thousands of homes were constructed on soil or in locations where calamity would be bound to ensue. It did.

Much of the soil in California (and elsewhere) has its own distinctive tough-to-deal-with characteristics. Some of it is expansive, which means it swells when it gets wet and dries into mud cake and cracks when it is dry. Other soil is viscous so it slides and slips out from under foundations or slabs when the moisture content is increased. This may happen when shrubs are planted next to the foundation wall of a house and flooded with water to make them grow. Most soil erodes easily, so it flows with moving water, and when erosion starts, it can fill a backyard, gutter, brow ditch, or channel in no time. Some soils are corrosive and will destroy plumbing or reinforcing rod if the conditions are right. Interestingly, certain soil creeps, inexorably rupturing roots, toppling fences, rending cracked, leaning houses uninhabitable. To compound the problem, many of the subdivisions developed in post-World War II California were built on fill; hilltops were graded into trash-filled canyons and compacted by mechanical means, too frequently not adequately. The buildings on this type of fill settled differentially, (i.e., one end of the building settled more than the other end), rendering them unfit for occupation.

Don't ask why, but most soil and foundation engineers and excavation contractors have their most junior people monitoring these tricky fill jobs. Bring all of these soil peculiarities together, build without proper compaction or adequate soil analysis, and you may be sure of land instability. The interesting thing is that this geological nightmare is ubiquitous in the United States (maybe world-wide). Just look at the yellow pages in Denver, Dallas, or Atlanta under "Contractors, Foundation Repair," and you'll find people are having soil problems almost everywhere.

By 1963, because of these conditions and the gigantic numbers of claims arising out of land failures, most soil and foundation engineers lost their professional liability insurance, and many civil engineers found it such expensive coverage that they opted for going uninsured. The AMICO professional liability insurance program started in April 1963, but soon our underwriting constraints, in view of loss history and frequency of losses, began to make residential subdivision engineering work taboo. After five years of experience (from 1963 to 1968), losses growing out of residential subdivisions made it eminently clear that insuring soil and foundation engineers or civil engineers involved in subdivision work was folly. So we didn't.

In 1968 the problem of insurability, largely because of residential subdivision failures, had become so acute with soil and foundation engineers that insurance companies around the world said, "You won't find us interested in your risk." It was in this environment that we recommended formation of ASFE as a loss prevention organization (see Chapter 9). Even the insurance plan we established excluded or had an extremely high deductible for those soil and foundation engineers who persisted in doing that type of work. There were many.

In 1968 the Supreme Court of the State of California handed down a ruling that was to have far-reaching impact on the residential development business. In *Connor v. Great Western Savings and Loan Association*,[1] the Court held that the savings and loan association that made a loan on a house later wracked by soil problems was responsible for the loss! The court said the S&L had an independent duty to buyers of homes to exercise reasonable care to protect them from damages caused by soil. The court ruled that every test for establishing such a duty had been met and the savings and loan institution's duty to the buyers of homes was to see that there had been adequate engineering precautions taken and that the soils had been properly tested. It went on to say that the buyers of dwellings upon which loans were made were to be protected from defects in design or construction by the savings and loan association since they were the best equipped to make such a determination! This case hit the savings and loan business like a sputtering grenade. It devastated the S&Ls' comprehensive general liability insurance. Who'd want to insure an S&L that had such a duty and no real expertise to make a judgment? No one, or almost no one. Overnight the savings and loan institutions became uninsurable because of comprehensive general liability claims that might arise out of building failures.

There was more to come that had bearing on this dramatic enigma. In 1969, another case blew the subdivision developers into a severe predicament. In *Kriegler v. Eichler Homes, Inc.*,[2] home builders were saddled with strict liability. Strict liability is a doctrine that finds a manufacturer of a product liable for damages that arise out of the product if it had a defect in it at the time it was sold to the consumer, whether the manufacturer has been negligent or not. This doctrine had been applied to automobiles, aircraft, hammers, machine tools, water heaters, but in this case, the District Court of Appeals of California, First District, found it applied to homes as well.

Eichler Homes, Inc., a popular Palo Alto, California home builder, constructed Kriegler's house in 1951. The concrete slab flooring had been lined with radiant hot water tubes to heat the house. Galvanized steel tubing had been substituted for copper, due to the shortage of copper during and after the Korean War. By 1959 the tubes corroded and failed. Kriegler sued Eichler Homes. In 1969 the District Court of Appeals found that there was, indeed, strict liability, and Eichler was liable even in the absence of the proof of negligence (relying heavily on *Schipper v. Levitt and Sons, Inc.*, 44 N. J. 70, 207 A. 2nd 314 {1965}). The Court said in part, "There are no meaningful distinctions between Eichler's mass production and sale of homes and the mass production in the sales of automobiles." The second bombshell hit the subdivision development industry blowing it into disarray.

That same year, 1969, the District Court of Appeals heard another case, *Avner v. Longridge Estates,*[3] in which they upheld the Kriegler finding of strict liability as to the developer and went on further to state, "It was reasonable to hold a developer strictly liable for a defective lot, and possibly any engineers who participated in the development of the lot might share in that liability." Those were dark days for anyone who earned a livelihood from residential development.

We at RAR were contacted by our soil and foundation engineer friends and the members of the California Council of Civil Engineers and Land Surveyors who were involved in residential subdivision work in early 1970 with a plea, "What can we do?" It did not seem like selling more liability insurance was the answer. We had to take the soils failure problem off of the public's back with trade-offs. To me the losses were very similar to losses that are normally insured by specialty insurance companies. For example, boilers and machinery are insured against failures that cause losses, both liability and property. After a thorough examination by a boiler and machinery engineer, many insurance companies will provide broad coverage for property damage or bodily injury caused by exploding boilers or failing machinery. Why not land failures? Could we get buyers of homes to agree to a loss prevention maintenance program and agree to take the responsibility for all land failures that were caused by their laxity in implementing the loss prevention recommendations?

We asked our clients if they could get a group of interested parties together from all of those organizations involved: CCCE&LS, ASFE, Associated Home Builders (AHB), and the California Savings and Loan League (CSLL). We set up an urgent meeting, because time was of the essence. It had been a wet year and homes were bound to start cracking, slipping, and sliding off their foundations, or down from a spectacular view to a grim one.

The meeting started off on a rancorous note. We of RAR opined that the enormous number of failures in residential subdivisions were the result of runaway mercenary instincts (greed). The public was sick of reading about slides, cracking foundations, and shoddy work. We advised the developers, savings and loan people, and engineers that the unfettered zeal for profit had to be curbed if the problem of land failure was to be controlled, at least by insurance. Most of those at this meeting did not like hearing such blunt criticism, and some drifted out saying, "To hell with you and your lofty ideals!"

Nonetheless, things came out of that meeting that convinced us we were on the right track. We found that far more property damage was done to residential property in California by land failure than by fire! It wasn't as visible, but it was there in the form of sticking doors, cracking slabs, and settling foundations, and most of it was due to inadequacy of expenditure for engineering. It was common gossip that soil testing was done on only one lot out of hundreds upon which homes were to be built. We were given extremely convincing proof by a staff engineer from the Los Angeles County Building Department, Chuck Yelverton. In 1963 the county of Los

Angeles had passed a grading ordinance. This ordinance was extremely strict on how much engineering, and what type, was necessary before a permit would be issued for the construction of a dwelling. The grading ordinance worked. Land failure losses ceased in properties built after 1963 in Los Angeles County. This gave us impetus to form an insurance company that would write insurance to protect homeowners against all types of land failures. The keystone would be strict adherence to the Los Angeles County Grading Ordinance of 1963. In addition, a far-reaching program of public education would be started.

Art Sherman and Herb Cooper of Cooper-Sherman Engineers were instrumental in getting the CCCE&LS to give monumental support to this effort. They also became one of the largest single financial investors, once capital and surplus were sought. They were both skilled businessmen with an entrepreneurial bent that made forming an insurance company an exciting challenge to them. The CCCE&LS produced a wonderful document that was to be posted in every new home, not in the garage, advising the owners about what to do and not to do, in order to avoid land failures. For example, "never irrigate hillside slopes, keep brow ditches free of debris, do not plant shrubs or trees close to the house's foundation." It is still a valid document, worth its weight in gold for any first-time home buyer.

Key in making a plan of the sort we had in mind was adequate spread of risk, which meant coverage would have to be purchased on virtually every new dwelling (that qualified) built in California. That way, we would not only get spread of risk, but preclude the chance of adverse selection (a process whereby someone purchases a type of insurance because he anticipates he is going to have a loss, such as a ship's master buying marine coverage when he knows the ship's hull is leaking badly). In providing coverage for land failure, we had to be careful that adverse selection would not happen, and that could be assured only if all new developments were insured, without regard to location. We didn't want some developer to insure only what he or she viewed as a "dangerous lot."

Dozens of meetings were held with the various groups during which we explained the concept of reducing losses with strict engineering control and spreading the risk through mandatory insuring of all developments. The members of the Association of Home Builders showed the greatest reluctance to commit to what they viewed as an additional expense. One of their number, Gordon Hanson, president of Challenge Development Co. and highly respected by his colleagues because of his quality in construction and ongoing success, said to them, "Come on guys. If this costs everyone the same amount, where's the penalty? We know these claims are coming in droves, and we know we are strictly liable for virtually any failure, so shouldn't we insure against this risk?" We also had support from Allan Fuller, another quality-oriented home builder, who, like many, thought the engineering requirements were long overdue. "We should be ashamed of ourselves for letting this soil problem get so far out of hand. I think it's time we did something about it," Allan said at an Association of Home Builders meeting.

It took several months to get consensus from the leaders of the various groups, but one step remained before we could begin raising capital and seeking reinsurance: A documented commitment from the members of the CSLL that they would make the coverage mandatory on all new residential subdivision loans. Joe Cowan of California Federal Savings and Loan was elected chairman of the new company, named Land Stability Insurance Co., and he spearheaded the effort to get the CSLL to pass the necessary resolution. The CSLL met at Quail Lodge, in Carmel Valley, California, in April 1971 and, after lengthy discussion and some strident challenges to the idea, voted unanimously to pass a resolution to require Land Stability Insurance Company (LSIC) coverage on all loans made after January 1, 1972, for single family dwellings. This turned out to be a Pyrrhic victory.

With CSLL's resolution in hand, I flew to New York to arrange reinsurance. I found reinsurance companies eager to participate. We were ecstatic that things worked out—or so it seemed. We hired Chuck Yelverton to do our engineering examinations in Southern California and Earl Buckingham, a retired civil engineer, formerly with the City of Oakland, to do them in northern California. They commenced making surveys in anticipation of the coverage we were going to bind. Policies were issued, but the flood of applications we expected didn't even form a trickle. What was wrong?

In 1972 the home building industry experienced a dramatic slowdown. This affected the halcyon days of the savings and loan industry by curbing the flood of loans they had been able to make in the preceding decade. The world had been good to them. All of a sudden, they were in a financial quandary: What to do about shrinking cash flow? Some of them went into the development business. They shouldn't have since they really did not know as much about it as they thought. Others began making commercial loans on condominiums, another bad move. What they did not do, and felt they couldn't do, was require LSIC coverage on all loans for single-family dwellings. They said, "The competition is just too great."

"But, Joe," I said to our LSIC chairman, "you guys gave your word that you would require the coverage."

"I know we did, Ed," Joe answered, "but we're not going to, so you know what that makes us." (We all know what eventually happened to the S&L business.)

In this milieu some of the A&A management and I became uncomfortable with one another and, by mutual agreement, I bought RAR. We both felt this would give me greater freedom to work on industry-owned insurance companies and other nontraditional insurance methods.

Although LSIC failed, we got an amended certificate to write property and casualty insurance, changed the name to The Fairmont Insurance Company and wrote a little bit of coverage through the Canon Insurance

Agency, Inc.* It was run by a very capable man, Bill Rosenfeld, but selling insurance in competition with the giant insurance companies was not a good move. In 1976, Fairmont was sold at a slight profit to a group who wanted to write workers compensation insurance. It is still extant.

The Binnacle

Once RAR was separated from A&A, I began getting calls from some of the other insurance brokerage alphabet houses† that had an interest in either captive insurance companies or industry-owned companies. One of these came from Steve Petrakis, who was with Frank B. Hall, Inc. at that time. Steve introduced me to Fred Galbraith, one of those grand old insurance people who does things right. He had a client, Red Stack Towing, a tugboat company owned by Thomas Crowley, Jr. They felt their marine insurance premiums were all the traffic would bear rather than what their loss experience would justify. The main market on their risk was London. For a guy raised in the workers compensation arena where we could compute a rate to a hair's breadth it did seem that marine insurance rates were somewhat excessive. Fred hired RAR as a consultant and we put together a California domiciled company, the Binnacle.‡ The ploy worked. London's rates dropped and the Binnacle fared well.

Other Inquiries

Our reputation grew as each profession went through a travail of professional liability claims, loss of coverage, and subsequent formation of a company or insurance plan. We did work with the various bar associations, but the lawyers found our demand for a loss prevention program vexing. After all, attorneys could not be doing many wrong things, could they? They did not like the ideas we propounded about their business abilities, which we found to be the worst of all professions; but then their high incomes made up for that, and they were not willing to consider any deportment that might impinge upon their cash flow. Can you blame them?

We were even invited to make proposals to various medical associations. They, too, did not like the suggestions we made that might cure their medical malpractice problems, such as, "Humanize your business deportment. You are treating your patients in a patronizing way that alienates

---

* A general agent, i. e., an insurance agent who may sell coverage through other insurance agencies, keeping a portion of the commission.

† Called the alphabet houses since a letter acronym is usually used in place of their actual name, such as, A&A for Alexander and Alexander, Inc., or M&M for Marsh & McLennan.

‡ The housing of a ship's compass located where the helmsman can read through a glass in the binnacle to see the compass.

them. Then when something goes wrong, they sue you in a vengeful way." The medical people felt we were wrong, and maybe we were, but they were being sued more and more frequently until it was called "a medical malpractice crisis." From our point of view it was more like a human behavioral crisis and still is.

AIR, Ltd.

One group of professionals we thoroughly enjoyed working with were the members of Assurex International, an association of independent insurance brokers who had formed their organization to give themselves a national presence. This enabled them to compete with the geographically diverse alphabet houses. By and large, the Assurex members were medium-to-large-size insurance brokerage firms whose extraordinary business acumen had placed them in a category of successful. For the most part, they had sterling reputations. We liked working with them because, in addition to being successful, they were very nice people. They met twice annually, and at a meeting in early 1976 we heard shocking tales about their professional liability insurance problem. We countered with the recommendation that they needed an ongoing professional liability loss prevention effort. They did not hesitate and commissioned RAR to produce an insurance agent's and broker's loss prevention manual and a semiannual seminar training program, the Institute of Professional Practice/Insurance Agents and Brokers Section. (We had started an Institute for Professional Practice for the soil and foundation engineers in 1974, see Chapter 12.)

By this time my brother, Richard P. Howell, Jr., whom we had been hiring on an as-needed basis from his consulting firm, joined us to work on loss prevention materials. He helped with the research and development of the insurance agent's and broker's manual, *Targeting in on Professional Liability: An Action Course for Insurance Agents and Brokers.* Richard had a wealth of knowledge, having been with Stanford Research Institute for a number of years before going into his own business, an economics consulting firm.

If you are not privy to the dark side of the insurance business, it may come as a shock that many insurance brokerage companies and some insurance companies are run on a crisis management basis. Bewildered by the overwhelming flow of paper, everyone just deals with the most pressing problems and lets the routine matters take care of themselves. This type of management often leads to claims of breach of professional duty, bad faith, fraud, and a host of other claims aimed at bringing order out of chaos. The truth is that it is usually none of the claimed departures from honesty or care, but just poor business management. While the members of Assurex were relatively free from claims, they did have some, and the underwriters who had magnanimously provided them with unreasonably priced coverage were turning deaf ears to their pleas for greater pricing equity. They decided to do something about it.

Assurex chose as chairman of a professional liability insurance committee the highly regarded Arthur H. Kindler of Kindler, Lauci & Day of San Francisco. Art is one of those rare people who can analyze a problem with great rapidity, then with lightning speed sort out a series of potential answers. He and Fred Clifton, who headed one of San Francisco's most admired insurance brokerage companies, Clifton & Company, knew of our success with other professional groups and came to RAR with their problem. We explained the formula of the loss-prevention-effort-offshore-company to Art and Fred and they instantly saw the logic of the rationale. Art and an elected board of directors helped us establish the company in Bermuda—Assurex International Reinsurance Co., Ltd. (AIR, Ltd.) The board of directors elected Art as president, Edward D. (Ted) Howe of Fred C. Church and Company, Boston, as first vice president, Charles F. S. Ryan of Charles, Ryan & Rivers, Los Angeles, second vice president, and John M. Sommers of Warren & Sommers, Inc., Denver, third vice president. All of these men had built outstanding organizations that betokened their business savvy.

Kemper did not feel they could be the professional liability insurance policy issuing company for AIR, Ltd. because of the conflict with their own agency force. The Assurex members knew many people at the St. Paul Insurance Company. Their president, Paul Drake, introduced us to their risk management department manager, Warren Bessler, and his coworker, Bill Walsh. Within 30 days, we were issuing St. Paul Insurance Company professional liability policies for insurance agents and brokers.

Sometimes the insurance business is fiercely competitive, almost territorial, with the writer of certain types of insurance slashing out at any competitor who dares enter his or her field. So it was with insurance agents' and brokers' coverage. Within a year and a half we found that the insurance companies that had been providing the extremely expensive coverage prior to the advent of Assurex International Reinsurance company cut their rates and pushed their sales and marketing with a vengeance. From our viewpoint, they were following the kamikaze approach to management, that is, getting suicidally too little premium for the risk. In the spring of 1979, we advised the AIR, Ltd. board of directors that it did not make sense to continue issuing coverage in the current rate-cutting climate, and we gave them five alternatives for the company's future, one being to go dormant. They decided to put AIR, Ltd. on the shelf in case there was a return to astronomically high rates or loss of market sometime in the future. This was done in October of 1979. Assurex Association took over AIR, Ltd. and gave it a rest.

ACG, Ltd.

About six months after we started AIR, Ltd. one of the insurance brokers, Fred Burns, of John Wortham & Sons, Houston, who participated in AIR's formation, called and said that they had a client who was in the chemical business and was having trouble buying product liability insurance. "Ed, our client belongs to an association, Affiliated Chemical Group, Inc.(ACG), and it is going to entertain proposals from the alphabet houses, J&H, A&A, and others to set up an offshore company to write their coverage. We would rather see you act as their consultant, if you're interested. They have scheduled a meeting for April 1977 to receive the proposals. Would you be interested?" Fred asked.

"Heck, yes," I responded. "Sounds like it might be fun."

"Well," Fred went on, "I don't know about being fun, but you're going to be butting your head with the big boys. They have some of these chemical companies as clients, and they don't want to lose them. So they'll be pulling out the stops. You better have a strategy."

Well, the simple truth is that I didn't have a strategy other than the one I had been using, that is, sell loss prevention and downplay the importance of the insurance. One other thing I knew was that the big insurance brokerage companies liked to sell feasibility reports. The purpose of these was to impress the clients with the thoroughness of their evaluation of the plan for an offshore insurance company. I had always taken the position, "If you can't buy the insurance, what's there to study?"

I traveled to Houston and met the CEO of John Wortham & Sons, Buddy Carruth, a charming guy, who said, "Y'all make yourself at home. Treat this office as your Houston office, ya heah?" I looked around their shop and marveled at the military precision of their operation. They were doing a huge volume of insurance business. Fred Burns took me to the site of the ACG meeting, where I was to be number three in the presentations. We got there just as two producers from A&A were leaving. I said, "Hi," and they looked at me with expressions that asked, "What in hell is he doing here?"

The meeting was in the boardroom of Dixie Chemical Company, and by the time I got there the air was blue with cigar and cigarette smoke. I gagged and blinked trying to get accustomed to the stench. Chairing the meeting was W. D. Bain, Jr. of Moreland Chemical Co., Spartanburg, South Carolina.* They said they didn't want a formal presentation but, in the interest of time, would ask questions.

Don Bain was to be the spokesperson, and he started out with, "We'd like to ask a series of questions. We've asked the same questions of the alphabet house brokers and now we'd like your answers. I must say, none of us has ever heard of Risk Analysis and Research Corporation nor Design Professionals Insurance Company, but Wortham says you were the guy As-

---

* Others in attendance were Francis P. Allen, E. F. King & Co., Inc., Norwood, Massachusetts; Norbert A. Bremehr, Petrolite Corporation, St. Louis, Missouri; George W. Kramer, Kramer Chemicals, Inc., Clifton, New Jersey; Ernest H. McCall, McCall Oil & Chemicals, Inc., Portland, Oregon; Edward N. and Dolores Mills, Milwaukee Solvents and Chemicals Corp., Butler, Wisconsin; Jerry Priest, Dixie Chemical Corp., Houston, Texas; William F. Schierholz, Chemtech Industries, Inc., St. Louis, Missouri; and Edward A. Wex, Hydrite Chemical Company, Milwaukee, Wisconsin.

surex International picked, so we'd like to listen to your answers. First, if we were to decide to set up an insurance company just what would you do?"

I drew in a smoke-filled breath and answered, "I guess you'll find our approach wholly different from the insurance brokers. For one thing, I think we should start with a claims and losses survey that would give us a feel for how bad your experience might be. The data will also give us a basis for rate setting since the past losses paid will develop an expectancy level for the future."

"I hope you understand," Don broke in, "that we don't think our experience has been that bad. We handle innocuous stuff like benzene, acetone, hydrofluoric acid, ammonia, and the like. All safe if you do things right. We admit that our industry may have one horrible loss every five years or so, but by and large, we just don't have day-to-day losses. In auto, sure, we deserve to pay more, but in general liability, including products losses, we think we're doing okay."

"Sure," I said, "but a confidential questionnaire will bring out anything that might be hidden in the woodpile. We need to *know* before we go to reinsurers or an issuing company. Insurance is based upon trust. We have to be able to lay out the dirty linen with the clean with reinsurers, excess insurers, and any issuing company that may assist us."

"Wait a minute. Wait a minute," Jerry Priest, President of Dixie Chemical Company, Houston, started. "Excuse me Don, but I don't know what he means by 'issuing company.' What's that all about?"

"You guys are working throughout the United States," I replied. "You need to file certificates of insurance with customers, agencies, and municipalities. It can't be a certificate from a little company in Bermuda, the Cayman Islands, or Liechtenstein. You need a solid, licensed-in-all-states underwriter that has a household name. We can try to arrange such a company, but they have to be privy to everything in your closet, good or bad. A confidential questionnaire seems the best way to go. Have the questionnaires returned to us and we'll tabulate that data and put it in workable form. Their confidentiality is paramount if you want to get honest answers. You guys will never see the results except as overall numbers. From that data we will develop rates and submit them to you for approval, and we'll show you how we developed them.

"The same information will enable us to plan a loss prevention program, which is a keystone to every one of our companies. Without a highly active loss prevention effort, we are not interested, even if the insurance brokers are. One other thing, please don't count on cheap insurance. Our rates will reflect your losses over the past five years, plus a factor for catastrophes. Keep in mind that you have to stick with this coverage once you've signed on. We can't set up an operation that will be torn asunder by the prosaic insurers coming back with low rates once we're operative. And they will. We promise only stability sustained by fair rates, based upon your actual losses."

Don raised his eyebrows and asked, "How much do you charge for the feasibility study?"

"What feasibility study?" I asked.

"Well, the brokers said that the first step would be a feasibility study that would take from six weeks to 90 days. They said that only then could they think about an offshore company and all. How about you? How long? How much?" Don queried.

"It seems to me," I answered, "that you are without a comprehensive general liability (CGL) insurance market for some of your group right now. Right? Setting up a CGL insurance company for your group in such a distress situation shouldn't take six weeks of study. You'd better, by gosh, get at it. Time is important. I think if you told us, 'Go,' it might take us six weeks before the first policy went out the door. That, of course, is dependent on how quickly your members can get the claims confidential and loss questionnaires back in our hands.

"We charge two-and-a-half times our actual employees' payroll. That's what many consulting engineers charge, and we think it's fair in light of the fact that employee fringe benefits run about 35%. Then there's rent and other overhead. And, oh yes, a slight profit. We charge for all out-of-town expenses. I guess to get the ball rolling, our fee will be under $10,000. We'll need a deposit of half that when you give us the order. So what do you say? We can start right now," I told Don, wiping the stinging smoke from my reddening eyes and trying to smile at the same time.

"We have to think about it. How about if I contact you in, say, about a week?" Don said, raising his eyebrows in inquiry. "Man, you sure don't operate like those insurance brokers, do you? I don't know if that's good or bad."

"I don't either," I offered, and got up, waved good-bye, and left.

When I got back to my hotel, the phone was ringing off the hook. When I answered, an excited voice said, "We decided to go with RAR! Why should we wait a week? How soon can we see the questionnaire form?" It was Don, and I guess they decided to eschew the feasibility study as a waste of time.

"How soon will you be back in Spartanburg?" I replied, "I can have the form to you by day after tomorrow, plus a letter of transmittal to go with every questionnaire, which you can sign and return to us, with your board approved questionnaire. The data collection packages can go out early next week. You need to appoint a committee to get on the phone to urge prompt action from the ACG members."

"Okay, okay, gotcha," Don countered. "And, oh, Ed, your straightforward approach without all the monkey business is what sold us. That's neat. Who wants to pay $25,000 for a dumb old feasibility study? We know we need the coverage. It wouldn't be feasible to go without it."

When I got off the phone with Don, I immediately called our San Francisco office and asked for Florence Whitmire, who had joined us in 1971, slogged through every job in the organization, and quickly rose through the ranks to become a major player in our company. She had worked her way through the University of California and had been an important employee in San Francisco's largest patent law firm, Townsend and Townsend. Her penchant for doing jobs in a timely and accurate way earned her an officership in RAR. Florence knows how to organize. Her more important trait on this day was her ability to deal with crisis situations in a cool, efficient way. The ACG program was, to me, a crisis. Renewals of existing coverage were coming up in just a few months; the ACG people needed replacement coverage post haste. I told Florence what we needed—questionnaire, form letter signed by W. D. Bain, Jr., return envelopes, registered mail—and she organized the effort with a "No problem." She always did things right—a good characteristic. Her unique capability seemed to be an outgrowth of her positive attitude. Everything was neatly and efficiently done on time.

The data were returned within 10 days, and they were a complete surprise. What they had said about their claims histories was true. They just did not have all that many comprehensive general liability claims. Plenty of auto losses, but the chemical companies were a good risk in the workers compensation and comprehensive general liability exposures. I remember that one of the automobile losses involved an acid-tank delivery truck that backed up to a likely looking down-pipe, took off the cap, and began pumping acid. The fact that it was the wrong pipe and the acid was being pumped into a fuel tank created all sorts of damages that came to rest at the automobile insurer's feet. (A strange and wonderful thing about automobile insurance is that it not only covers claims that arise out of the vehicles movement, but the loading and unloading of the vehicle at its destination or origination.)

Our survey made it look like the ACG could have a very successful insurance company with the right reinsurance. That made it incumbent upon us to try to find a reinsurance company that would be willing to share the exposure with them and provide excess coverage for the once-every-five-years large loss. We targeted one million dollars as capital and surplus.

By then (1977), Jim Koehnen was the President of American Re-Insurance Company in New York. I called Jim and said, "Hey, Jim, I have another group I'd like you to look at as a possible risk. Their loss record looks pretty good, but what they do might make a run-of-the-mill underwriter blanch. Can I come back next week?"

"What do you have this time, Ed, asbestos manufacturers, hydrogen balloons, football helmet manufacturers?" Jim asked facetiously.

"Close, Jim, chemical manufacturers and distributors," I replied.

"Oh, my gawd, Howell, how can you even suggest such a thing? But come on back. We'll at least take a look," Jim retorted.

So back to the jungle city of New York I went. Jim brought in one of his senior underwriters, never-a-dull-moment Jim White, a guy who was on center stage at all times, with a big grin and a joke for every situation.

After looking at the data, the two Jims admitted that their first impression of chemical manufacturers and distributors was probably wrong and that there did seem to be an underwriting profit possible. Most underwriters are like the rest of us, leaping to conclusions based upon common knowledge rather than statistical facts. It was fortunate for us that the two Jims recognized this tendency and reconsidered their conclusions.

"All right, Ed," Jim Koehnen said, "we'll go with you on this if you can find an A+ AAA company to be the issuing underwriter." He may have been thinking, "Who in hell would do that?"

It took some doing, but since Kemper Management Company, Ltd., Bermuda, was going to be manager of the company, they agreed to issue the policies using the AMICO. They agreed to this only if the policies would be 100% reinsured by American Re-Insurance Company, which would have the first $100,000 100% of any one loss reinsured 100% by ACG, Ltd. This meant that we had to get a letter of credit from our bank, running to the American Re-Insurance Company to guarantee their assumed liability on the first $100,000. To do this we needed money. We took the ACG board to the Newstead House in Bermuda, formed the company, ACG, Ltd., and started to raise the capital and surplus to make ACG, Ltd. a viable entity. In due course, with monumental urging from the ACG, Ltd. board, the chemical manufacturers and distributors made their investments, and the company, ACG, Ltd., was ready to issue policies through AMICO.

The company began writing coverage in July, 1977. Scott McKown and I flew all over the country taking applications and examining premises to make certain that safety measures were in place. RAR acted as its consultant for underwriting and claims until 1982 when John Wortham & Sons took over. ACG, Ltd. has been a winner from many points of view.

Pacific Surety Reinsurance, Ltd.

During our formation of LSIC, one name kept popping up in our contact with the Los Angeles area developers— James Econn & Associates. "Old Jim handles all of our insurance. If you want to have anything done with Land Stability Insurance, you contact Jim," was what we heard time and again. This piqued our curiosity since it seemed that he had amassed a large cadre of clients with whom we would be working. His clients were so laudatory about Jim's insurance expertise, integrity, and his high level of professional service that I told myself, "This is one guy I've got to meet." LSIC came and went, and only one agent put much premium on our books, Jim Econn. All of the other agents groused about the low commission level (5%), but not Jim Econn. He said, "The percentage is irrelevant if the volume is high enough. I intend to have high volume of that type of coverage. My clients need it."

Shortly after RAR had helped put Assurex International Reinsurance, Ltd. together I got a call from a man named Bob Howie. "Ed, this is Bob Howie. I'm the head of a group of insurance agents and brokers called Insgroup. We have joined together to compete with the alphabet houses. Each of our members is in a different geographic location, kind of like Assurex, and they cooperate to provide insurance markets, plans of coverage, and service outside of the geographical sphere of the originating producer. We've heard about your consulting on offshore companies and we would like you to speak at our next meeting here in Denver. We might want to hire you to set up a company for us. We think we should have a company for some of our most difficult lines. Are you interested?"

"Sure," I responded. And that's how I got to meet Jim Econn. He was a member of Insgroup and chairman of the Captive Insurance Company Committee. After my presentation, he came up to get acquainted and to tell me about his particular problem with his clients. He had a large volume of land developers' insurance and bond business. Besides having a terrible land failure exposure, the developers also had to post expensive subdivision surety bonds on every subdivision with local government agencies before a permit to build would be issued. The bonds were to make certain that the developer put in things like parking strip trees, proper drainage, gutters, and street lighting. Once the development was completed, the governmental agency would make an inspection, and if the work had been properly performed, release the bonding company. If not, the agency would call for the sums in the surety bond in order to have the work properly done.

Jim told me, "We have been placing our clients' bond coverage with various companies, none of whom will give us the type of rate they deserve. Their loss ratios are in the 2% area; really, almost no losses in the last seven years. See, we know our clients real well from years of working with them and, in addition, we have an accounting firm audit our surety bond buyers to see if they are financially solid. (In surety, the three C's are the determining factors in underwriting: character, capacity, and capital.) If they say they are solid and we know they are honest, we arrange bonding. If not, we don't. I personally look at every risk. Something really unusual would have to happen before one of our bonds would become subject."

"The way I see it," Jim went on, "it doesn't make a lot of sense for our clients to pay the bonding companies all that money when the bonds never make any loss payment. Why can't we set up a company to take the premiums, get the investment income, and pay losses if they ever occur? What do you think, Ed?"

I didn't have to think for long. "Well, it certainly sounds like that might be a good thing to do. Have you talked with any bonding company about some type of retrospective rating plan on a group basis. You know, the developers pay a deposit premium and anything not used to pay losses, taxes, and costs of doing business goes back to them in the form of a dividend at the end of three years?"

Jim frowned and said, "We've tried that approach, but the companies just said, 'No.' Not 'No, because . . .' just, 'No.' They wouldn't even discuss it. Besides, think of the investment return that we're missing out on placing this 'no lose' line with a company that doesn't give us credit for the superlative experience. Some of these subdivisions take up to five years to complete. I can multiply five times the current prime rate and come up with a whale of a lot of money—money that just sits there, and the return goes to a company that is taking very little risk. That isn't right, is it? Should we be giving all that money away? You see what I mean?"

I did. The Insgroup members were not cohesive enough for an off-shore company. Their business was too diverse. Many of them wanted cheap insurance for their clients, which is not a good and valid reason to form a company. We bowed out and went to work with James Econn & Associates.

Jim Econn is one of the best businessmen I've known in the insurance industry. He built his solidly based clientele by long hours of hard work and always keeping the best interests of his clients uppermost, regardless of the money involved. He is dedicated to their needs and sees that his firm delivers the best bond and insurance coverage possible at a fair price. He abhorred the cut-rate underwriters that would insure today but run out on you tomorrow. He wouldn't use them. When I'd call his office the calls went through without an annoying third-degree, "Who's calling? What's it about? Will he know you? What size shoes do you wear?" Rather, I'd receive a pleasant, "Yes, sir." His people were quick to tell you when he would be back if he were out. His whole operation was a giant cut above most insurance agents or brokers. You see, Jim and his people knew that they were in the service business! They weren't doing the clients a favor by being in the insurance business. The clients were customers and were treated as such with pleasant, responsive politeness. For him, this service-oriented dedication to his customers and constant polite demeanor worked.

Besides knowing it is good business to be nice to people with whom you work, Jim's agency performed as perfect intermediaries. They stood between their clients and the insurance companies and made certain that both got a fair shake. Clients and companies alike benefited from this protective role the agency assumed. Jim's agency checked his clients thoroughly for credit, attitude, business savvy, and reputation. The companies with whom he dealt reported that he had never sullied their doors with problem risks. That's smart business thinking.

Pacific Surety Reinsurance became a reality in spring of 1978 at a meeting in Bermuda. Conyers, Dill, and Pearman had our file ready and waiting.

Design Professionals Pacific Reinsurance Co., Ltd. (Depac Re, Ltd.)

Some insurance companies are volume driven, that is, they believe (probably mistakenly) that the way to financial success is through increased premium volume. This leads to cycles in the pricing of insurance. Rates are cut to acquire more premium volume, which leads to adverse underwriting results, followed by makeup rate increases. One wag described the insurance industry as "a yo-yo business." It happens to be close to the truth. The ups and downs are pronounced.

In 1979 DPIC was being pounded by competitors that were sharply cutting rates to increase their volume and, at the same time, increasing commissions to agents hoping this, too, would increase their premium volume. We could not do that; it would be contrary to our philosophy. So we decided that a new strategy was in order, one that would give our agents greater incentive to place coverages with our company but would allow us to maintain a stable, adequate rate structure. "Why not set up a reinsurance company owned by our agents?" we thought. "This company would be a profit center for the agents, thus necessitating no commission change for the agents." Our board of directors thought that might be a good idea. Our reinsurers had been making a fine profit from our business, and it seemed logical that a new company could be formed to take advantage of some of this reinsurance profit. We hoped this profit would revitalize our agents' loyalty and interest in our company. These thoughts led to our forming a new reinsurance company, DPIC Pacific Reinsurance Company, Ltd. (Depac Re, Ltd.).

It may seem strange to those who vacation there, but we had become bored with Bermuda. It was no longer fun to fly to New York, try for the 59th Street Bridge, go to Newark, and fly to Bermuda, and do the attorney, accountant, and manager things. But what to do? We needed a new jurisdiction, one with an adequate infrastructure, gentle on taxes, and fun to visit. Risk Planning Group, in one of its newsletters, mentioned Vanuatu (once the New Hebrides) and Hong Kong as possible alternative insurance jurisdictions. So it was "Hong Kong here we come."

Hong Kong looked attractive. It was a sophisticated, metropolitan city with all of the financial amenities we needed. We had conversations with the Orient Department officers of the Bank of America and they assured us that all of the necessary elements for forming an insurance company were readily available in Hong Kong. They even gave us the names of two law firms with whom we could correspond in order to get things rolling.

We wrote to one of the law firms and received a polite reply saying that they would be glad to serve us, they thought we should have no difficulty with the registrar of companies, and that they were appointing Caroline K. Crumpetor, Esq. (not her real name) to handle our file. They advised us that she would get everything ready for us to visit in April 1983 and hold a formation meeting.

I called Peter Kelly in Hartford, who had given us such enormous help with limitation of liability, and asked him if he would join me as our attorney on a trip to Hong Kong to get the company established.

Hong Kong is an exciting place to visit. They have excellent hotels, good restaurants, and an adventure a minute. Our first adventure was with our attorney. We called her and set up a midmorning Thursday appointment so we could leave the following Sunday. We arrived at the appointed time and she began with a British accent. "I'm sorry to say, actually, but you see, emm, emm, you cannot possibly do what you want to do. Dreadfully sorry. Hope you understand."

Peter looked at me, I looked at Peter, and I was about to blurt out, "What in the name of hell are you talking about, lady? I've come all the way from San Francisco, and Mr. Kelly even further, and now you say we can't do what we came to do?" Peter must have known what was on my mind because he held up a restraining palm, looked at her, and calmly said, "Please explain this late development."

"Well, actually, there has been a change in the law, you see? The Insurance Companies Ordinance has been revised, with Chapter 41. I've discussed it with the staff of the Insurance Authority, and it is their opinion that the Insurance Authority will not grant your application. Sorry, don'tcha know?"

"Well, have you discussed it with the Insurance Authority himself?" I broke in.

"No. He's a very busy man!" she retorted with a look that was meant to make things final.

Peter said, "Maybe we'd better give him a call. What's his name and how do I reach him?"

"His name is Archie Lam, and I can assure you, you will have to wait a long time for an appointment," the bespectacled lawyer replied.

We called Archie Lam, explained to his secretary that we were to return to the United States on Sunday, and asked for an early appointment. "How about 1:30 today?" the secretary replied. We arranged to meet our lawyer at Archie Lam's office and went off to a fine Chinese lunch, with shark fin soup followed by dim sum.

We arrived fifteen minutes early and were ushered in immediately. Our lawyer had not yet arrived. Mr. Lam was very gracious and said, "Welcome to Hong Kong. We would be most pleased if you would establish an insurance company with this jurisdiction as its domicile. One million dollars U.S. will be fine as capital and surplus. We understand that no risks will be located in Hong Kong, nor coverage written for Hong Kong domiciled companies, so we believe that will relieve you from paying our flat 15% income tax. You see, income earned outside of Hong Kong is not taxable. What else can we do for you?"

We said, "Nothing, thanks. It's been a pleasure dealing with you."

The lawyer arrived just as we were leaving. She looked very flustered when she saw our faces wreathed in smiles and asked, "Actually, emm, emm, what happened?"

Peter said, "We'll tell you outside." When we were outside, Peter again unlike my inclination, was gentlemanly. He looked at the lawyer and said, "We will not be requiring your services. You may bill us if you wish, but if you do, your action on this matter will have to be made public, particularly to the bank that recommended your firm. Do you understand?"

She nodded assent and wandered off, studying the pavement.

Chapter 10

Controlling the Scourge

All's well that ends well: still the fine's the crown;
Whate'er the course, the end is the renown.

—*Shakespeare, All's Well that End's Well*

Author's Note: Although the scenarios in this chapter are fictitious (except for reference to Andersen-Bjornstad-Kane & Jacobs, Inc., in Seattle) the events described were taken from the claims files of the insurance company that is Different by Design. The purpose of the depicted scenes is to show that professional liability claims are not the result of matters beyond the control of the parties involved. The tragedy is that design professionals and their professional groups still do not recognize that they are capable of controlling their future professional liability destiny. It is hoped that the events described and their outcomes will serve as incentives for design professionals and their insurance agents to thoroughly involve themselves, individually and as groups, in professional liability loss prevention efforts.

Look, There Are Other Architects

Spence Davis reflected about the regional office building that they built in the Big Bend River Valley and how much better it went than the wastewater treatment plant they'd done five years before. "Regional office" was a misnomer. Actually it housed most of their top executives and should have been called their home office. Legally, their home office was in New York. At least that is what their corporate papers said. Most of the top executives, including the chairman, had, one-by-one, taken up residence in the Big Bend River Valley. They wanted to be close to the action.

Five years after the Yellowstone Paper Company wastewater treatment fiasco, its top management had decided to build a headquarters building. Because they were under tight budgetary constraints they felt they had to pull out all the stops to save money in construction.

They heard about an architect who had an excellent reputation in the Big Bend River Valley, and Spence Davis, vice president of plants and facilities, was given the task of interviewing him to see whether he should be selected as their prime design professional on the regional headquarters building. Their first meeting was uneventful. The architect, James T. Bowes, said, yes, he would like the assignment and he felt that he could come in within the budget. He showed them photographs of a few of his past jobs to give the Yellowstone Paper people a feel for the type of work he would do.

They liked them. Bowes was simple in his approach, and yet there was a certain amount of strength in the designs he conceived. As a consequence, Spence Davis was told to proceed with the appointment of Bowes as the architect on the job. Once this decision was made, everyone became excited, and the urgency for completion became overwhelming. The chairman of the board urged Spence Davis, "Get things rolling as rapidly as possible. Inflation being what it is, every day we save in time is money in the bank!"

Spence Davis approached the job on a crisis basis. His first order of business was to get Bowes to sign the contract of hire. He had their legal department draw up the contract, and he sent it to Bowes with a covering letter requesting that he sign it immediately and return it so that the work would flow.

The next day he received a telephone call from Bowes who said he would like to get together to discuss the contract. He also wondered whether they had given any consideration to using a standard AIA form modified for their special needs.

Spence Davis took sharp exception to this suggestion: "Look, Mr. Bowes, we are a big corporation. We have a full staff of attorneys, competent in determining what should go into our contracts. They are not about to use some standard form that might be fine for a hot dog stand but cannot cover the eventualities we might have in a building of the size we are contemplating."

Bowes replied, "I understand your concern about doing the job right. As a consequence, I believe it essential to get together with you and discuss some aspects of our agreement that I think will be important to you. There may be some things that your attorneys have not contemplated that you may wish to include in the document. They may even save you money."

That last consideration did it, but the meeting was agreed to grudgingly. Spence Davis invited Douglas Kurd, a Yellowstone attorney, to join them. At the last minute, the chairman of the Yellowstone Paper Company, hearing of Bowes's request, said he would like to sit in on the meeting. He felt the initial meeting was important, for it would set the tenor for future activities connected with the design and construction of their office building.

They met in Bowes's office. The people from Yellowstone Paper were struck by its austerity. The conference table was a simple rectangle made of straight grain Douglas fir. They sat in wooden straight-back chairs. The look on the face of the chairman of Yellowstone Paper must have betrayed his feeling, for James Bowes felt compelled to say, "We architects are good at creating environments for others. When it comes to our own facilities, our income limits us to that which is strictly utilitarian."

They sat down, and Yellowstone Paper's attorney, Douglas Kurd, began by saying, "Look, Mr. Bowes, I went over that agreement last night. It has everything in it we want. You're a busy man. We are busy, too. If you have some editorial changes you would like to make, we will listen. But for my part—from the legal point of view—that contract is written on the basis of what will work. So why don't we save a lot of time and get this thing over in a hurry."

Polite Persistence Pays Off

Jim Bowes was unperturbed. He studied the faces of the people at the meeting. They all returned his gaze in a cold, unflinching way. He responded, "Well, Mr. Kurd, I appreciate your position. However, I am afraid that we have a long way to go before we will have that agreement in a condition that will be useful to both of us. I am still of the opinion that we should start with the standard AIA form. It has been used successfully on thousands of projects. We can make modifications to it to serve your needs."

Kurd interjected, "No way! We know about the standard AIA form. I can just see those guys drafting a contract that is one-sided—all in the favor of the architect. It is utterly ridiculous to think we might use it."

Bowes remained calm and said, "I do not believe that is the way it is. The contract was drafted so it would serve owners with a wide range of needs. It would defeat the interests of the architectural profession if it were unfair or lacked mutuality. Nonetheless, if you are adamant, I will be glad to use your contract as a base, but there are many changes that need to be made."

Kurd snapped back, "Look, there are other architects. While you and I have been sitting here, the interest rate on the funds for our building has gone up. We do not have a lot of time to waste on what I consider a trivial aspect of our building program."

Bowes hunched forward in his chair, looked intently at Mr. Kurd and stated, "Douglas, when I do a job, I do it right. That includes matters relating to the contract as well as to the architectural services. It is true that there are other architects. It may be that if the most important thing to you is getting a signature on a contract that contains burdensome and inequitable clauses, you should go to another architect. On the other hand, if you want a professional working on your job who is going to show extreme care and concern over all aspects of his services, you might do well to listen to me and contemplate the changes I think are necessary."

At this point the chairman of Yellowstone Paper broke in and said, "Come on, Doug, cool off. Let's give him a chance to say what he has on his mind."

They all sat looking intently at Jim Bowes, waiting for him to enumerate the changes that he wanted. "Since I am not a lawyer, I have used the standard AIA form as a guide. In addition, my insurance company has prepared a manual that contains information relative to the contracts we sign. I listen to what they have to say; they are interested in reducing the amount of litigation in construction; by doing that they help you as much as me. First of all, your contract refers to me as a 'Contractor.' That is confusing. I will not be doing any contracting work. As an architect, I provide professional services. With your permission, I think we should change the term to 'Architect.'" The others nodded agreement.

"Secondly, it requires me to provide 'any and all architectural and engineering services necessary to complete the regional office building for the Yellowstone Paper Company.' I do not believe that is correct. I will provide professional services for the project in accordance with the terms and conditions of this agreement. It may be that this will not include certain activities such as landscaping, soil and foundation engineering, or other types of work that might have been included in your 'any and all services'."

The others nodded agreement and Bowes went on. "Your payment provision is just fine. And the section that calls for additional compensation for additional services is in order. However, the section that states that the plans and specifications are to be owned by Yellowstone Paper Company causes problems. Architects render a service, just like lawyers. When we produce plans and specifications, we have a common law copyright in them just as attorneys do in their briefs. They are not unlike works of art. They carry with them responsibility. If we were to transfer ownership to you, we would be selling you a product, not rendering services. This raises liability problems. I am not even sure that my professional liability insurance would follow them if title were transferred to someone else. Therefore, I suggest that that portion be stricken from the agreement."

At this, Attorney Kurd said, "What? What difference does it make? What if we want to build another building somewhere else? Why, then we could use those plans and specifications."

Bowes smiled and said, "My point exactly. Are you expecting me to be responsible for the adequacy of plans and specifications that might be used on another structure? That's not fair. You are trying to get something for nothing."

At this the chairman of the board of Yellowstone broke in and said, "Come on, Doug. We do not need to own the plans and specifications. The eventuality that we will try to use them again is so remote that it is not even worth consideration."

Bowes went on, "You stipulate that 'time is of the essence.' My attorney and my professional liability insurance carrier advise me that that is a legal phrase that may place me in jeopardy. The only thing I can say is that

I will 'perform to the best of my ability and in a timely manner.' I am afraid of the phraseology you use. It seems to me that making time of the essence might be an assumption of liability under contract that could cloud my professional liability insurance, since my policy has an exclusion for liability assumed under a contract or an agreement. You would not want that, would you?"

Kurd responded, "O. K., strike 'time is of the essence' and put in that you will 'perform in a timely manner.'"

Bowes looked relieved and continued, "Your hold harmless and indemnity clause is a bit harsh. In addition, my insurance agent advises me that it is not insurable in its present form." At this point Spence Davis broke in and said, "What? We have used that on other jobs. Why is it not insurable?"

Bowes answered, "It seems that professional liability insurance policies have exclusions in them. One policy exclusion stipulates that the company will not insure for liability assumed in a contract or agreement. What they mean by that is they will not insure for liability beyond that provided for in common law. As a consequence, an agreement to hold someone harmless from and against any and all liability of whatsoever kind arising out of the performance of the work is not insurable. To be insurable the hold harmless and indemnity clause should be limited to the negligence of the architect."

Kurd blurted, "No way! What if you do something on purpose that causes damage? What about your willful misconduct that might lead to damages?"

"Well," Bowes went on, "it seems to me that I would be liable for those anyway and perhaps it is not a good thing to put something like that in a contract if it will cause any trouble with the effectiveness of the insurance. Don't you gentlemen agree?" Spence Davis shook his head affirmatively and said, "I think you are right. I think we want there to be no question about the insurance being in place. After all, we pay for it indirectly. To have its benefit clouded in any way is not good business."

"In that regard," Bowes went on, "your insurance provision is drafted in a way that will cause both of us real insurance problems. I am able to provide you with the limits that you request, the contractual coverage (if you will alter the hold harmless and indemnity clause) and the underground, collapse, and blasting coverage. However, it is not possible for me to name you as an additional insured on my policy."

At this Spence Davis broke in and said, "Why, we have had quite a number of contractors get us named as an additional insured on their policy. It's common in the construction industry."

"True," Bowes responded, "but they were contractors, not professionals. My most important insurance is professional liability insurance. It is a very personal thing. It insures against my negligent professional acts. If you were to be named as an additional insured and one of your employees performed some professional duty in connection with a job I design, an allegation might be made that the coverage was in place for them. The insurance company does not want to have to argue that in court. As a consequence, they are not willing to name you as an additional insured.

"It may be that they would be willing to name you only in the general liability portion of the policy. You see, I have my professional and general liability coverages written in a single policy form. This prevents there being any question about coverage, should a loss ensue. Some architects will insure with two different companies, one writing professional, and the other writing general liability. Inevitably, in case of a loss, there will be an argument between carriers. This is especially true of a loss of a questionable nature—I mean questionable as to whether it is professional or general in nature. I have obviated that by covering both eventualities in one policy."

"It would be my recommendation that you talk with your insurance broker about an owner's protective policy. It may be that one could be purchased for your company that would protect against liability arising out of the performance of the work and give you the limit of liability you want."

Spence Davis nodded agreement and said, "Well, I am convinced if the rest of you are. I have been handling the insurance on our projects and was not aware of the professional liability problem. I guess we can see our way clear to buying the owner's protective coverage ourselves. I simply cannot understand why some of these points haven't been brought to our attention before."

Bowes looked at Spence for a moment and said, "It has been my experience that many insurance companies sell coverage but don't render much service. Our carrier has given us advice on these matters as a professional and general liability loss prevention measure. At first we thought that their insistence on 'doing things right' was nitpicking. We have since found that their attentiveness to these details has saved us needless embarrassment with valued clients. The company was originally started by design professionals in private practice. They decided from the outset to render services that would reduce losses. They patterned themselves after the workers compensation mutuals that looked to loss prevention to make the line successful. My agent tells me that boiler and machinery carriers did the same. In fact many of the insurance companies formed in this country developed plans of loss prevention as the foundation for their being. My carrier strives to do the job right! By the way, my insurance agent gets a majority of his income from design professionals; he knows our needs and that works for your benefit as well as ours.

"One other thing I would like to ask," Bowes said, "and that is to be named on the builder's risk 'all risk' insurance policy that you or the contractor purchases. You see, I will have considerable work product tied up in the project before it is completed. If it is lost due to fire or some such thing, I would like to be able to recoup my loss along with the rest of you. In addition, it may save me from being the butt of a subrogation claim if a windstorm or some other thing causes damages to the project and the insurance company attempts to subrogate against me on one pretext or another. That has happened, and as a consequence we architects like to be named as additional insureds on the builder's risk policy. It normally does not cost anything extra."

"I don't see why not, do you, Doug?" said Spence Davis.

"No," responded Doug Kurd.

"I noticed that you have a warranty clause in the contract, Mr. Kurd," said Bowes. "Again, that creates a tremendous insurance problem for me since it is an assumption of liability that is not insurable. In addition, we architects are not able to act as guarantors. The only warranty we can give you, either express or implied, is that we will perform to the best of our ability and in accordance with generally accepted architectural practices within the community in which we work. Anything beyond that would be too odious a burden and would place us in the position of being guarantors—which we can never be."

Kurd broke in, "Well, if it is insurance again, I guess we can take that out. By the way, that insurance company sounds like one hell of a good company." Then he glanced at the chairman and said, "But we are going to demand a guarantee from the contractor!"

"Well, that may be," replied Bowes, "since contractors are often asked to guarantee their work as a condition of getting the work. You also make arbitration the sole and exclusive remedy in the event of a disagreement or dispute. I do not think that would be in your best interests or mine either. It may be that if we have a dispute we will want to take it to arbitration. This would be over any disagreement concerning the terms and conditions of this contract. But if there is a tort liability situation and we need to draw in other parties, arbitration poses a problem. It does not make it possible for us to join suppliers and others who have not signed arbitration agreements with you. Then, too, discovery is not as easily done in arbitration as it is in litigation, particularly in our state. I am certain that if we had a disagreement, it would be to all of our advantages to have the opportunity to review each others' documents."

At this point the chairman of Yellowstone Paper Company was glaring hard at Douglas Kurd. He slowly asked, "What is the idea, Doug? It does not sound to me like arbitration should be the sole method for resolving a dispute."

Kurd squirmed and said, "Well, we can take the arbitration clause out. I am not particularly in favor of it. I think you will find it is in the AIA agreement."

Bowes said, "Yes, that's right, but it is not something that cannot be deleted from their standard agreement. And I do so when I use the AIA form. Even the AIA acknowledges that arbitration may not always be appropriate and advises architects to consult with their attorneys regarding its use."

"Well, is that everything?" asked Kurd.

"There is the limitation of liability clause," said Bowes with a benign smile.

"What is that?" asked the chairman of Yellowstone Paper.

"Limitation of liability is an agreement between the client and the architect that the client will limit the architect's liability to $50,000 or his fee, whichever is greater, in the event of a professional error, omission, or negligent act. The owner, in turn, requires that a similar limitation be passed on to the general contractor and subcontractors who perform the work on the project. The limitation affects damages only between the parties and does not apply to third party claims. The inclusion of the limitation of liability clause is important because we architects have had a problem similar to that of doctors, lawyers, and accountants. We are continually being sued over inconsequential matters, and our resultant costs for defense and nonproductive time are enormous."

"Out of Your Mind"

Kurd rose from the table and was obviously angry, "You have got to be out of your mind. If you think our company is going to hold you harmless for your errors and omissions, you are wrong! We simply are not going to get involved in any tricky scheme like that!"

Bowes responded calmly, "I am not asking you to hold me harmless. I am asking you to limit the amount of liability I will have for damages that might be caused to you by some professional or alleged professional negligence on my part. Like you, I know too well that should something happen, it is a lawyer's strategy to escalate the alleged damages to use as bargaining power. This forces the defendants to accede to settlements that they would not agree to otherwise. The limitation of liability clause gives protection from that type of legal harassment. Besides, I would think that you as a company would be interested in seeing limitation of liability fostered. You produce a product, Furfir, from your waste bark. It is a good product. It has high insulative qualities. It is clean, fire resistive, lightweight. It has everything going for it. The only trouble is you are not selling very much. I suspect that the reason you are not is because it is an untried, innovative material that design professionals are simply afraid to specify because they will be sued if they use a new material and it does not perform exactly as anticipated. Limitation of liability will remove a certain amount of that fear from an architect's or engineer's mind. It enables him to do his best for his client and to rely upon innovative means to cut the cost of the job. You people are under a strict budgetary restraint. I know of several areas where I might try new building materials that could have a major impact on the cost of your building. If I use those new techniques and they work, you will be the beneficiaries of considerable dollar savings. On the other hand, I would be foolish to do so because of the risk involved. Shouldn't the risk of using highly cost effective new things be borne by the person who will greatly benefit from them? I believe it should."

Bowes went on,"Limitation of liability is a way of saying we recognize construction is risky and that the owner has to bear the largest share of the risk. The limitation I am asking of you is the amount of my fee. On your building it will be something in excess of $300,000. That to me seems like it could cover a lot of sins. It in no way limits the amount of coverage I will have in place with respect to third parties, should they make claims against you or me because of my professional negligence."

Kurd looked perplexed and asked, "What about the contractor? Are you going to make him responsible for your errors and omissions?"

"In no way!" replied Bowes. "I am merely saying to the contractor, who has a limitation of liability clause in the general conditions of his contract, that he is limiting the liability of the owner and the architect to damages to him on account of professional errors or omissions; the limitation is a rather substantial amount! Look at it this way, there have been billions of dollars of construction done with the limitation of liability clause used; our insurance company, that monitors such things, knows of no instance where limitation of liability placed a contractor in jeopardy."

The chairman of Yellowstone Paper broke in, "I don't think I understand that. What do you mean ?"

Bowes stood up and strode to a chalkboard. "What I mean is this: I will be fully responsible for damages to others that might be caused by my errors in design, but there will be a limitation to the amount of damages the contractor can claim against me because of direct property damages to him." At this point Bowes drew figures on the chalkboard that related the flow of damages. He pointed out that should there be injury to third parties, he would be fully liable on account of his errors or omissions, but there would be a limitation of slightly more than $300,000 should the contractor claim that errors caused damages to him.

"About the only place that I can think of where limitation of liability would adversely affect the contractor is if he were to bid the job too low and later allege that his low bid was the result of errors in the plans and specifications. In such an instance, his claim would be limited contractually to the amount of my fee. Most competent and honest contractors should not object to that. However, if the contractor is one of those guys who gets jobs by dishonest low bidding, he had better watch out! Also, if he prepares his bid in a slipshod way, he may be in trouble."

Bowes paused and looked at all three faces. They seemed intent, but still slightly distrustful. Kurd in particular had a negative expression. His mouth was pursed as if he were tasting something bitter. Bowes continued, "One way you can look at this is that it protects *you* from contractors who are not completely forthright in their bid or who are careless. Keep in mind that limitation of liability is widely used in our commercial world. Most of the large turnkey and design-construct firms have it in their contracts. Liquidated damages in a construction contract is a form of limitation of liability; it limits the amount of damages that can be claimed to a stated amount. It is used by patent attorneys. Financial advisers use it commonly. It allows the conduct of commerce that might otherwise be jeopardized by the enormity of risk being assumed in light of the consideration received. That is the way I look at it. I think it is good for you, for me, and for honest and competent contractors. Why, I have had contractors tell me they would not bid on certain jobs where they knew that certain other contractors were bidding because they knew that they would be low balled. Limitation of liability makes that difficult."

The Chairman of Yellowstone Paper looked intently at Bowes and said, "I think I buy what you are saying."

"Now wait a minute!" Kurd interjected, "I can't put my stamp of . . . ."

"Please, Doug," the chairman responded, "this is a business matter, not a legal one. I think I am beginning to sense why we have had so much market resistance to Furfir. I am also beginning to sense we might save substantial sums of money if we remove the threat from our design professional team that they will be involved in a litigation nightmare. Remember our wastewater project. A lot of that was our fault."

"Thank you, sir," replied Bowes, "I think you are doing the right thing."

Spence Davis now rose from the table and said, "Well, I guess that finishes everything."

Bowes looked at him imploringly and said, "Not quite, Spence. There is one important matter that needs to be addressed, having to do with the construction review. Your contract stipulates that your engineering department will perform the *construction inspection*. First, it would be our recommendation that you change the word *inspection* to *review*. Our local chapter of the AIA did some research on the word *inspection*, and found that there was no substantial difference between the services of *superintendency* and of *inspection*. The word *inspection* has a broader meaning than periodic observation and may imply that one who is *inspecting* is overseeing the performance of the work. I am certain you do not mean that whoever has this function will be overseeing the contractor and his methods of construction, superintending the work, or being responsible for job safety; that simply is not the function of a design professional, or even one of your staff, at the jobsite.

"What we prefer to believe is that the duty will be to observe periodically the work to determine its compliance, in general, with the design concept. This does not include superintendency of the work, methodology, or being responsible for safety. Therefore, our local chapter of the AIA and, as I understand it, a number of engineering societies prefer to describe the fieldwork as *construction review*. With the choice of words out of the way, I must advise you that I simply cannot perform professional services in your behalf without providing the full scope—this means doing the construction review as well as the design."

What's This?

The chairman of Yellowstone Paper leaped to his feet and practically yelled, "What's this! I'm trying to save money on this job, not spend it on needless services! We have an excellent engineering department! They should know all there is to know about building. We have compromised on every point that you have brought up. This seems to be one where you should give a little. The hourly rate we pay our people is less than half of what we would pay you. I simply do not see the point."

Bowes smiled at him and said, "Sir, professional service has a beginning and an end. If it is interrupted at any one point before completion, there is a change in continuity that can have dire effects. Our profession is one of developing concepts and committing them to paper. The concepts committed to paper are, in part, abstractions subject to interpretation. If an improper or incorrect interpretation is given to those concepts, it can result in needless expenditures, or even worse, major building deficiencies. Further, I have to admit that I have human frailties. In each set of plans and specifications that I produce there are errors."

At this point Douglas Kurd rocked back in his chair with an "I told you so" look on his face that showed a Cheshire cat grin.

Bowes went on, "But those errors are easy to rectify once the construction process begins if we are there to observe the progress of the work. If someone other than those who have worked on the design concept perform this work, there may be a breakdown in continuity that can lead to trouble. Then, too, there might be missed opportunities to make certain changes in the job, during construction, to capitalize on conditions not previously recognized. What I am saying is so commonplace that our professional liability insurer, started by design professionals, has an underwriting prohibition of those firms who have construction review performed by someone else. Alternatively, they will not insure design firms who do the construction review on someone else's plans and specifications. They take this position because it has been an area of high frequency and severity of claims. Thus, what I am saying is this: In the long run, the small amount of money you might save by doing your own review will be far offset by the increased risk of loss you would be assuming, and it would increase the likelihood of liability claims against me to a greater extent than I am willing to undertake."

Spence Davis looked at the chairman and said, "Do you remember Tom Smith?" The silence that followed was thick enough to drown out all argument.

The three executives from Yellowstone Paper sat in a contemplative mood for a moment. Spence Davis finally broke the silence and said, "I have to agree. I have seen it happen. I think we would be better off if we had him do the complete job from stem to stern. Even though our people are good, they really aren't able to interpret the architect's intentions, and they will not be able to rectify some of the unexpected problems that occur on every job. We don't want another fiasco like the wastewater treatment project."

The chairman of Yellowstone nodded agreement.

"Now," said Bowes, "if you will give me a few days, I will prepare a contract in accordance with what we have been talking about. Then, Mr. Kurd, I hope that you will excuse me if it has a strong flavor of the standard AIA form."

Kurd winced and said, "Of course."

Seven months to the day following their meeting, construction was ready to begin. Bidding by contractors had been very light. One out-of-state contractor, whose main base of operation was 2,000 miles away, balked at the limitation of liability clause and did not prepare a bid. One local contractor, who had been involved repeatedly in litigation, also withdrew. Bowes was highly pleased that the award went to O'Brien Construction with whom he had never worked, but which had an excellent reputation for integrity and organizational ability. It was this reputation that got it the job, because, even though its bid was not the lowest, it was selected for the work.

Bowes had called Tim O'Brien, president of O'Brien Construction, a week before the excavation was to start and said, "Tim, this is Jim Bowes. I would like to get my team and your superintendents together prior to commencement of the work. I have some things I would like to go over with everyone; that is, to explain how we are going to work."

O'Brien countered, "What's up? What do you want to say to them? Why do we have to do that?"

Bowes retorted with a laugh, "Well, just say that you are humoring an old man. I have a procedure that I have used on other jobs that I would like to try on *you*. It may save us all a lot of trouble later on."

So a few days later they all met at O'Brien Construction's office. Present were Bowes, his field representatives, the mechanical, electrical, and structural engineers, O'Brien's superintendents, and a superintendent from each of the subcontractors. Bowes began the meeting by telling everyone who he was and that he was happy he was going to be working with them. Next he described what Yellowstone Paper was trying to accomplish by building their building in the Big Bend River Valley. He had a model that would come apart a piece at a time. He introduced each of his employees and told what their responsibilities were to be. By the time he had finished he had conducted an old-fashioned organizational meeting. Following the organizational meeting, he asked if they would all mind staying another fifteen minutes to look at some drawings he had prepared. He took a flip chart and slowly turned the pages over one-by-one to show them how the building might be sequenced. It was a technique he had learned from a structural engineering firm in Seattle, Andersen-Bjornstad-Kane-Jacobs, Inc. (ABKJ). This technique had enabled ABKJ to accomplish near miracles in construction: it had shortened construction time materially, since everyone knew exactly what the sequence of construction was going to be and how the various components and disciplines would work together.

He could tell that O'Brien's people were impressed with the entire procedure. This was especially true of Tim O'Brien who came up to him after the meeting and shook his hand and said, "Gee, Jim, I enjoyed that. It sometimes helps to work with an old pro." Jim Bowes smiled and felt good about the fact that the technique seemed to be working again. Tim O'Brien said, "By the way, I ran into something that perhaps we should think about."

"What's that?" asked Bowes.

"Well, it is something I learned from an architect in Phoenix; he got it from his insurance carrier, the same one that writes your professional liability coverage. It is called formal, nonbinding mediation (FNM). You know I don't like arbitration. Every one we've been involved in has been expensive and didn't accomplish what it set out to do. This new dispute resolution technique seems to cure the problems I ran into in arbitration. It requires that everyone on the job participate in the FNM procedure if they supply or perform services in excess of $5,000 on the job.

"FNM is a combination of the best features of mediation and arbitration. Disputants are required to bring all unresolved conflicts with other parties to the work before a mediator at the jobsite. This is done on an instant basis, or at least within a few days. Where necessary, those in disagreement must submit all documents they are asked for by the opposing parties. This gives them something equivalent to discovery in litigation.

"When the required documentation is produced, the disputing parties sit at a table and explain their side of the situation. The mediator tries to settle the dispute through persuasion. If they cannot resolve the dispute through a mediation procedure, the mediator's recommendation can be admitted in court; of course, all parties must agree to that before the start of the job.

"We used this procedure on a tennis complex that we built in the Middle West. It worked! I'd like to suggest it to you. It's not that I expect disputes. But it surely tends to minimize disagreements if you know that you will have to take them to this outside party who can resolve them instantly if you are not able to do so."

Bowes looked at him thoughtfully. He pursed his lips and whistled softly, "I did see the information our underwriter sent out on that procedure. I'll have to admit that it sounds pretty good. It seems you young upstarts come up with some pretty useful ideas from time to time. I'll present this idea to the Yellowstone people. Their attorney may balk at it, but their chairman is a very enlightened gentleman. I think he'll buy the idea that this might be a good procedure to institute at this point. Have you got any ideas about who the mediator might be?"

"Well," replied O'Brien, "don't laugh when I say this, but my dad would be a good one." He stopped and searched Jim Bowes's face for a moment, broke into a grin and said, "I even think we might get him to do it on a reduced fee."

Bowes smiled and said, "Well, I don't know whether the Yellowstone Paper people would go for your dad as mediator, but maybe we can find someone like him. I know he knows construction, but I am afraid if his boy were in trouble, he would have a fairly prejudiced point of view. Let me sleep on it, and after I have talked with the Yellowstone Paper people, I'll get back to you with some suggestions. They might have their own idea of who would be the best mediator, but we'll give it a try."

The construction ran smoothly for seven weeks. The FNM clause was drafted as an amendment into the contract documents, and a highly respected retired contractor was appointed as the mediator. He was someone who said he "had spent a lifetime fighting with architects and owners," and felt he "could represent everyone's interests on an unbiased basis."

It was not until the seventh week that he got his opportunity. The Big Bend River Valley was visited by an unusual storm. It started with heavy rains, followed by sleet, and then deep-freezing weather. This was very unusual for that section of the country. It got cold in the winter, but it never went down to the temperatures they experienced following the heavy sleet and rains. The steel had been erected and closing in had begun. But the effects of the frigid weather forced the job to stop for one day just before a long weekend. When the crew returned on the Tuesday following the vacation holiday, they were astonished to find one of the box columns that had been erected weeks before badly deformed at its base. It appeared as if a huge hand or weight of some kind had pushed down on the column; it had been unable to withhold the strain and had bulged out at the bottom like an elephant's foot.

The contractor's superintendent on the job contacted the architect immediately and said, "Man, your design must be way off. The column hasn't begun to have the load on it that it's going to. It's giving already."

Jim Bowes's field representative had been trained in such situations to gather as much information as possible and avoid any comment. He quickly set about taking Polaroid pictures of the deformed column and then hurried back to his office. When Jim Bowes saw the bulging steel, he could hardly believe his eyes. He called his structural consultants right away and followed that call with a call to his professional liability insurance carrier. They had a program of preclaim counseling that was to be used in those situations where it was evident that someone might make a claim of professional liability. Fortunately Jim Bowes and his structural consultant were both insured by the same company.

The structural engineer reviewed his calculations, plans, and specifications and found everything to be in perfect order. The insurance carrier's investigator visited the site with Bowes and was amazed at what he found. The insurance company contacted an expert it had used on other jobs and informed him of what had happened. He arrived in a matter of hours and was at the jobsite by 6:00 A.M. the day after the discovery. Of course, the structural portion of the job had been stopped since there was a concern that the whole structural system might be plagued by inadequacy. By noon the insurance company's expert had an answer. It seemed that the box column had a diaphragm plate at its base. In each corner of the diaphragm, next to the column wall, there were some weep holes which were there to permit escape of air should the column heat up, or of water should it somehow condense inside. During the unexpected inclement weather there were periods of alternating rain and freezing. Ice had formed in these weep holes and had stopped them up. After the stop-up, a considerable pond of water had collected in the column due to a drainage pattern from the floors above. Over the long weekend, during the exceptional freeze, ice formed and caused the column to deform. Just like the the high school physics demonstration in which a cast iron tube is fractured by freezing water.

When Bowes and his structural engineer heard this explanation their jaws went slack. It seemed like the sort of thing that just could not happen. They called in Tim O'Brien who called in his steel erector, who responded by saying, "Don't look at me. I did my job. The cost is someone else's." Tim O'Brien called his builder's risk "all-risk" underwriter. He said, "Read the exclusion relating to frost and freezing. We don't cover for damage of that nature unless it's the result of frost or freezing caused by fire, lightning, windstorm, explosion, hail, riot, etc."

Spence Davis said, "I don't think the expense should be ours. After all, Jim, you're our architect, it was your design that led to the loss." Jim Bowes looked at his structural engineer and laughed. He knew his response would be that the responsibility was not his because he had designed in accordance with generally accepted practices. There was nothing wrong with the design. At this point they called in the mediator. Henry Frederickson, the mediator, was a man with a bounce in his step that belied his 75 years. His skin was deeply coursed with wrinkles that evidenced a constant exposure to the elements. He didn't talk much, but was an attentive listener. He had called all parties connected with the steel problem into the construction shack and admonished them that they needed to resolve this matter quickly so the important work of construction would not be impeded.

Spence Davis showed up at the meeting with Douglas Kurd. Henry Frederickson reacted quickly by criticizing Spence, saying, "The whole idea of FNM is to do away with the litigation process. By showing up here with your attorney, you have created an imbalance. It would only be fair now if all of the rest of these gentlemen had counsel at their shoulder; thus, legalese would be introduced into the communications process. With your kind permission I think we will excuse Mr. Kurd." Douglas Kurd gave a questioning look at Spence Davis, but as all eyes turned on him he could see there was unanimous resolution to abide by the ruling of the mediator.

Once he had left, Henry Frederickson said, "Gentlemen, if you will please sit down with me, we will get this thing resolved. I would like each of you to explain your relation to the damages that were the result of the freezing. I understand there is no dispute about the facts. You have all agreed this was an uncontemplated event. You have all agreed the construction was properly done. You may or may not have agreed the design was proper. Let me point out to you that we will resolve this matter this morning. If there are those of you present who are representing large organizations and you would like to refer our decisions to them for committee action, forget it! Your FNM agreement explicitly places the responsibility with me to prepare a court admissible document in the event you, yourselves, cannot come to a satisfactory conclusion. Now, let's start with Mr. Bowes's structural consultant. What have you got to say, sir?"

The structural consultant looked surprised that he had been called on first. He cleared his throat, looked at everyone around the table and said, "I was following the standard detailing in the design of that diaphragm. It has been used in thousands of columns and is in accordance with everyone's idea of what is right and proper. The design may not have anticipated the extraordinary weather we had. I have been informed that we haven't had a similar freezing snap since they started keeping weather records in our state. Then, too, I think it was unforeseeable that the drainage pattern on the upper floors would have caused concentration of water at the head of that column. Had the contractor put on column caps, the loss would not have happened."

He looked to Jim Bowes on his immediate right who said, "I go along with Perry (the structural consultant). I can't fault the design, nor can I fault the fabrication. I don't like to use the term, but I think it was an 'act of God.' Something totally unforeseeable."

It was now Tim O'Brien's turn, and he hunched forward in his chair, looked directly at Spence Davis and said, "The contract documents were silent on who would be responsible for those things not covered by builder's risk insurance. The contract did stipulate that you, as the owner, would provide builder's risk 'all-risk' completed value form coverage. You named me, the subcontractors, and the design team on the policy. From my vantage point, since you are silent about responsibility for unexpected events, and since you assumed the responsibility for providing coverage for disasters, it appears to me that you, the owner, should be responsible for the uninsured damages."

"Why Us?"

Spence Davis perceptively winced and searched the face of the mediator. He did not seem to find any comfort there, because he looked back at Tim O'Brien and said, "Why us? We hired a design team and a contractor to build a building. That's what we want. You should have foreseen that something like this would have happened and protected the job from inclement weather." While he spoke Spence Davis's eyes showed that he was not fully convinced of his own words. As a matter of fact, the sense of guilt welling up inside of him was only tempered by his fear as to what he would say to his boss if he relented on this point.

Jim Bowes must have understood since he started giving Spence a crawl hole. He said to him softly, "Now, Spence, I think I know how you feel about this. It was a totally unexpected thing, something outside the realm of probability. In the absence of any clearly delineated agreement concerning responsibility, it seems that a major share of the cost should rest with the owner."

"What do you mean major share?" shot back Spence Davis.

"Well," replied Jim Bowes, while giving everyone at the table an imploring look, "I would be willing to pick up the cost of remedial design, if everyone else will help share in the cost. The steel fabricator would refabricate the column at his cost, and Tim would replace it on a direct cost basis. That would leave you paying for labor and materials, but no profit or overhead."

Tim O'Brien beamed, "You've got a winner, Jim. I'm willing if everyone else is." They all nodded in assent.

"Well, why did you call me in?" groused Henry Frederickson.

As a matter of fact, there was no occasion again during the balance of the job to call him in; when disputes arose, and there were several, the parties would get together and hammer them out among themselves. Lurking in the back of everyone's mind was the fact that should they be called into a mediation session, someone who was completely dispassionate would be settling their arguments for them.

All went well on the job until close to completion. Then it became evident that specifications and details concerning necessary hardware and equipment to close up the service area had been left out. One of those details can create an architect's nightmare. Jim Bowes's field man reported to him that the contractor felt there should be some plan to close up the facilities; there was not a thing shown in the plans and specifications. Everyone in Bowes's office was stunned. Their plans had gone through a quality control check that would have made a nuclear power plant designer green with envy. Still, they had missed all of the hardware connected with the rolling doors at the service entrance. The cost of the units was substantial. Jim Bowes called Tim O'Brien and explained that there had been an omission and that it would have to be rectified.

"Well, what do you want from me? Is this one of those things where I get stuck on the limitation of liability?" Tim asked in a defensive way.

Bowes replied, "No, limitation of liability would have no effect in this matter. The omission did not create damages to you. The damages, if any, will be to the owner. I'll discuss this with Spence Davis immediately. They will be using the lower floors at the outset, and it will be necessary that they secure the service area at night."

Jim Bowes was plagued by a nagging doubt in his mind on how to approach the people at Yellowstone Paper. He had heard rumors that they were being financially hurt by inflation and that every cent used in the construction of their building was deepening their financial problem. He reflected on the situation for some time and then decided to call his professional liability insurance carrier. He thought that their preclaims counseling system might assist him in making a tactical decision.

His gut feeling was that Yellowstone Paper would be extremely unhappy that a costly component had been omitted. That he believed they would have no legal claim against him was not important—damage to his reputation might be severe. This was on the eve of the completion of a job on which all had gone well. The relationship with the client had been extraordinary and now there was a likelihood that things would disintegrate. He hated to ruin the good opinion they had of him but could see no recourse.

Jim Bowes's professional liability underwriter was very prompt. The person they sent to see him had to be termed "an old pro." He had spent his entire business career handling construction claims and during the past 10 years had specialized in professional liability claims against consulting engineers and architects. He listened to Jim Bowes thoughtfully as the history of the job was related and the eventual omission revealed. He was attentive while Jim went over the details.

Then he pushed his chair back from the table, contemplated the ceiling for a long period and began to speak slowly, "Very interesting, Mr. Bowes, but not unusual. In my job we deal with hundreds of architects and consulting engineers. It is a rare job where something is not overlooked. It's always disappointing to the design professionals, but not usually as damaging to their reputation as you might think. People expect things of this nature to occur. It's provoking to them only when there is an attempt at cover-up or concealment. What they like to see from their design professional is evidence of complete integrity. As a consequence, our advice in a situation like this is to bury your sense of guilt and make a straightforward approach to the client with very little in the way of apology and a lot of explanation on how things will be righted so that their scheduling will not be thrown off."

"How about the expenses? I mean, won't they think that I should pay for the cost of adding these components to the job?" asked Jim Bowes.

"No, I don't think so,' replied the preclaims consultant. "These guys are businessmen. They understand unjust enrichment. I think they'll see right through to the heart of the matter. If they don't, you can keep in mind something I learned way back in the 1950s from a case that was adjudicated in the District of Columbia. It was called *Henry J. Robb, Inc. v. Urdahl, et al.* In that case there was an error in the plans and specifications for a heating system. The error was discovered prior to the time the system was put together. The question was whether the design professional was responsible for the additional cost of rectifying the error. The court said that the owner would have had to pay for the omitted item if it had been properly specified. Hence, the owner would be entitled to recovery of only the cost of performing the work out of proper sequence. Otherwise, the owner would be unjustly enriched."

Jim and the preclaims consultant discussed other similar situations in which the preclaims consultant had been involved. Jim thanked him and called Spence Davis to set up a meeting.

When Jim Bowes arrived at Yellowstone Paper, the triumvirate—the chairman, Spence Davis, and Doug Kurd—were waiting for him. He laid out what had happened and braced himself for an explosion. He was startled by the benign attitude they all took concerning the omission. Jim was especially surprised that Douglas Kurd didn't take the opportunity to torture him with recriminations. As a matter of fact, Douglas Kurd seemed to be bored with the proceedings and excused himself for "a pressing engagement." The chairman of Yellowstone Paper and Spence Davis told Jim to do whatever was necessary to get the facilities in place as soon as possible. They said that they were pleased with the job and its progress. They were especially pleased with the areas where creativity in design had resulted in dollar savings. One had been the use of a one piping loop for both sprinkler heads and a hydronic heat pump system, a creative idea of the mechanical engineer that had saved almost $1 per square foot of construction cost. The mechanical engineer had made other similar savings that had pleased the Yellowstone Paper people enormously.

Not All Fun and Games

"You know," said the chairman of Yellowstone Paper Company, "I sensed that you were really nervous when you came in this morning, Jim. I guess being an architect isn't all fun and games. I've thought many times about your discussion about professional liability and how it has been affecting your profession. I'm a marketing man. As a consequence I tend to think in terms of price-return ratios. I wonder whether you architects get enough for what you are doing. One thing seems evident to me; you are allowing someone else to set the price on the value of damages for your liabilities. One thing we always say in marketing is don't let the customer determine your price; set it yourself. I don't know anything about professional liability, but it seems as if the lawyers have taken the ball away from you, and they are setting the price on the settlements that are being made. From a marketing man's point of view, I would say, Hey, that's the wrong way to do it.

"Your limitation of liability approach is pretty good, but maybe it isn't finite enough. When I was in the field, selling paper, a contract of sale always had a 'damages' clause that set forth what the damages would be if we failed to make delivery on time. It seems to me that architects and engineers might do well to think about setting up some kind of damages clause, so that when anything went wrong the pricing wouldn't be set by someone else. Remember, I'm just a marketing guy, but I have seen how your FNM and limitation of liability have worked in our favor. I think they have meant real dollars to us! I just wish that more could be done to take the professional liability monkey off your back. It would mean real dollar returns to your clients and a more satisfying life for you." He then rolled back in his chair and looked at Jim as if he were expecting some kind of retort.

Jim Bowes got up from his chair and began pacing back and forth in front of the chairman of Yellowstone and Spence Davis. He said, "I'll have to be frank. I used to enjoy the profession a whole lot more than I do now. Before the early 1960s we weren't all running scared. We had a team spirit on every job we got involved in, and it was fun to see the job go together and the construction evolve. Slowly but surely, the rules of the game have changed so drastically that one of our profession's major considerations now is our professional liability. It shouldn't be that way. It's not only bad for us, it's bad for society.

"Architects and engineers are creative people; creative people probably do not perform well under extreme stress. In my opinion, professional liability threats have made it virtually impossible for us to perform to the best of our ability. Sad, but true. I am not wise enough to know what causes it. I do share your opinion that the profession should take control of the costs of alleged errors in design and not leave it to the legal fraternity. They have their own agenda which, because of human nature, creates an incentive for them to gain from our plight. Not a good situation at all."

All three men then sat thoughtfully for a moment or two. Jim Bowes rose and said, "I do want to thank you for your understanding in this situation and I appreciate your empathy. We should have your job completed on time, and I hope you are pleased with the outcome." The chairman of Yellowstone Paper rose, as did Spence Davis, shook hands warmly with Jim Bowes and thanked him profusely for having done an admirable job.

Chapter 11

Discovery: Professional Liability Loss Prevention

A lawyer without history or literature is a mechanic, a mere working mason; if he possesses knowledge of these, he may venture to call himself an architect.

—*Sir Walter Scott, Guy Mannering*

In 1959, Arthur Hailey, the now well-known author of such books as *Hotel* and *Airport*, wrote *The Final Diagnosis* (Doubleday, New York, 1959). It is about a pathologist, Joe Pearson, whose job was to do postmortem organ studies to make certain that the certified causes of death in the hospital where he worked were correct. You learn in this book (as well as from friends who are doctors) that the stated, obvious causes of death in medicine are often mistaken and that many reasons for death are wholly overlooked by a hospital's medical staff. Perhaps Hailey's book influenced my thinking to a great degree, because I became convinced that the conventional wisdom surrounding the causative factors leading to design professional losses may not have been properly identified. There were, in my judgment, components creating claims besides the much heralded "errors and omissions." What were they?

If we can accept that human civilization is walking around with a veneer of humanitarian civility covering a lurking hulk of potentially aggressive simianlike animal, physiologically programmed to attack under certain circumstances, what then? First we must know what may set off the aggressive behavior we find so pathological in today's professional world. What are they? Edward O. Wilson[1] suggests some seven situations likely for the honor of being stimulators of professional liability causing aggressive behavior. They are:

1. Defense and conquest of territory
2. Assertion of dominance
3. Sexual aggression
4. Weaning termination
5. Predation
6. Defense against predators
7. Moralistic aggression to enforce societal rule

Joe McQuillan was a vice president in RAR when we started our quest for loss prevention methods for design professionals in private practice in 1969. He had over a dozen years of experience as a consulting engineer (mechanical) and now had his Juris Doctorate from Lincoln Law School. With our claims involvement and with Joe McQuillan's engineering field experience, we zeroed in on *predation* as being one element that needed examination. We had several professional liability claims that seemed to be predatory. In one case, the chairman of a hotel chain had told one of his employees (who told our claims manager), "I never pay my architects or consulting engineers what I owe them. I can always find something wrong with their work and threaten to sue them. They always drop their claim for fees." He had sued one of our insured mechanical engineers on the flimsiest pretext. Isn't that a predatory practice? Was this sort of thing happening often? Often enough.

In our simple way, we thought the best defense against predatory claimants might be an elaborate fence. Not a fence made of wood, wire, or brick, but one constructed of legal blocks, business ploys, personnel management schemes, legislative efforts, and communications improvements designed to shield our vulnerable design professionals from easy attack. We thought it made sense to make the claimants overcome a series of hurdles before they could bring claims against our insureds. Making it tough to make a claim might discourage the predacious types, who like an easy kill. We had nine choices that we could try.

1. Include exculpatory clauses in the design professional contracts of hire.
2. Use defensive language on their plans and specifications.
3. Use strict guidelines in client selection.
4. Carefully draft contracts of hire enumerating what services were to be performed and what services would not be performed (i. e., the design professional will not be responsible for matters of job safety; safety is the sole responsibility of the contractor).
5. Train all personnel, not just technical people, how to deal with a conflict situation or an accusatory statement.

6. Have top management screen all proposals to ascertain that they do not overstate the capabilities, duties, and responsibilities of the design firm.
7. Check the financial condition of the owner, contractors, and subcontractors.
8. Set up an in-house training program aimed at improving all communications with clients, owners, contractors, government agencies, and others. Implement professional culture educational programs to stimulate bonds of loyalty to the profession.
9. Have the prime design professional draft the general and special conditions (the contractor's contract) clearly delineating the fact that the contractor will be responsible for job safety, liability to the public for the work being performed, and protection of the work from fire, windstorm earthquake, and such.

Another antecedent event that may trigger claims (aggressive) behavior against design professionals (really, all professionals) would be *moralistic aggression to enforce societal rules*. Time and again we would have plaintiffs' attorneys say to us (see Chapter 8), "What the hell! These guys deserve to be sued. They are doing absolutely nothing to police their own profession (lawyers included). If it weren't for us, they would be running roughshod over the public. So don't give us that starry-eyed claim that they are being persecuted." It was hard to argue with their logic. After all, a profession is supposed to be a group of people who have a systematic theory that is taught at a university, which they are then granted authority to practice (usually by state license). For this they are given community sanctions (a monopolistic control over the profession, including such things as accrediting schools), in exchange for maintaining levels of performance and ethical code enforcement. It is the last two elements where virtually all professions had fallen into ruin. None of them were doing much to maintain levels of performance nor enforcing ethical conduct. This appeared to be a major flaw in the professions and perhaps a crucial element in the burgeoning professional liability-malpractice phenomenon. A real tragedy!

Defense against claims stimulated by *moralistic aggression to enforce societal rules* is considered to be justified by the assertion that the plantiff's attorneys are bringing suit as a vital service for society because the professional societies are not requiring proper performance in their calling. It would take a major revision in certain mind-sets to overcome this rationalization. It would require enormous help from the design professionals' societies. Would they be willing to give it? We, in RAR, figured that a monumental job like this would require 10 years and an on-going program to stabilize any improvement that might be made in the professional culture.

Certain accounting firms had faced this problem, so they instituted a plan of peer review. That is, a review of a firm's business and technical procedures to make certain that they were in conformity with the technical and ethical standards of the profession. We thought the idea of peer review would be worth introducing to the members of ASFE, so we arranged for a partner of Arthur Young & Company's (now, Ernst & Young) Los Angeles office, Hugh Grant, to give a speech on their experience at one of ASFE's semiannual meetings. The members of ASFE gave a very positive response, even though there was grumbling like, "I'm not letting my competition into my shop!" So the start was slow. Some of the cooler heads volunteered to be reviewed and within two years the floodgates opened and ASFE members had a majority of the members' firms peer reviewed. Lee Lowry, of Lowry & Associates, Sacramento, said, "It was the most rewarding business experience of my career." We thought, "If only other design professional groups would adopt a similar plan."

Eugene B. Waggoner, past president of ACEC and Jim Stratta, past president of CEAC saw the sense of peer review. Even though they tried to interest their colleagues, it took some years for ACEC to adopt peer review as an association service. Now, they and other design profession organizations, are working at peer review diligently and it is having a major impact on the psychological well-being of the reviewed firms and improving their claims status.

Ethics are still not a subject of active pursuit by the design professional organizations, probably because the federal government has clamped a hammerlock on the engineering professions by saying that they cannot have codes of ethics that make bidding for the awarding of work in contravention with the profession's standards.[2] Isn't that strange? The federal government has a prohibition against the practice of awarding federal engineering jobs on the basis of price, but they will not allow the National Society of Professional Engineers (NSPE) to have a similar nonbidding clause in their code of ethics. Such an ethical standard would protect the public from low-balling by less skilled design professionals who garner work by being cheap. The Justice Department has taken away one of the most important elements for maintaining professional standards. Why would the Justice Department do that? They contend that such an ethic is in restraint of trade, but that doesn't seem likely because the nonbidding clause was in the code of ethics for years and competition was keen. It certainly is not in the public interest because it encourages doing "cheap" professional work. Will it take the collapse of a major structure to bring enlightenment to the Justice Department?

In the design professions, renewal of the professional ideology was not practiced because, once graduates left their sequestered academic institutions, they were on their own to make a buck the way they saw fit. This seemed to be a major flaw. Oh, the professional societies have Fellowships, but Fellowships are awarded the old guys, usually because they have done well in business. The rank and file of the design professions really did not have programs (circa 1971–1972) aimed at raising the level of their technical proficiency and cementing their bonds of loyalty with their profession. This was also true of almost all professions, that is, medical, dental, legal, theological. Many times, the relationship between the professions' associations and their constituents was essentially *business need* rather than a professional maintenance effort. *Marketing of professional services* became the main focus of the professional societies, not "Let's improve our systematic technical abilities and strengthen our loyalties."

In the company that was trying to be Different by Design, we felt that, if progress in elevating the design professions from the status of "just business men, seeking a dollar" to that accorded professional people as at the turn of the century, much had to be done to enrich the self-esteem of the professionals and to create strong bonds of loyalty between the individuals and the profession.[3] In keeping with Lorenz's ideas, and in coincidence with hundreds of society's institutions, in the design professions there needed to be a cooperative group undertaking such as continuing education, followed by public recognition. This would require a new concept, perhaps an institute that would not only reinforce loyalties, but fill important voids in design professionals' business and social education. Engineers seemed to need inculcating in professional values and training in basic business law, defensive strategies, skills in communication, techniques of conflict resolution, history of engineering, and modern personnel practice. Why not an Institute of Professional Practice?

It was April 1972 in Louisiana. It was so muggy and overcast, our San Francisco-type suits were stifling and dripping wet. At the New Orleans Roosevelt Hotel, the highly acclaimed Dr. Sam Krull, a professor of Human Behavior at the University of California, gave a soaring presentation for the ASFE membership that gave them new insights into what makes businesspeople tick. Then, RAR got its chance to make a proposal for starting a profession-building, loyalty-enhancing effort for the soil and foundation engineering (now called geotechnical) professionals. Our proposal called for the founding of the ASFE/Institute of Professional Practice (IPP). This, we suggested, would be a six-week home study course followed by a two-day seminar, during which the participants would be called upon to present a paper on a randomly assigned subject. The curriculum of the home study portion would include History of Engineering, Professionalism, Economics of Engineering, Business Law, and Risk Management. If the participants succeeded in passing the home study portion (open book tests), derived from graduate level books, they would attend the seminar and present their papers. Paper presentations were to be graded by the audience. If they passed both portions, they would receive a Certificate of Completion from ASFE/IPP and presumably public recognition (this last item never reached fruition).

The ASFE members were almost silent after they heard the proposal for IPP. You could not tell from their eyes what they were thinking, because they were looking at their notes, or the floor, the ceiling, or out the window.

We told them what we thought it might cost (a large sum) and they whistled and looked bewildered. We forgot that these guys (no women in those days) had spent all of their lives, from high school on, in technical engineering courses with only a tiny smattering of the social sciences or English. Now, we were telling them, "Hey, if you want to save your profession from perdition you have to wake up and learn something about the social sciences, business, and communication. Your succeeding generations deserve to have the profession renewed." In the back of each ASFE members' mind (they told me later) were the thoughts, "Gee, I've got to go back and explain to our management team why they should make a sizeable investment in making our guys renaissance people. How in hell can I do that?"

There was a fair amount of grumbling about the cost and one member from Pittsburgh suggested that we (RAR) were trying to feather our own nest, "You just are making more consulting work for yourselves! I say, to hell with this idea."

"If you think that, why not hire some experts in education to develop the curriculum and program ideas?" I countered.

That's what they decided to do. They put William H. McTigue of Haley and Aldrich, Cambridge, Massachusetts, in charge of a committee to implement our concept. He was to be president elect of ASFE in two more years and this new responsibility gave him the advantage of getting to know the ASFE members better and to show how well he could perform. Bill McTigue was one of the younger members at the meeting. A graduate of MIT, class of '54, and extremely bright with darting eyes and an inquiring mind. "Explain that to me, please" was his frequent phrase. Fortunately for IPP, Bill became a zealot about IPP. He nurtured a sincere belief that the profession needed revitalization and that the younger generation deserved the cultural inculcation that IPP would bring them. He stumped hard for the funds to get IPP launched. It was tough. The only thing that made it possible were large block pledges of tuition for the first classes, which they hoped could be launched in a year.

Bill McTigue found an organization in Boston that said they could put the IPP together and have it going in a year. The trouble is, they couldn't. Bill gave the consultant RAR's phone number, so we could answer any questions they might have and to help them get oriented. We would get calls from them with questions like, "Say, what do these guys do anyway? And what's a triaxial shear test?" or "What kind of construction do these guys do besides tunnels?" A year came and went and it was obvious the consultants had hit a snag. A big snag. At the end of 18 months Bill McTigue called and said, "Ed, we're ready to eat crow. I don't care what the others say, I'm in charge and I want RAR to take over and make IPP a reality. It's just too good of an idea to let it die. Will you guys at RAR do it for us?"

"Well, we will certainly try. I'm not so sure that we'll be the best in the world for you, but we'll do our best. Please send us an advance."

I didn't know if we had the muscle in our personnel to put together the necessary material and staff to make it what we had envisioned, but we certainly would try. A bit of serendipity came our way, however, which made things all right. We had an organizational I-can-do-anything expert working for us, Florence Whitmire. About two days after Bill McTigue called, Florence came into my office, crashed into a chair and said, "I'm getting bored. I need more challenge. You told me when I was hired, if I could do all the jobs in the organization, I could move on to something with more challenge, more pay, and be part of the management. I think it's time. So, how about it?"

"Yes, I did say something like that. You've done an excellent job. Every position you've filled has been improved by your presence and you've set high standards for those who've followed you. That's really great. I've got something that will keep you awake nights, a challenge above your wildest dream." I then outlined the theory of renewing the bonds of loyalty in a profession, instilling the culture in a professional person and climaxing in public recognition. I could tell the concept excited Florence because her ears got red and her eyes shone.

"Gee, that sounds wonderful. I'm ready to start now," Florence answered leaping up from her chair.

Within two weeks she had the organization figured out. She was going to use outside consultants to collect program and study material in their specialized fields and then the same consultants would act as facilitators (individuals who would keep the sessions on the subject, without being participative) at the seminars. The programs would be largely carried by the consulting geotechnical engineer students through the presentation of papers and during a wide open, no holds barred, question and answer period. The theme would be "Learning by Doing," which meant that there would be role-playing sessions where one person would act as owner, another as adverse attorney, or irate contractor. As facilitators, Florence planned to hire A. Shapero, Jack Fordyce, Richard P. Howell, Howard M. Vollmer, attorney Jim Moore (Rochester, New York), Joe McQuillan (then practicing as an attorney), and Chuck Maurer, DPIC's staff attorney. Things seemed to come together rather well, until we were advised that there was still a cash shortfall. Some of the larger geotechnical firms, Dames & Moore, Woodward-Clyde Consultants, McClelland Engineers, D'Appolonia Engineers, Shannon & Wilson, Soil Testing Services, Inc., and Haley & Aldrich, were tapped again, and pledged more participants in order to try to make the programs self-liquidating (most of these firms required that the employees use vacation time to attend the seminars). Even so, we were too short of funds to make it a going concern. We talked with Bill McTigue and said, "How about if you let RAR own the copyright, and then we can reduce our fee? That way we might be able to get ACEC or some other group to buy the programs and keep us from losing money on the deal."

Bill checked with the ASFE membership and they said, "Sure." IPP was off and running.

Earl Sibley, currently president of Shannon & Wilson, said that he felt the IPP course was the most valuable experience he had in his business career. He graduated with "honors" because his performance on his assigned subject, insurance, was outstanding. His company has continued to send their key employees through the IPP course. Don Roberts, of Dames & Moore, was another outstanding student of IPP and his personal satisfaction with IPP was so high that he became the chairman of the steering committee when ASFE took it over. It continues as a valuable adjunct to the geotechnical profession.

The only thing that did not get realized were the public accolades that Lorenz thought so important for the loyalty renewal. I guess the management of the various firms thought it a boondoggle to throw a party for their employees. Maybe they were right.

By 1977 Richard P. Howell had put together the home study volume for IPP, *Nontechnical Aspects of Professional Practice*. It makes good reading by any professional person interested in improving his or her professional culture. Today, IPP is offered in 50 universities across the nation under the tutelage of Dr. Ronald E. Bucknam (formerly with Haley & Aldrich), a professor at the University of Washington.

RAR used the same format with insurance agents and brokers, but the IPP/Insurance Agents and Brokers Section never did expand. Nor have we been able to generate much interest in other professional groups. Professional societies just do not feel that their mission is to try to bring about a renaissance in their profession. If not them, who?

Wow! What Wonderful Legislation

A chronicle of the work that was done on getting legislation passed into law as part of the "fence" for protection for design professionals was given earlier. The results were not always as unrewarding as was depicted. In fact, the combined efforts of CEAC, CCCE&LS, CCAIA, and other organizations resulted in some very good law that went a long way toward protecting design professionals from predatory law suits. For example, we were able to get cooperation from the Associated General Contractors in getting two sections of the California Civil Code amended that improved the lot of people connected with the construction process.

Section 2782.5 stipulated:

All provisions, clauses, covenants, or agreements contained in, collateral to, or affecting a construction contract and which purports to indemnify the promisee against liability for damages for (a) death or bodily injury to persons, (b) injury to property, (c) design defects or (d) any other loss, damage or expense arising under either (a), (b), or (c) from the sole negligence or willful misconduct or the promisee or the promisee's agents, servants or independent contractors who are directly responsible to such promisee, are against public policy and are void and unenforceable; provided, however, that this provision shall not affect the validity of any workers compensation or agreement issued by an admitted insurer as defined by the Insurance Code.

Wow! What a wonderful piece of legislation. Now the worry about onerous hold harmless and indemnity agreements could be laid to rest. We had the AGC to thank for siding with us and lending their considerable weight to the passage of the amendment. Of course, it benefited their members as well as designers because they did not like being held accountable for someone else's negligence. The insurance industry gave considerable help also, because they did not like insuring policyholders who might be called upon to pay damages for a person or persons not insured in their policies.

Our battle was not over. At the time this legislation was being proposed, we were trying to implement limitation of liability. AGC had voiced great concern about its use, since they thought that we were trying to push the designers' negligence onto their members. The AGC formed a task force to look into limitation of liability, and they called a statewide meeting at the San Francisco Airport Hilton, with its coffee grinder sounding air-conditioning and blinking fluorescent lights. The mood was ugly. I was accompanied by John Beebe, executive director of CEAC, Eugene B. Waggoner, past president of ACEC, and Chuck Blair, a board member of DPIC. After the AGC guys got through venting their spleen on, "G— D— insurance nerds," we called for an unprejudiced hearing. It didn't seem like we'd get it until Gene Waggoner explained the difficult plight geotechnical engineers found themselves in relative to claims. The chairman of the AGC task force, Eugene Von Winning, then said, "Come on, you guys, listen up."

I explained to them how limitation of liability did not make the contractor liable for designers' errors. If there were errors in design and the contractor built in accordance with the plans and specifications, he would not be liable for the resulting errors; the designer would have to pay for them up to the amount of his limitation (usually his fee), and then the owner would have to pay. I told them that the only place I could see increased exposure for the contractor would be in his bidding. That is, if he bid too low and alleged that his too low bid was the result of errors in design, the most he could collect from the designers would be the limitation amount (roughly 5% of the construction costs). We all explained how low-balling contractors were a big problem for designers, and limitation of liability would put a stop to it. The AGC members were sympathetic to that argument and told stories about being shut out of jobs where their competition had low-balled the bid.

The AGC task force then called for a private meeting. The three of us went to the lobby and had coffee, chewed our nails, and waited for their decision. Eugene Von Winning came out after an hour or so and said, "We're just going to be neutral. We won't be against limitation of liability and we won't be for it. Just benign." It was a good decision on their part.

We were then in position to get an addition to the Amendment of Section 2782 by 2782.5 which said:

Nothing contained in Section 2782 shall prevent a party to a construction contract and the owner or other party for whose account the construction contract is being performed, from agreeing with respect to the allocation or limitation as between the parties of any liability for design defects.

It passed and we cheered! We now had codification of the legality of limitation of liability. Although there was a substantial volume of legal precedence upholding limitation of liability, it was nice to have something to point at if an errant attorney said, "Yeh, but is it enforceable?"

Another legislative coup that reinforced our "protective fence" was the result of the combined efforts of CEAC and CCCE&LS. They got a change in the Professional Engineers Act by the addition of Section 6703.1 which stated:

The phrase 'supervision of construction of engineering structures' means the periodic observation of materials and completed work to observe their general compliance with the plans, specifications, and design and planning concepts, and does not include responsibility for the superintendence of construction processes, site conditions, operations, equipment, personnel, or the maintenance of a safe place to work or any safety in, on, or about the site of work.

Although we had recommended for years that the consulting engineers put a similar phrase in their contract of hire, it was nice to have it in the Professional Engineers Act where it could be used as a defense against claims that sought to show that the engineers were responsible for things that were not part of their professional duties, such as job safety and equipment. Some similar law for architects would be a real help.

We were able to develop a number of professional liability loss prevention techniques, but they would be of little use if they did not become a part of the design professionals' practice procedures. In studying the history of loss prevention we looked at the methodology of past promulgators of loss prevention ideas to see how they implemented them. What we learned was fascinating. It seems there have been three main methods of instilling loss prevention concepts.

1. *Intimidation* is used widely. For example, in traffic control to reduce accidents, if a person fails to stop at a stop sign or red light, he or

she is subject to arrest, conviction, and fines; most people obey the law because they feel threatened. Bob in Chapter 2 said, "What this S. O. B. is trying to get across is, the next guy that has an accident is fired!" Three firings later, his employees were fearful for their jobs, and suddenly the accidents stopped. It is that *real* threat that brings conformity to loss prevention procedures. Vessel owners are threatened by the loss of their marine insurance if they do not conform to seaworthiness methods, so the captain is instructed to keep everything in accordance with the marine underwriters' dictates. In construction, failure to wear a hard hat on the job is ample reason for discharge. There are literally thousands of examples of *intimidation* resulting in conformity with loss reducing behavior.

2. *Incentives* are frequently employed to gain acceptance and usage of loss prevention measures. In workers compensation insurance, dividend plans are offered to employers if they will take loss prevention seriously. Some of our insured employers of railroad tie cutters paid their people a no-loss bonus on a monthly basis for goods delivered if there were no loss time job injuries. Fire insurers grant rating credits to those building owners who install sprinkler systems. In construction, it is common practice to give construction teams bonuses for no loss completion of the work. (Workers compensation paid to an injured worker is only about 25% of the total loss to the employer, so bonuses make fiscal sense.) Truck fleet owners are awarded lower insurance rates by underwriters for use of time-lapse odometer devices that keep drivers on 10 hours or under a day schedule. Jewelers receive large reductions in their burglary insurance rate if they install intrusion alarm systems. So, *incentives* do work to affect loss prevention measures.

3. Perhaps the most efficient, and least recognized, tool in implementing loss prevention is the use of *identity*. Modern psychiatrists refer to *identity* as a coherent sense of self, which depends upon the awareness that one's endeavors make sense, that they are meaningful in the context in which life is lived. *Identity* depends upon stable values and upon conviction that one's actions and values are harmoniously related. For loss prevention purposes, it regulates one's deportment in such a way as to make the adoption of loss prevention techniques inviolate if the action is chosen as a person's word picture of himself. It is the compulsion that makes an 85-year-old retired Marine shine his combat boots every morning before leaving his home. It is what makes master craftspersons turn out flawless violins, works of art, or piano concertos. *Identity* is what makes a person become a Presbyterian, Catholic, Buddhist, or Black Panther. It is the element involved in peer review, the IPP, and other things related to the self of a person. It is the ingrained behavior that is the result of a belief. How many things do we do because

"It's just our way"? Maybe hundreds. Affecting *identity* is something to strive for in loss prevention, since if a loss-reducing activity becomes part of a person's *identity* one need not worry about its being used. It will be.

In the company that is Different by Design we had the three methods for making professional liability loss prevention work for our insureds. *Intimidation* was not something that we could resort to, since we didn't have the necessary power. We did have policyholders say to us, "That application for professional liability insurance kinda threatens you, doesn't it? I mean if you answer 'No' to some of those questions about whether we use certain loss prevention measures, does that mean you don't get the coverage?" That was not the intent of the questions, but perhaps it did cause a subconscious sense of guilt in applicants that makes them use the recommended procedures. Who knows? We do know that some of the insured design professional firms used intimidation with their employees to make certain that claims were thwarted by proper procedures.

Our best course was through the medium of *incentives*. For this we used dollars. We instituted a plan of home study for the key employees of an insured firm. The curriculum was on things that improved design professionals' business practices, hopefully, reducing claims exposure. If they would take the home study courses, and pass the test, we would reduce their professional liability insurance premiums by a percentage. The credits given on this plan have exceeded $10 million! Incentives work well. In addition we started a rate credit program for the use of limitation of liability in contracts of hire. If a certain percentage of contracts contained such a clause, the insured might earn as high as 25% in rate credits. Many firms were able to earn the highest possible credit. The effect on claims was dramatic when limitation of liability was used. Claims simply did not materialize! It may not have been the legal effect of the clause, but the fact that the parties were talking about the things that can go wrong in construction before the fact, not after the fact. They understood at the outset that when the unexpected occurs, it is not the sole responsibility of the designers. Risk is openly discussed and the sharing of it becomes part of the agreement.

We believe that the clause calling for nonbinding mediation has a similar effect; the parties are forewarned that things do happen during construction that no one anticipated, and they must be dealt with on a shared-risk basis. If the policyholders of the insurance company that is Different by Design have mediation clauses in their contracts they may have as much as half of their deductible (up to $12,500) paid by the insurance company!

Another major *incentive* we built into our Different by Design company has been a monumental success. It has to do with the need for early warning that something might be going wrong on a construction job that might involve one of our policyholders. We have told our policyholders,

"If you will give us early warning of potential disputes, conflicts, or job trouble, we will open a loss prevention file, which unlike a claims file, will not run against your deductible nor the indemnity limit of you policy. That way, on a no-cost-to-you basis, we can hire technical experts, legal counsel, mediation personnel, or whatever else is needed to avert an actual claim." The results have been dramatic. For example, a large midwestern state university was building a new administration building. The contractor on the job noticed what he thought might be an inadequacy in the design. He told our insured about it, who notified our claims people. A loss prevention file was opened and an expert was hired to review the plans and specifications. A serious discrepancy was found that would delay the job by two months for remedial work. Opening of the administration office of the school in the fall would be seriously hampered by the delay. When the design flaw was explained to the president of the university, he reacted without rancor, and thanked the engineer for his candor. The remedial work was done, all at no cost to the insured engineer. We looked on the outcome as a real loss prevention victory.

This type of thing has resulted in a major shift in reporting from policyholders. They no longer wait until there is proclaimed trouble, but report things before they become unmanageable, name-calling donnybrooks. This *incentive* has worked as if magic.

An early, and possibly heroic, effort of the company that is Different by Design was the conducting of an on-going series of seminars aimed at instilling limitation of liability into the *identity* of design professionals. Starting in 1973 a team was developed—Jim Rush of Schmidt, Smith and Rush (Minot, North Dakota); Gene Waggoner of Woodward, Clyde Consultants (San Francisco); Jack Fordyce, independent psychological consultant (Portland, Oregon); and Peter G. Kelly, Esq., of Updike, Kelly and Spellacy (Hartford, Connecticut). This indefatigable group gave seminars on limitation of liability and other *identity*-enhancing loss prevention subjects at least two dozen times. A new team was developed, and even though this is a very expensive activity, the effort continues even now. *Identity* is important in professional liability loss prevention.

Identity with the loss prevention steps is not easy to establish. It was interesting to note that certain design professionals instantly made professional liability loss prevention part of their firm's personality. Henry J. Degenkolb, a highly respected structural engineer and eventually a board member of DPIC, had one of those firms so imbued. Henry and his technical management team seized every loss prevention recommendation and made it "theirs." No argument, it just became the way they practiced. I'll never forget how they faced down a contractor who balked at having a limitation of liability clause in the special conditions. The job went to another contractor whose bid had been closer to reality. The rebuffed contractor threatened law suit, but it never materialized.

Ed Martin of Albert C. Martin & Associates (now Martin Associates

Group, Inc.) took the idea of advising the owners about unexpected events that might occur. He put in their contract of hire a clause, which I can only paraphrase, but said something like, "Our plans and specifications do contain errors, omissions, and inconsistencies and it will be up to the owner, contractor, and subcontractors to identify them so that they can be rectified during course of construction." Talk about preparing the parties for the unexpected!

An architect in southern California, Ebbe Videreksen, AIA, surprised us by saying he had been using a clause like our limitation of liability clause for years, having started using it in 1967. His read:

The Client agrees to limit the Architect's liability to the Client and to all construction contractors and subcontractors on the Project, or any Third Party, due to the Architect's negligent acts, errors or omissions, such that the total aggregate liability of the Architect to all those named shall not exceed $100,000 or the total amount of the fee in this Agreement, whichever is greater.

Here, we had thought we had invented limitation of liability for design professionals, but this architect had been using it for some years, with no complaints from clients or contractors. It was his *identity* showing. He, also, had a clause pointing out that there would be errors, omissions, and code conflicts that should be dealt with when found. That man has to have a very high opinion of his profession to have done something like that. It, in turn, makes others think that his professionalism is sterling.

Dozens of architects and engineers showed a similar inclination to adopt the loss prevention recommendations as their normal practice procedure. To reinforce the feeling of *identity* our premium credit program encouraged home study courses, peer review programs, and we put on dozens of regional seminars aimed at imparting the professional liability loss prevention techniques into the persona of design professionals. Frequently, these seminars would be sponsored by CCAIA, CEAC, CCCE&LS, ACEC, and AIA. We featured speakers like Albert Shapero, Jack Fordyce, Milan Radovic, Harry Strassberg, Arnold Mitchell, Peter G. Kelly, and one or more of our staff attorneys. In 1979, the company that is Different by Design conducted 63 seminars throughout the United States. Most were at no charge to the insured attendees. This type of activity is still being conducted by the company that is Different by Design as a mainstay.

People have as a part of their natural psychological makeup a revulsion for treatment they consider lacking in integrity or appropriateness. They will react to such treatment in a recriminative way, often with a vigor that transcends the perceived wrong, if they feel that they have been deceived, demeaned, or insulted. Anything that runs counter to one's belief in truth will stimulate strong reaction and aggressive action. That is why better communication is perhaps the best protection against professional liability claims.

During World War II, a major breakthrough in information theory was developed by Claude E. Shannon of Bell Laboratories, who many equate with Newton or Einstein as respects his contribution to science. He used the second law of thermodynamics, sometimes called the entropy law, as the basis for his hypothesis on information theory. The entropy law* says something like, "Every system left to itself changes, rapidly or slowly, in such a way as to approach a definite final state of diffusion of materials or energy from an area of high concentration to low; such as the passage of heat from a hot to a cold body; the oxidation of organic substance by the atmosphere; and the increase of randomness and chaos in human cultures." (In information theory, as in the transmission of messages, the uncertainty of the message being received as was transmitted is measured.) Shannon suggested that redundancy in messages impedes the transfer of information, much as "noise" does on transmission lines. He thought it would be better in information transfer (communications) to package the message better rather than trying to improve the transmission lines.

This brings us to design professionals in private practice. We felt that changing design professionals (the transmission lines) into *Great Communicators* may not have been possible. Look at us (insurance people): Our talk is loaded with undecipherable, redundant words. We use buzzwords, jargon, and acronyms in insurance verbiage: CGL, ISO, XCU, object, general averages, co-insurance, floater policy, "all risk," POP, inland-marine, Inchmaree, "risk" to mean several different things, and more, none of which convey a meaning (seemingly) to anyone not skilled in insurance (arcane) parlance. This type of information transfer should have insurance in deep

---

* A droll story illustrates this communications breakdown due to the entropy law that goes something like this: The President called in the secretaries of the army and navy and said, "I have some serious news. We have intelligence that indicates the Japanese may make a surprise military attack. We don't know exactly where, so we should be prepared at all major military installations. Alert your commanding officers. I suggest we use the new British invention, radio detecting and ranging (RADAR), to provide aircraft detection. While not tested, it has served the British well and it might be of use to us. We will continue negotiating with the Japanese in case this intelligence proves to be erroneous."

The secretaries of the army and navy told their commanding officers, "The serious President is intelligent. He says it wouldn't surprise him if the Japanese made an attack with military forces on our installations. It may be Alert Bay. The exact time of their attack will be negotiated with the Japanese. Tell your majors. Use the British radio, since they will be detecting them with a device tested with their planes. We will try to prove this intelligence is erroneous."

The commanding officers advised their wing and division commands, "The President wants us to be serious about the Japanese. They are negotiating a surprise that doesn't take much intelligence. The British majors are detecting radio frequencies that may be erroneous, but we don't know where yet. When it is tested, we'll let you know. Inform your noncoms to be alert."

The noncoms wrote home, "Dear Folks: This is top secret, and comes from our intelligent commanding officers, so don't tell anyone except Uncle George and brother Billy. The Japanese have negotiated with the British to build a radio thing. We don't know what it is, since it hasn't been tested, so the officers say don't pay any attention to it. I get to operate it next Sunday. At least we can sleep in on Sunday, December 7th and we don't have to be on the alert. YVT, Tech IV, Sam."

communications trouble, but it does not. Why? Maybe it's because insurance idioms are almost all standard form. That is, policies of insurance, endorsements, binders, settlement agreements, literally all the elements of communication are issued by insurance company bureaus, and the sameness of them is assured. They have been tested in courts of law, argued about endlessly as to intent, so much so that the outcome of any dispute is readily predictable. While Shannon's entropy law theory of information may not be directly in point, it does seem that insurance has hewed to the concept of packaging the information in an efficient, concise manner used by almost all insurance companies and this has kept the messages clean and understandable. What kind of deep trouble would insurance people be in if they tried to devise a different contract for their many policyholders?

This suggests that design professionals would be well advised to persist zealously, in using standard AIA, ACEC-NSPE, and ASCE forms of agreement, which have been tested in court, argued about endlessly as to intent, and now explain the design professional's role in their profession with a high degree of common understanding. The sense from these standard agreements should be less susceptible to the ravages of entropy than those that are cooked up in dingy law offices where understanding of construction is suspect. Other than this, about the best that can be done is to warn design professionals repeatedly that failure in information transfer is at the heart and soul of their professional liability problem.

We can hope that they, as intelligent individuals, will do something about it. So far, they have.

Chapter 12

The Guys and Gals
Who Make It Go

On my honor I will do my best
To do my duty to God and my country
and to obey the Scout Law;
To help other people at all times;
To keep myself physically strong,
mentally awake, and morally straight.

—Boy Scout Oath

"I always thought we had the best agents ever, but I have to say, you seem to have the most professional group of agents I've run into. There isn't a sour apple in the bunch. How do you do it?" Hiram L. Kennicott, Jr. of AMICO had cornered me after an agent's meeting in Oakland, California in April 1967.

It was our practice to meet once a year with our agency force to bring them up to speed on new coverage provisions, professional liability loss prevention developments, insurance management changes—anything that might help an insurance agent or broker dealing in a difficult program. The agents began calling this meeting the "annual brainwashing." We weren't really that good at it, but our professional liability loss prevention-insurance formula and extensive field underwriting demanded tremendous effort and dedication by our agency force. They deserved extraordinary help to bring about our plan to do more than provide insurance coverage. They had to go out and talk face-to-face with the policyholders and be prepared to answer questions about coverage. "We don't do soils investigation, but if we get sued for a soils failure, are we insured?" When you are asked questions like that, you couldn't say, "I'll check the manual." You have to look clear-eyed and halfway intelligent and respond, "As long as you are not receiving fees for soil work, we will delete the exclusion for work in connection with subsurface soils failures, at no cost, and you will be covered." A good agent would then run back to the office, check the manual to be absolutely certain and then draft a letter that committed his or her statement to writing.

At these annual powwows, we often had our best defense attorneys talk to the agents about new and original strategies to defend claims. In that particular meeting, Landon Morris, of the law firm Morris & Polich of Los Angeles, gave an outstanding talk on the importance of being sensitive to the claimant's position when defending claims.

Kenneth W. S. Soubry, executive vice president of A&A (and soon to be chairman), gave an erudite speech about the role of the agent (broker) in specialty insurance programs and how important it was to communicate the correct message to the client. Our attending agents* agreed, since our choice of agents was largely governed by the Boy Scout oath. After all, our role as insurance people was to do our best and help others at all times. Or is that more altruism?

In Chapter 5, it was explained how we looked for three things in an agent or employee: (1) A good first impression and an awareness of the social amenities, (2) evidence that the individual had exercised a significant amount of self-discipline at some time during his or her life, and (3) indications that the prospect had given selflessly of his or her time and energy for others, working for Hospice, the United Way, SPCA, and similar organizations. Going a step further, it would be nice to find that he or she had been trustworthy, loyal, helpful, friendly, courteous, kind, obedient, thrifty, brave, clean, and reverent, just like a Boy (or Girl) Scout. I think that was what Hi Kennicott recognized in our chosen agents, that they fit the scout mold. Instead of earning merit badges, though, they took home commissions. We adopted our three-point procedure in the AMICO program and kept it with DPIC. It seems to have worked rather well.

Following our appointment of Hurley, Atkins & Stewart in Seattle, I went to the October, 1965, CEC meeting in Denver. In attendance was Don Gray, of Ken R. White and Company, a large, highly respected civil engineering firm. Don listened to what we said about professional liability loss prevention and called his insurance agent the first thing next morning .

"Hello, Rollo. Listen, I have some good news and some bad news. Let me tell you the good news first. There's this guy, see, Ed Howell, who talked to the CEC of C last night at the Denver Athletic Club. He's got a professional liability insurance program going in California with the AMICO, one of the Kemper companies. It is based on loss prevention, just like we use in workers compensation. Anyway, Orley Phillips, Harvey

---

* In attendance were Jim Hurley and Jim Atkins of Hurley, Atkins & Stewart, Seattle; Rollo E. Jacobs, Jr. of Steele, Jacobs & Gardner, Denver, Colorado; Peter Hawes and Hugo Standing of A&A, Los Angeles; George Hallmark of A&A, Dallas, Texas; Douglas Kincaid, A&A, Baltimore, Maryland; and Scott McKown of Wirt Wilson & Company, Minneapolis, Minnesota.

Kadish, Nick Carter, and others are trying to get him to expand to Colorado. That's the good news. The bad news is, if he does, and you're not his agent here, we might just have to jerk our coverage from you. I'd call him, if I were you, and see what your chances might be. Hello, Rollo? Rollo? You still on the line?"

Rollo E. Jacobs, Jr. did call me. His message was waiting when I returned to San Francisco. He was worried about his best engineering account. He asked to meet with me and offered to fly out at once. Because there were several other agents in Denver who had shown an interest in our plan, I set up appointments with him and the others the following month in Denver. The other interested agents had been recommended by insurance people, and, frankly, I was prejudiced in their favor. I mean, insurance people would know the best agent, right? Not in this case. I saw at once that Rollo fit our imaginary scout model perfectly. Although he didn't need to, he was helping others (by teaching Dale Carnegie courses) because he empathized with those who experienced the same difficulties he'd once had.

Rollo could be a fighting demon for his clients' interests. He would do battle with large corporations who were bent on hog-tying consulting engineers with odious legal language. Usually, his persuasiveness would prevail. He was politely persistent, wearing down the financial guy or corporate attorney who was trying to take advantage of *his client*. If they didn't relent, he wouldn't give up, but would call me into the fray. Rollo and I often visited risk managers or attorneys of giant Colorado corporations to plead with them to be more reasonable. Except for one company, they all saw reason and modified their hold harmless and indemnity agreements or other burdensome clauses. (This was fairly easy because we could point to the exclusion of coverage arising out of liability assumed in a contract or an agreement. We would ask the engineer's client, "Would you rather have your engineer fully insured or not?") Rollo was profoundly loyal to our programs and worked unstintingly at professional liability loss prevention education. Without a doubt, we sought to duplicate his dedication and persistence in our other agency choices.

Employees

In our hiring practices we used the same three-point evaluation as for agents. In addition we adopted a consultant's recommendations. In his seminars for consulting engineers and architects, Dr. Albert Shapero used to say, "The most important thing you do as managers of professional organizations is to hire people. After all, the only things you have to work with are people and information. The richer either of these sources of income, the greater your profit."[1] We applied this advice to insurance company management as well. One of the first things we did when we could afford it was to hire a top-notch, full-time librarian, Annette Gaskin. Slowly and methodically, Annette built a reservoir of printed and recorded information that would make it easier for our researchers and underwriters to gather information. Our underwriters, in particular, needed her skills (she had a masters in library science) to help them learn the nuances of construction (what is a triaxial shear test anyway?). The worst mistake a manager can make is to assume that employees somehow know the same things management does. It doesn't work that way. Mrs. Gaskin helped us aid our employees to become more knowledgeable. At Employers of Wausau they said, "Knowledge is earning power" and they were so right. In time, we had one of the finest insurance industry libraries in the city of San Francisco.

As for hiring and retaining employees, we must have done something right. We were able to put together a team of highly motivated people who did superior work. Motivation was the secret and I would tell you how we did it — if I knew. I think our people were highly motivated because of a number of factors. One such factor had to be the nature of our cause. When hiring, we stressed that we were on a crusade to try to help some other people who were in desperate trouble. We believed that, and gave it top priority in the conduct of our business. It was at the core of our corporate persona. We did not *have* to fight for the institution of limitation of liability or the other difficult-to-sell professional liability loss prevention measures; in fact, as our competitors pointed out time and again, our profits would have been greater if we had ignored the problem. They'd say to me, "Hell, Howell, you're just tryin' too hard. You don't have to do that." Our belief in helping others, however, and our conviction that it was *right* must have influenced our employees, because they were excited about participating in the crusade to help our policyholders. They worked hard toward our common goal.

Successful organizations and their employees are interdependent. Employees depend on the organization for fair treatment, opportunity, and recognition for their contributions. The organization reaches the company's objectives via the employees' efforts. "If you take care of your people, they will take care of you," my father used to tell me. Our management team and board of directors believed that and we tried to make certain that our people had opportunity, fair compensation, and recognition for their service. It was our policy (taking Dr. Shapero's advice) to pay for any educational courses employees wanted to take to better themselves. Several were awarded CPCUs under this program; one graduated from the Dale Carnegie speech course; still others took courses in computers. We also purchased any book, periodical, or training aid employees thought would help them do their job (this policy was never even slightly abused). We hired from within. If a job opportunity came up, it was offered first to existing employees. It was a good system, because we knew about people before they took on a new job. This was interdependence working; we helped them and they helped us.

When hiring, once again we used Dr. Shapero's advice:[2]

Get your employees to recommend someone, The 'network' is by far the best source of good people. Your employees will not endorse someone who will make them look bad, no matter how friendly they are. Thus, the applicants are pre-qualified. Then too, the applicants will know more about your company than you do, because their friends will have briefed them. Newspaper ads are the worst source for employees. You won't have time to interview all the applicants that come to you from newspaper ads. Use a headhunter as a last resort to the network.

We followed his advice and did one additional thing. If someone who had been recommended by one of our trusted employees came to us, even if we did not have an opening, we would hire them and put them in "training" until we needed them. We always did. This, too, worked well.

Our pay was above scale. The insurance industry had a reputation for "hiring cheap." It could be argued whether this was true, but we chose to pay slightly more than other insurance companies. When we wanted to hire someone, after making certain they met our criteria, we would ask them what salary they required. We always paid the amount they said they needed. True, sometimes they wanted more than we could afford and in those instances we did not hire them. Trying to beat an employee down on what they wanted would make them feel they were being treated unfairly. Not a good start.

In my early years in the insurance business, it was my observation that women did not receive fair treatment. If you graduated from Stanford, had your MBA, and were female, you could almost be assured that you would be pounding a typewriter in your insurance company job. That was before the women's movement, but it continued until fairly recently. We decided that was wrong and we hired a lot of bright women to do our special tasks, paid them as much as men, and gave them opportunities for management positions. Underwriting, in particular, seemed to attract women. Long the sacred territory of male employees, underwriting was challenging, took perceptive ability, and could be rewarding for those who were highly motivated. We were criticized by other insurance people for this move, but we were never sorry. Our female employees were motivated. They could see we were different—Different by Design. They knew that women in underwriting were rare and they worked hard to prove we were smart to have given them a chance. We may have overdone it a bit at one point because the underwriting department (of about 10 people) became totally female. For us, it was a winner and our agency force and policyholders did not object. Fortunately, today women are filling many slots that used to be reserved for men. Giving people a fair chance is a great motivator.

"Money alone won't motivate people" was the cry of the management gurus of the early 1970s. Even so, our bonus system was configured so that everyone in the organization, not just the so-called key employees, could earn a merit bonus based upon performance. Everyone in our company that was Different by Design was considered a key employee and participated in the bonus pool. There was no such thing as an unimportant job. We knew it and we told the people who were doing what some called menial tasks that their work was just as important to the organization as the

CEO's. Take filing, for instance. I once worked in an organization where they were hamstrung because they had demeaned the filing lady; she retaliated by "firing" the management and doing only what she wanted to do, which wasn't much, because she was given to understand that her job was not important. Boy, did she show them!

The DPIC board of directors created a bonus pool based upon progress and profit. Most employees were pleasantly surprised by their bonuses; they were larger than the industry thought necessary. The amount was left to their immediate supervisors, subject to equity review by the management team; at no time did we have any complaints about unfairness in bonuses. It seemed to motivate people in spite of what the management experts were saying. Employee turnover was almost nonexistent, less than 5% per year compared with more than 20% industrywide.

We may have overlooked Dr. Shapero's advice when it came to recognition, however. We tried to tell people how well they were doing, but there were times when the press of business crowded out that important duty.

The company that is Different by Design succeeded because of the people who were associated with it. Agents, employees, reinsurance people, and support personnel alike worked to help others because it was the *right* thing to do. Although we had some failures in this regard, in the main, we had a really fine bunch of people working with us and it showed when surveys were done by the various professional societies. Our company was always given the highest rating of any company providing our type of coverage, and our management knew it wasn't something management was doing. It was our people our policyholders appreciated.

Chapter 13

Transition

All is well that ends well.

—John Heywood (c. 1497–1580)

The company that is Different by Design came very close to not being born, as was explained in Chapter 6, largely because of ugly, primal politics in all of the organizations involved with its formation. In the end, the imperative for a stable source of professional liability insurance for consulting engineers overcame political considerations and the company was formed. In fact, all but one of the companies formed by RAR went through severe birth pangs brought about by struggles of individuals for dominance. All ultimately survived, possibly because the alternative was the lack of one form of badly needed insurance or another. Without that as an overriding impetus, the companies started by RAR probably would have ended up like most good business ideas that simply wither and die. It is reason enough to believe that the best insurance ideas grow into businesses because of overwhelming need, rather than financial gain sought by the founders. (This, or because the founders are having so much fun, an esprit, doing their thing — as in the electronics and software industries, that came into being because the founders were having such an entrepreneurial thrill.)

Infancy

Infancy was a grand time for the company that was. The long hours, constant challenge, the "How do we write coverage in Wyoming with the insurance commissioner so dead-set against claims made policies?" (we went in as a surplus lines writer) "How long will it take us to get licensed in Texas?" (two weeks with magical, political help from CEC of Texas Executive Director Ray Lewis and assistant Katie Whitaker) kept us in a constant state of euphoria. Our premium volume exceeded all of our projections, almost doubling annually the first few years, and the cry for coverage from virtually every state became overwhelming. One of our board members was so smitten by the numbers that it numbed his reasoning. "Why, I should quit engineering and sell insurance. Better yet, how about if we appoint my wife agent in my state?" That did not seem like a good idea.

Our cooperation with Kemper continued and the workers compensation program envisioned by Hi Kennicott grew along with the comprehensive general and professional liability insurance writings. At one point, the combined coverages provided AMICO with the single largest source of business for their commercial casualty business, according to John Roscich, then an AMICO underwriter in the commercial casualty department. We were stumbling over our own feet trying to keep up with the demand for professional and comprehensive general liability insurance. New agents were being sought to service the accounts in virtually every state. About 50% of our management's time was spent in travel to open new markets, to appoint new agents, to lead professional liability loss prevention seminars, and do research for new professional liability loss prevention measures. It was an exhausting existence.

The Teens

The company zipped through its early childhood. Then one day in late 1974, we entered a new transitional phase, the teens. This was not because of our age, but because it was time to face the upcoming years and the facts created by prodigious growth. We knew that our capital and surplus (unassigned earnings) ratios were getting close to being "questionable," that is, the ratio of capital and surplus to the premiums being written. The California Department of Insurance did their triannual audit and I received a call from their financial analyst, Christie Armstrong, who pointed out that the ratio was thin. "Yeah, but our cash flow is strong and our settlement time is almost five years. So, we have time to earn a cushion with investment return," I told him. He relented but suggested we seek additional capital.

Liability Insurance Accounting

Neither statutory nor GAAP Accounting can be relied upon to give an accurate picture of a long tail liability insurance company's financial condition. It takes a complete analysis of the claims files in order to determine what the actual condition might be—not something easily done.

Our board looked at the problem of inadequate capital and surplus and proposed to raise capital by a common stock offering to the design professional community. They reasoned, "This is the way we did it before, so it may work now, too." We were advised by financial people that raising additional capital for a company that had no in-house management would be tricky at best and perhaps impossible. Because RAR managed the company, the idea of merging RAR with DPIC to give it a management was discussed and seemed like the logical answer. "Worth" became a hotly contested issue. How much was each entity worth relative to the other? We in RAR, whose stock was wholly owned by employees, believed we were the going concern, with an agency force, reinsurance connections, underwriting and claims know-how that was extremely valuable. Some of the engineers, however, were of the opinion that it was the insurance entity's capital that was valuable (the old divide-the-pie syndrome). It was paramount that the issue be settled before merger could be contemplated. To sidestep a finger-wagging, profanity-ridden revolution, DPIC's board of directors decided that an outside expert was needed to formulate a rational determination.

The best-known organization capable of doing the appraisal was the world famous insurance company rating organization, A. M. Best Company, of Oldwick, New Jersey. The board agreed unanimously that Best's findings would be honored by the two entities. It was hired and its vice president, Patrick Greene, came to San Francisco. He analyzed our combined financial data and did a survey of RAR to see how we were operating.

"I know what we said, but we're not going to abide by his decision. We're going to take this to the stockholders," was the response from a few of the board members who did not like Mr. Greene's findings. This meant that at the very time we were trying to build cooperation in raising capital, DPIC had a stockholders' battle on its hands. In an attempt to placate the dissidents, RAR relented by reducing its value by 25% from the amount that Mr. Greene proposed, but to no avail.

There followed almost a year of conflict dominated by the politics of ACEC, with regionalism largely determining how stockholders felt. It was New York City against California, with the states in between divided on the correct course of action. It appeared that there was a major split in the stockholders' opinion about whether a merger between DPIC and RAR should take place at all. In fact, it seemed the Different by Design company might be doomed. Proxies were prepared and sent out to stockholders. The stockholders' meeting was held in connection with the ACEC annual convention. When the votes were counted, the merger was approved by a wide margin.

In 1978, with the merger behind us, we were in a position to raise the badly needed additional capital. Because we were a national company, we were anxious to have investments from a wide quarter. The company's lawyers, God bless them, ran up mountainous bills in connection with our new stock issue, and the accountants did their share of hourly billing as well. The total cost to the combined companies was close to $100,000. This would have been fine, except that when we counted all investments made from our new stock issue, it barely came to $250,000.

We solicited investment from architects as well as consulting engineers, but they simply did not have spare money. Except for a few of the very large firms, investments from architects were almost nonexistent.

The failure of the issue to meet expectations left us in a tenuous position. The Department of Insurance was breathing down our neck, and it appeared that we might have to retrench to stay within the ratios sought by the Department of Insurance. But wait! Terra Insurance Ltd., domiciled in Bermuda and owned by geotechnical consultants, wanted DPIC to succeed. (DPIC was issuing its policies to the geotechnical community and managing Terra's business affairs.) In an heroic gesture, Terra invested $500,000 in DPIC and saved the day. DPIC was pulled back from the brink and could continue to issue policies of insurance.

The company that is Different by Design surged through its adolescence. 1979, 1980, and 1981 were banner years, and the company came to full adulthood in 1982. The 1982 Annual Report of the Design Professionals Financial Corporation (DPFC, the company that managed the merged companies) contained a letter signed by the chairman and president which stated in part:

Adulthood carries with it immutable responsibilities. One of these is to be caring about people who depend on you; another is to concern yourself with your community's development; a third is to be fair and honest in dealing with all people you contact. It is difficult to say when DPFC/DPIC reached adulthood. It was plain during the infancy of the company, we grasped for ways to do things better. A period of explosive growth followed, not unlike human adolescents who bloom into maturity to face the responsibilities of adulthood.

It is with a sense of pride that we now face the future as a seasoned, mature insurance complex. Our values remain firm: We regard the quality rendering of risk transference and management services as uppermost. The company continues to recognize its duty to act vigorously in behalf of its clientele and the design professional community. Many services are rendered to architects and engineers as professional bodies, without regard to the ultimate financial impact, simply because we see their individual and collective welfare as inexorably intertwined in our own.

We were conscious of the transition in our company's identity when we passed this milestone. We had taken many major management steps to prepare ourselves for the challenges that lay ahead. One of the most important was to recruit a cadre of insurance specialists to help us maintain our elevated service and business momentum.

In March of 1982, Peter B. Hawes was elected executive vice president of DPFC and president of DPIC. (You may remember his name from earlier chapters. He was the salesperson A&A assigned to work with me on the AMICO program.) Peter had stayed with A&A, and had risen to the position of vice president of western region special projects. In 1977, he left to join Dinner Levison Company, a fine San Francisco insurance brokerage organization, as head of operations. Then he went on to ISU Companies (an insurance franchising company) in 1979. Since I had known Peter in the early 1960s, he had acquired his CPCU and four kids. He came aboard as the heir apparent.

While in high school in Palo Alto, I had known a guy who was a constant entertainer, Bill Breeden. He could tell jokes like a pro. He could regale a classroom into unruly disorder, and often did. I had lost track of him during World War II, but when A&A went public in 1969, it began acquiring medium-size insurance brokerage companies throughout the world. One was Charles W. Sexton & Co. of Portland, Oregon, and who was on their management team? Bill Breeden. Because of his awesome insurance knowledge, Bill soon became head of the A&A Portland office. He had graduated from Wharton School of Business, majoring in insurance, and had worked for Kemper in Philadelphia and San Francisco honing his insurance skills. When we began to expand our team, I remembered Bill and thought, "Why not? We need brains. And a joke now and then would be nice." I was in Portland in late 1981 making a speech before the Association of Engineering Geologists (who were all excited about Mount Saint Helens, which had erupted on May 18, 1980). I called Bill to see if a cup of coffee was in order. It was. "Hey," I asked, "why don't you throw over all of this rain, pain, and no gain and join us in our move to sunny Monterey?"

We put Bill in charge of Peninsula Excess Insurance Brokers, a subsidiary company of DPFC that sold excess insurance (policies of insurance that have limits in excess of the limits issued by the primary insurer). It was a good thing, too. Through Bill's efforts, Peninsula Excess became a remarkable success. As is his nature, Bill worked unstintingly, maybe even compulsively, and seemed to enjoy what he was doing, but he really didn't get in all that much golf. A pity. Bill is a living, breathing example of the truth of Employers of Wausau's motto, "Knowledge is earning power." He retired in the spring of 1993 after a very successful career. Peninsula Excess was an outstanding example of things being done *right*.

James V. Atkins, Master of Business Administration from the University of Washington, CPCU, had been one of our agents in Seattle, along with his partner, Jim Hurley, in the brokerage firm Hurley, Atkins & Stewart. They'd done an excellent job for DPIC. They had won the trust and friendship of the Washington-Oregon design professional community and had trained a second generation of sales and servicing people in our Different by Design approach. Jim Hurley, whom I described earlier as one of the greatest insurance men that ever lived, had died on December 17, 1980. We were all devastated; he had been the quintessence of honesty and integrity and had lived strictly by those beliefs. "It's like the end of an era," Atkins said after Hurley's demise. He began to question his lifestyle, the leaden skies of Seattle, and felt he needed a change. We invited him to join us in Monterey. It took him some time to make up his mind, but his wife helped to hurry the decision. So they left beautiful Seattle in June of 1982 and Jim joined us as head of our marketing department.

These three guys referred to themselves as "The Class of '82."

1982 was another banner year. The company that was Different by Design had assets of close to $40 million and growth continued to be tremendous. Professional liability loss prevention had caught on in the design professional community and our claims management results had improved so much it looked like we were going to show even greater profits.

In the late summer of 1982, the California Department of Insurance started their routine triennial audit. We felt confident since everything was going so well. We had certifications from our own auditors, Arthur Young & Company (now Ernst & Young), that said our reserving was adequate and other financial factors stable and in good condition. Everything seemed fine until December 31, 1982, when the Department of Insurance wrote a terse letter that disallowed an intercompany receivable and opined our reserves were understated by 10%. Not 9.3% nor 11.1%, but a flat 10%. (My statistics professor would have said, "Whoa! What's with this flat 10%?") Had they said our capital was thin and needed beefing up, we would have agreed, since we knew that and would have proceeded to seek additional capital. Arthur Young & Company stuck by their audit and so began a battle with the Department of Insurance that lasted almost a year. We should have known better. Such disputes can hang on incredibly arcane opinions. The upshot was that we were forced to seek an investor or buyer for the company; in other words, find an entity capable of replenishing our capital and surplus.

Peter Hawes and I talked with a number of money brokers, venture capital intermediaries or investment bankers (depending on how they wanted to be billed), realizing all the while that we were weak in their arena. Those guys are in a cutthroat business— and it's your throat they want to cut. Their fees are stratospheric. After they have explained their fee structure, and you're still gasping, they are quick to add, "No guarantees, you understand. We'll do our best, but don't count on anything. And by the way, we require a retainer—$20,000 ought to do." Yes, we were weak in the money acquisition scene.

We talked with a number of these merchants of dough and became thoroughly discouraged. We were what they called "small potatoes," since our needs were fairly modest compared to huge corporations. The "big guys," $100 million plus, would really inspire the money men because they could get rich on a merger deal. They just couldn't get exited about a little, highly specialized insurance company.

It was described in Chapter 9 how RAR set up a specialty insurance company, Land Stability Insurance Company, whose name changed to the Fairmont Insurance Company and was then sold. After Fairmont's sale, the new management had to raise capital in order to write a high volume of business and they were able to do so, even though they were writing workers compensation, a tough line of insurance. Because they had been successful in raising capital, we talked with their CEO and he told us of the person who had helped them, Joe Dowling, of Dean Witter Reynolds, Inc., of Westport, Connecticut.

Peter Hawes and I contacted Joe Dowling and arranged for a meeting in Miami prior to our DPFC board of directors meeting in December 1983. Dowling said he'd like to help us and gave us his fee requirements. Again, we gasped—it was becoming a habit. Although we had the impression that we were not going to be a top priority item on his agenda, we agreed to his deal. Then we waited, and waited. Nothing seemed to happen. I called Dowling's office in December 1983 and got hold of a Mrs. Nancy Funt. I explained that the Department of Insurance was about to stop the issuance of new and renewal insurance policies and we sure would like some action. She said, "Let me look over your file."

A few days later, she called back and said, "You're really a diamond in the rough. You have tremendous potential, strong cash flow and I'm sure we can do something for you. The thing is, I'm about to have a baby and I'll be out for six weeks or so. Can you wait?"

In mid-February, 1984, Nancy Funt returned from maternity leave and gave me a call. "Mr. Howell, I have a man who would like to talk to you about your company. His name is Alan Gruber. He's chairman and CEO of Orion Capital Corporation of New York City. He said he'd be interested in taking a look at your company. Would it be all right if I had him call you?"

"That would be just fine. And, er, congratulations on the baby," I responded.

Two days later, Alan R. Gruber gave me a call and said, "Nancy Funt has explained your situation about the Department of Insurance. I've made some inquiries about you and your company intrigues us. Could we see you and your financial people 10 days from today in California? I'd like to bring our team to your offices."

"Well, let's see. Yes, that would be fine. We'll be ready for you."

Their team had come from many locations, and we met at the SFO Airport Hilton. The meeting went well. So they chartered a plane in San Francisco for the trip to Monterey. When they began pouring out of the airplane in Monterey, it reminded me of those film tricks that show about a dozen people getting out of a Volkswagen. Out came Alan Gruber, followed closely by Ed Hobbs, president of Orion Capital Corporation, David Searfoss, chief financial officer, Bill Crandall and Jack Welch, underwriting and marketing, Stan Miyao, actuary, Mike Maloney, corporate counsel, and attorney Lou Rushon.

Back in our offices, Alan Gruber had told us about Orion Capital Corporation. His narration went something like this:

Orion Capital Corporation was born (or, perhaps, reborn) on March 31, 1976, as the reorganized successor of Equity Funding Corporation of America. Equity Funding had filed a Chapter X bankruptcy petition on April 5, 1973, after the disclosure of a massive financial fraud. The court-appointed trustee, Robert Loeffler, managed the estate of Equity Funding and developed a reorganization plan which received the approval of a diverse set of creditors three years later.

Based in Los Angeles, Equity Funding started as a sales organization representing independent mutual funds and life insurance companies. Equity Funding developed programs for combined sales of such products that employed so-called funding arrangements under which the mutual fund shares were used as collateral on loans to pay the life insurance premiums. In principle, if the fund shares performed well and interest rates remained low, the funding program could become self-funding in a fairly short time, but this was not usually the case. Equity Funding later developed, largely by acquisition, its own proprietary mutual fund and life insurance products, and also broadened its activities as a "fully integrated financial services organization" to include a savings and loan, oil, cattle, and real estate investment partnerships, a securities brokerage-dealership, and others. On the basis of its reported financials, Equity Funding appeared to be a prosperous and rapidly growing organization. At its zenith, the market capitalization of Equity Funding's common stock was about $750 million.

In fact, however, starting in 1964, the year that Equity Funding went public, more than 100% of the company's reported yearly earnings came from phony accounting entries. Without bogus income, Equity Funding would have reported a loss in each and every year of its operation as a publicly owned company.

A great deal has been written about the Equity Funding fraud and much of the literature seems to characterize the fraud as the brainchild of computer wizards. Although certain of the fraudulent financials did come from computer printouts, the recording of phony assets and the hiding of liabilities on a massive scale could have been done in the quill pen era. The fraud was essentially a securities fraud, doubtless motivated by the desire to inflate the price of Equity Funding stock.

It appears that some 50 to 75 people had at least an inkling that things were not as they were represented to be. Of this group, 22 people were convicted of criminal involvement in the fraud with all but 3 pleading guilty.

The trustee succeeded in what at first appeared to be an impossible feat—to hold the pieces together for three years while putting together a plan of reorganization that reconciled the interests of diverse bank creditors, indenture trustees, and other claimants, with various parties having conflicting claims on various assets. For example, at the time of the bankruptcy, there existed outstanding share certificates representing 300% of the capital of a key insurance subsidiary, with a bank group having 220% of the stock as loan collateral and the other 80% free of any lien. Other parties could potentially seek recision rights. The resulting plan has rightfully been called a triumph of diplomacy.

Alan R. Gruber, Orion's first, and thus far, only CEO, joined the trustee in January 1976, to aid in planning so that the transition out of bankruptcy would be smooth. Mr. Gruber was also appointed by the court as president of

Equity Funding, a position that had been vacant since the resignation of Stanley Goldblum in April 1973. An early chore of some importance was the selection of a name for the company— and a name change was certainly in order. Those who haven't done it may not appreciate how difficult it is to find a name that doesn't create confusion. Sitting in Equity Funding's office on Avenue of the Stars, at the corner of Constellation Boulevard, in Los Angeles' Century City development, Mr. Gruber considered quite a variety of heavenly names. The first likely choice was Aegis, which has the right "protective" connotation and which also has the same Æ ligature as does Aetna; Aegis was rejected because some found it hard to pronounce while the lawyers thought Aetna might not appreciate the connection. Orion then came to the fore, and when Mr. Gruber read a textbook description of Orion as "a mighty hunter of great beauty and enormous strength," he was convinced; it was just right!

In any event, Orion Capital started on March 31, 1976, with a melange of untainted assets, an onerous loan agreement, and a brand new board of directors made up of people who had been approved by the various creditor groups, the Securities and Exchange Commission, the FBI, and the United States District Court. In fact, the first meeting of the new board of directors was held in the Los Angeles court room of Judge Harry Pregerson, who presided over the reorganization.

The principal initial operating assets of Orion Capital were two traditional life insurance companies, Northern Life of Seattle, and Bankers National Life of Parsippany, New Jersey. In addition, a large assortment of nonproductive assets were targeted for liquidation—ranging from cattle ranches in South Dakota, Colorado, and Iowa, to some small oil and miscellaneous investment interests. Orion's first postbankruptcy audit was qualified by the auditors because of material contingent assets which couldn't then be evaluated with sufficient accuracy, a most unusual qualification.

Shares of Orion Capital were distributed according to the reorganization plan to various classes of creditors, including the shareholders of Equity Funding, who were allowed to become junior creditors as fraud claimants. After the new company had circulated pro forma financial information to its new shareholders, the SEC permitted over-the-counter trading of the shares to begin October 19, 1976. The initial trades were at $4.25 per share. The shares of Orion Capital were listed on the New York Stock Exchange on December 27, 1978. An original shareholder of one share would, by the end of 1995, have owned 2.74 shares, adjusting for 1992 and 1993 stock splits and assuming reinvestment of cash dividends; this would be the equivalent of about $119 in market value.

One of the important residual assets of Equity Funding was a large net operating loss carryforward (for tax purposes) which arose from the writedowns realized in the bankruptcy reorganization process. A peculiarity of the federal income tax laws existing at the time of Orion Capital's start was that life insurance companies were taxed under a singular set of tax laws and could not file consolidated federal income tax returns with affiliates in other lines of business. Thus, Orion Capital was in a true Catch 22 situation—it had the ability to shelter large amounts of taxable income arising from any domestic business other than the one it happened to be in. With this tax situation in mind, the company embarked on an evolutionary process of selling its life insurance units and reinvesting in other businesses. It selected the property and casualty insurance business as a promising field in which to make its mark. That evolution was already well along when the opportunity with DPFC-DPIC was presented to Orion Capital in early 1984.

Hara Saikaku (1642–1693) once said, "To make a fortune some assistance from fate is essential. Ability alone is insufficient." So it was with our situation in March of 1984; fate was to take a hand. In Chapter 4, it was explained how Ron Seaver of AMICO had quite fortuitously stumbled into A&A's San Francisco office looking for "large, challenging lines of insurance." This was at the very time I was desperately searching for an insurance market for the members of the CEAC. Just fate? Again it seemed like a profound stroke of luck to have run into a vice president of underwriting at the American Home (AIG) who was a civil engineer and who understood my belief that civil engineers were, in the main, honorable men. Some sociobiologist might say that what we view as good fortune or luck may be genetically programmed into us, like a salmon going upstream to spawn, or birds flying south in the fall, but regardless of the explanation, fate was to step in again. The company that is Different by Design had an extraordinary turn of good fortune in the person of Alan Gruber.

Born in Brooklyn, he felt the dramatic sociological changes that pervaded the United States in the years between the Great Depression and World War II. His father was an accomplished designer of women's clothes and his mother created a happy, wholesome home, later working as a bookkeeper when her children were grown. From the time Alan was very young, he showed a keen and competitive interest in anything mathematical, particularly the challenging game of chess. When he was 15 years old, he graduated from Townsend Harris Preparatory School, a school for gifted students, and was admitted to Massachusetts Institute of Technology (MIT).

Within two years (1945), under a program of advanced standing courses allowing one to proceed at one's own speed, Alan had earned his S. B. in engineering and in another year his S. M. By the age of eighteen, he was a teaching fellow. He taught mechanics and thermodynamics. During his undergraduate stint at MIT, he also ran the school newspaper with an editor's eye that was unforgiving over a misplaced comma or error in syntax. He still has that eye.

Alan then went to Harvard to work toward his Ph.D. and, by 1948 at age 20, had earned an M.A. and completed all courses and qualifying exams for his Ph.D. He needed only his thesis for the degree, but fate intervened. The next summer, he took a summer job on a program run by MIT for the Atomic Energy Commission studying the feasibility of nuclear-powered flight. There he met some fellows who were starting a nuclear consulting company, Nuclear Development Associates. They asked Alan to join them. The two main principals of the company told him, "Okay, we don't like accounting, legal, or running the shop. So, in addition to your technical engineering duties, you get to do that, too." They made him chief engineer and treasurer. He worked six or seven days a week, often into the wee hours. When he took the job, he invested $100 in the new company; that sum eventually grew a thousand fold. The company blossomed with venture capital support from the Rockefeller family and others. Alan never went back for his Ph.D.

Ten years went by and Alan decided he needed a change. A challenge presented itself in the form of Roy Marquardt of San Fernando, California. Marquardt was running an aerospace organization, with a major division concerned with events at the Nevada test site. Marquardt made Alan an attractive offer, so the Grubers (Alan, his wife, and three children) moved to southern California. The job was technical, and meant explaining (or trying to explain) things to Air Force generals. It also gave Alan an insight into how big corporations operate. It was a disturbing view.

Alan's experience at Marquardt created a new opportunity. He found that he liked to "straddle the fence," to work in an environment in which he could use both his technical and business knowledge. After a job with a small venture capital group in Los Angeles, Alan was hired by Boeing as a consultant to examine technical companies with an eye toward acquisitions. Instead, Boeing decided to bet the farm by building the B-747.

He was next hired by Xerox in 1967 as head of planning. While this job was partly technical, most of his efforts went to business, particularly corporate acquisitions. It was this stroke of fate that prepared Alan for the day he met with DPFC, because he looked at several insurance company acquisition candidates (much later Xerox became a big player in the insurance industry). He learned that the statutory accounting used by insurance companies and mandated by states' insurance departments could not always be counted on to give an accurate picture of an insurance company's real worth. I can only speculate that his reasoning ability, learned in playing chess, also gave him an intuitive ability to look beyond the facade of statutory numbers displayed by a company when making an evaluation for possible acquisition.

Alan left Xerox and moved to Heublein (Smirnoff Vodka, Kentucky Fried Chicken, etc.) as head of acquisitions, research and development, vineyard financing, and so forth. From there he went back as a business troubleshooter for the Rockefeller family in New York where he had been some years before. Eventually, the executive search firm of Korn-Ferry approached him with the intriguing task of trying to reorganize Equity Funding. The bankruptcy judge, trustee (Loeffler), banks and lawyers all thought he would be just right for the job. He was.

It was evident to us in DPFC that there were some within Orion who objected to the acquisition of our company. One of their number looked me right in the eye and said, "Well, if we buy your company, we will not run it as an eleemosynary institution." I can only assume that he was making reference to our considerable expenditures for loss prevention that many insurance people viewed as wasteful. Another Orion dissident had previously been on the underwriting team of an eastern underwriter whom we had approached for excess reinsurance. They hadn't wanted to participate, a decision that later proved to be a mistake because the underwriter who did made large profits.

Despite the naysayers, the meeting went off without a hitch. By noontime the next day we had an agreement in principle that would ultimately lead Orion Capital Corporation to be sole owner of DPIC, DPFC, and RAR. The agreement included Orion's adding additional capital to meet the demands of California's Insurance Department. I would be chairman of the board of those companies and Peter B. Hawes the president.

Plumbing the Future

The company that is Different by Design wasn't a fluke. Instead, its evolution followed a path similar to the thousands of insurance companies that have been formed over time. All of those companies required some innovation on the part of the founders. They started out to do things that had not been done by other insurance companies, to employ creative ideas such as loss prevention, new claims management techniques, or new insurance concepts. Businesspeople who had an insurance need, like the timber and pulp manufacturers around Wausau, Wisconsin, formed the Employers' Mutuals of Wausau, using new and untried timber harvesting loss prevention ideas to reduce claims. The lumber dealers of Illinois formed Lumbermen's Mutual Casualty Company (Kemper), used strict underwriting practices, accepted only good, experienced insureds, and enforced stringent loss prevention measures. The founder of the Fireman's Fund Insurance Company,[1] Captain William Holdredge, came up with a particularly intelligent innovation. His scheme was to write fire insurance only in cities that had fire departments made up of well-trained volunteer firemen. From the profits of his insurance company, he paid 10% to the firemen's charitable funds in the cities in which they provided insurance. Because of this financial incentive, the firemen's zeal for extinguishing fires quickly rose, and the Fund was able to make a good profit from an otherwise marginal line. Nor was that the end of the Fund's creativity. In 1872, after disastrous underwriting results from insuring whaling vessels, they wrote coverage for whaling vessels when all other insurance companies had given up. How? Captain Willisstun, a member of their marine insurance committee, noticed that most of the losses took place within the Arctic Circle after October 1, so he suggested warrants* on the marine insurance policy that re-

---

* A warrant on a policy of insurance is a statement of a fact or condition of the subject insurance which, if untrue, will void the policy. Usually the application for insurance must be made part of the policy in order for the warrant to be enforceable.

quired the ships to be south of St. Paul's Island (Pribilofs) by September 15.[2] Their premium rate was a gut wrenching 16% of the value of the hull and cargo! In spite of this outrageously high rate, the whalers stood in line begging for the coverage. The insureds had consented to a reasonable limitation on their operations, to be south of St. Paul's Island by September 15 (shades of limitation of liability for design professionals). It worked, and the whaling industry survived (until displaced by fossil fuel petroleum) and the Fund made a handsome profit.

It is likely that thousands of insurance companies will be founded using the same DPIC-Employers Mutuals-Lumbermen's Mutual-Fireman's Fund model.

In the coming decades, there will be a genuine need for creative risk management and novel insurance plans. Pollution and environmental cleanup, for instance, will be major fields for the insurance specialist who can piece together the underwriting, claims management, and loss prevention techniques so these risks might be successfully insured.

Other challenges lie ahead. Workers compensation, for example, is a horrible mess. There is widespread fraud and, what's more, the intent of the law is largely ignored by state industrial accident commissions who seem bent upon giving away huge sums of money whether or not the claimed injury is job connected. This drift away from the legislative intent is a perfect example of misguided bureaucratic adjudication. There are things that could be done to bring this situation into balance and they need doing. (How about putting employees in the stream of dividends from low loss ratio years?)

Health care is another problem. If not addressed by the insurance industry, it will become the domain of government—and we know what that might mean. Our current president, Bill Clinton, attempted to develop a bold plan of government controlled health care that could have doomed the efforts of the insurance industry.

These problems, and many more, might be addressed by the same sort of techniques used by the founders of the company that is Different by Design and their predecessors. Future generations can apply similar methods to contain risk, correct existing problems, and support the new industries. Although it may be easier to use "in place" insurance facilities, this will not always be possible since many underwriters will not understand the new technologies involved, such as hydrogen fuels, laser medical devices, microwave transmissions, and will eschew insuring them.

Some insurers, such as Kemper, may be casualties of philosophical change. They announced in the chairman's letter (David B. Mathis) in their 1992 Annual Report: "We have decided to exit the property-casualty business. Although historically good performers, the property-casualty companies do not fit with our vision of Kemper Corporation in the years to come."

I feel sad about this change, but it is easy to see that it may be a good step for them, and I believe that it will create an opportunity for someone who wants to assume Kemper's property-casualty role.

Other insurance companies have followed different procedures and been financially successful, but is that enough? The reason DPIC adopted its Different by Design philosophy is that we found it led to happier policyholders, highly motivated employees, fewer claims, and greater profits for the insurance company and its agents.

How were we different from most other insurance companies? How did we succeed with a line of insurance that some said was hopeless? Here are some of our principles of business conduct. Although you may not think them different than those practiced by other insurance companies, you might agree that together they represent an uncommon way of doing business.

- Loss prevention will work. It is not, as many insurance people state, "mere window dressing." For it to work, the insured, his or her agent, and the insurance company must all be totally committed to it. Once loss prevention becomes habit, losses are dramatically reduced in almost any line of insurance and with virtually any type of risk. This includes such lines of coverage as medical malpractice, officers' and directors' liability, accountants' professional liability, veterinarian malpractice, chemical companies' products liability, and even group medical coverage.

- "Knowledge is earning power." The Employers of Wausau's motto is just as credible today as when they adopted it some 60 years ago. It is no mistake that many successful DPIC agents have CPCUs, CICs, or CLUs. They increased their insurance and related knowledge because learning is a major part of their job—it gives them a decided earnings advantage. Many of them attained advanced academic degrees or equivalents, like Rollo Jacob's mission with Dale Carnegie, that contribute to their service and earnings capability. Most understand that formal education only prepares one for the real learning that comes on the job or in a career-oriented library quest. It is the hunt for answers to clients' or policyholders' questions that is true career challenge. This validates the heart and soul of the motto: "Knowledge is earning power." Gaining that knowledge is just as much a part of the job as showing up on time on Monday morning, and it sure is fun!

- Communication: Policyholders want and deserve more from an insurance company and its agent than just a piece of paper with a lot of confusing words on it. They want information and understanding and it is the duty of the company and the agent to make certain that they get it. This puts an additional burden on the company, its employees, and agents. Seminars, bulletins, manuals, and training programs are a must in today's risk prone world. In the long run, any time spent in imparting information to your policyholders will be returned a hundredfold in policyholder satisfaction, loyalty, and profit. Again, it's fun.

- While it may be impossible to measure the worth of one business activity against another, claims management has too long been relegated to a subordinate status. Claims people deserve an extra measure of support since their activity, more than any other, reveals an insurance company's true identity. They can save the day! Advertising slogans are meaningless to policyholders unless their claims are handled in a fair and expeditious manner. Claims people should be accorded wide discretion in making decisions as they are best able to judge the circumstances of a claim and the best method for equitable settlement. Help the insurance industry; take a claims person to lunch!

- Insurance organizations work best if they are loose and comfortable, not rigidly structured or highly schematized. The best results seem to come when the personnel work as a team. The much imitated military organization model will not work in today's educated insurance world where people are capable of making informed decisions about profound matters. The days of authoritarianism in the insurance organization are gone! People must feel a strong personal identity with the enterprise in order to do their best. If employees feel like they *belong,* they will convey the organization's philosophy and identity; profit and satisfied policyholders will be the reward.

- Insurance companies and agencies are service organizations whose assets are information, people, and capital. Each of these elements deserves high priority treatment. Information should be made readily available to all agents and personnel; it is not good enough to be available *somewhere*—it must be close at hand. Service is our job! Employees need to understand that they owe a great debt of gratitude to the policyholders and that they should treat them accordingly. Good people can be garnered by looking into their histories; this will reveal whether they are capable of getting along with others, have exercised self-discipline in some matter, and are selfless. In return, they should be challenged by their employment and fairly compensated. Capital is the lifeblood of an insurance company. It requires constant attention to make certain it is adequate for policyholders' needs and regulators' expectations.

- Being Different by Design means the insurance agents and company personnel should be involved in the business community of their insureds. Specialization is in order. To work with any group of people, you must know the intricacies of their business and understand their problems and insurance peculiarities. In addition to gaining technical expertise about their business it may mean it is important to socialize with policyholders so that important truths can be revealed in a relaxed, social situation, providing the insurance person with much needed intelligence and the policyholder with a better grasp of the company's philosophy. Besides, it too can be fun!

Perhaps the two greatest obstacles to an improved culture in the insurance industry in the coming decade will be those impediments that have plagued it in the past—apathy and cynicism.

Nothing can kill an organization faster than apathy on the part of its participants. In the insurance industry, many companies suffer from a nine-to-five syndrome, characterized by employees who put in time, but who really don't care about the outcome of their effort. The policyholder is something that annoys them. The tasks that they perform are done grudgingly. The public sees this and reacts. It is sad.

It is easy to become cynical about the insurance buying public when fraud is so rife. The automobile body shop man who, when asked for an estimate to fix a dent, says, "What's your deductible?" and then suggests that he will pad his estimate to pay that amount, typifies the common insurance fraud. The public's perception of the insurance industry continues to be just as cynical, since it is not as fully informed as it should be about coverages and feels the insurance companies dodge their responsibility in claims matters. Nonetheless, this cynicism may be reversed with clear explanations of coverage and vigilance by claims people to make certain the claims dollars are honestly spent.

Public cynicism may also be remedied by dedication shown in a time of need. For example, in the summer of 1991, a freak hailstorm struck the city of Billings, Montana. It ruined almost every dwelling roof in that city. Within hours, the major homeowners' insurance companies swung into action. State Farm Mutual, Safeco, Allstate, Farmers Insurance Group, and others sent squads of adjusters from all corners of the nation to service the demands of the devastated homeowners. Checks were written on the spot to start paying for the damage; follow-up checks were issued when the repair work was done. The adjusting teams worked around the clock, out of vacant stores. The millions of dollars needed to repair the roofs flowed rapidly into the community and helped to rectify the worst disaster the city had ever experienced. The insurance companies worked cooperatively, as a team. The citizens of Billings are no longer cynical about the insurance industry.

When that type of response is demonstrated by so many insurance companies, this is a good time to be in the insurance business. There is something soul-satisfying about doing a good job for people who depend on you.

Source Notes

Chapter 1:

1. *Eisner Food Stores v. Industrial Commission*, 211, N. E. 2d 683 (Nov. 19, 1965), and *Laukkanen v. Jewel Tea Co.*, 222 N. E. 2d 584 (1966).
2. Samuel C. Florman, *The Existential Pleasures of Engineering* (New York: St. Martin's Press, 1976), 12.
3. Kurt Mendelssohn, *The Riddle of the Pyramids* (New York: Praeger, 1974).
4. Ibid., 79.
5. Ibid., 114.
6. Jacob Feld, *Construction Failure* (New York: Wiley, 1968), 4, 5.
7. L. Sprague de Camp, *The Ancient Engineers* (New York: Ballantine Books, 1960), 86.
8. Ibid., 86.
9. Petroski, Henry, *To Engineer Is Human* (New York: St. Martins Press, 1982).
10. Sextus Julius Frontinus, *The Water Supply of the City of Rome*, A.D. 97, translated by Clemens Herschel (Boston: New England Water Works, 1973).
11. Gosta E. Sanstrom, *Man the Builder* (New York: McGraw-Hill, 1970), 111 and various.
12 Anders Franzen, *Ghosts From the Depths: The Warship Vasa*, National Geographic 121, no. 1, January 1962.
13. M. Prawy, *The Vienna Opera* (New York: Praeger, 1970, plate III/3).
14. Ibid., 26.
15. Feld, *Construction Failure*, 95.
16. Henry Petroski, "Still Twisting," *American Scientist* 79 (September–October, 1991).
17. The *New York Times*, November 8, 1940, 19.
18. *Discover Magazine*, "The Great Bridge Controversy" (February 1992): 26.
19. Joseph Gies, *Bridges and Men* (Garden City, N.Y.: Doubleday, 1963), 245.
20. The *New York Times*, December 3, 1940, 19, and December 4, 1940, 29.
21. Paul Johnson, *Modern Times, The World from the Twenties to the Eighties* (New York: Harper & Row, 1983), 450, 451.
22. Ibid., 464.
23. Peter W. Huber, *Liability, The Legal Revolution and Its Consequences* (New York: Basic Books, 1988), 79–80.
24. James Patterson and Peter Kim, *The Day America Told the Truth* (New York: Prentice Hall Press, 1991), 25.

Chapter 4:

1. *Barraque v. Neff*, 11 So. 2d 697 (1942); *Bayshore Development Co. v. Bonfoey,* 75 Fla 455, 78 So. 507 (1918); *Beacham v. Greenville County,* 62 SE 2d 92 (1950); *Bloomsburg Mills, Inc. v. Sordoni Construction Co.,* 401 Pa. 358, 164 A 2d 210 (1960); *Capitol Hotel Co. v. Rittenberry,* 41 SW 2d 697 (1931); *Clark v. Smith,* 234 Wis 139, 290 NW 592, 127 ALR 410 (1940); *Day v. National U. S. Radiator Corp.,* 241 La 288, 128 So 2d 660 (1961); *Foeller v. Heintz,* 118 NW 543 (1908); *Gagne v. Bertram,* 43 Cal 2d 481, 275 P 2d 15 (1954); *Hale v. DePaoli,* 33 Cal 2d 228, 201 P 2d 1, 13 ALR 2d 183 (1948); *Inham v. Binghamton Housing Authority,* 143 NE 2d 895 (1957); *Montgomery v. City of Philadelphia,* 391 Pa 607, 139 A 2d 347 (1958); *Montijo v. Swift,* 219 Cal App 2d 351m 33 Cal Rptr 133 (1963); *Olsen v. Chase Manhattan Bank,* 10 AD 2d 539, 205 NYS 2d 60, 175 NE 2d 350 (1961); *Patorelli v. Associated Engineers, Inc.,* 176 F Supp 159 (1959); *Robb v. Urdahl,* 78 A 2d 386 (1951); *Scott v. Potomac Insurance Co.,* 217 Ore 323, 341 P 2d 1083 (1959); *Smith v. Goff,* 325 P 2d 1061 (1958); *Surf Realty Co. v. Standing,* 78 SE 2d 901 (1953); *United States v. Rogers and Rogers,* 161 F Supp 132 (1958); *Alexander v. Hammarberg,* 230 P 2d 399 (1951); *Ressler v. Nielsen,* 76 NW 2d 157 (1956).

Chapter 6:

1. Wallace R. Hansen et al., *The Alaska Earthquake, March 27, 1964: Field Investigation and Reconstruction Effort* (Washington, D.C.: GPO, 1966). Fergus Wood, *The Prince William Sound, Alaska, Earthquake of 1964 and Aftershocks* (Washington, D.C.: U.S. Department of Commerce, 1967).

Chapter 7:

1. For a wonderful summation of the fate of design professionals who get entangled in the legal process, see Meehen, Richard L., *Getting Sued and Other Tales of the Engineering Life* (Cambridge, Massachusetts: MIT Press, 1981, Chapter 9).

Chapter 8:

1. *Tunkl v. University of California Regents,* 60 C. 2d 92, 100 (1963); *Florida Power & Light C. v. Mid-Valley, Inc.,* United States Court of Appeals, No. 83-5506 (June 24, 1985).
2. Thomas H. McKaig, *Building Failures* (New York: McGraw-Hill, 1962).

Chapter 9:

1. 73 California Reporter 369 (1968).
2. 74 California Reporter 749 (1969). The plaintiff's attorney was the same Robert Wilhelm who had advised us to get rid of "approved" on shop drawing stamps.
3. 77 California Reporter 633 (1969).

Chapter 11:

1. Edward O. Wilson, *Sociobiology, the New Synthesis* (Boston: Harvard University Press, 1975).
2. *NSPE v. Department of Justice.*
3. See Howard M. Vollmer and Donald L. Mills, eds., *Professionalization*, Englewood Cliffs, N.J.: Prentice Hall, 1966, a variety of writings from Durkeim, MacIver, Carr-Saunders, Parsons Hughes, and Goods on the professions; Morris L. Cogan, "The Problem with Defining a Profession," *Annals of the American Academy of Political and Social Science* 297 (January 1955), 105–111; "Toward the Definition of a Profession," *Harvard Educational Review* 23 (Winter 1953), 33–55.

Chapter 12:

1. Albert Shapero, *Managing Professional People* (New York: The Free Press, 1985), 146–147.
2. Ibid., 42–43.

Chapter 13 :

1. Frank Morton Todd, *A Romance of Insurance* (San Francisco: H. S. Crocker Company, 1929), 29. A book about the Fireman's Fund Insurance Company.
2. Ibid., 69.

Index